THE WAY OF DIVINE UNION

BEING A DOCTYRINE OF EXPERIENCE
IN THE LIFE OF SANCTITY, CONSIDERED
ON THE FAITH OF ITS TESTIMONIES AND
INTRERPRETED AFTER A NEW MANNER

BY

ARTHUR EDWARD WAITE

Golem • Media
BERKELEY, CA
www.golemmedia.com

Golem Media

BERKELEY, CA

Golem Media
1700 Shattuck Ave #81
Berkeley, CA 94709
www.golemmedia.com

First published in 1915 by William Rider & Son, Ltd,
London. Golem Media edition, 2007.
Printed in the United States of America
ISBN 1-933993-55-3

PREFACE

OUTSIDE certain serious and a few excellent books on mystical religion belonging to the present day, and outside certain authoritative studies connected with it actually or artificially, there has grown up a disposition to address the man of ordinary thought, even that symbolical scapegoat called the man in the street, as if either could take up the subject and progress by easy stages to a given term therein. Whether this is the fashion of a moment or otherwise, there is not less than a call for intervention on the part of those who know the mystical work and that it is the most difficult enterprise which can be undertaken by the human mind. It is altogether necessary that it should be disencumbered of adventitious elements owing to the presence of which it is often relegated to a sphere of archaic research ; but those who pretend that there is an easy path to the state of consciousness in God only deceive themselves, while in both directions they may do incalculable harm unwittingly.

The true nature of the mystical experiment does not appear fully in any of the authoritative texts, and it has not entered into the heart of modern compilers and commentators, who are speaking therefore on the most momentous of all subjects with a very partial knowledge of its import. I am referring more especially to lay writers who are not in the Catholic Tradition, but though it should be otherwise in the Roman Church, as the fountain of mystical knowledge in the western world, the statement appears to obtain in all quarters, while in Latin Christianity there are further limitations attaching to traditional methods handed down from the past and assumed to be the only way.

I might have confined my inquiry in this volume to a delineation of the mystical work and left it to speak for itself as to those who are fitted for such a pursuit of sanctity. But on all sides of the science—in its history, classification and criticism—I have found that most modern writers miss things that are important, even if some of these are concerned only with the point of view and the approaches.

I do not wish to be understood as setting out on my own part with any hostile intentions towards others who are my immediate precursors on the path. Except in these prefatory lines, I am not seriously concerned with modern mystical writings, and they can be a subject of bare reference in a very few cases only. If it be worth while to say so, I believe that all have been written from a heart of sincerity ; that many are likely to be profitable when a certain needful equipment is brought to their reading ; and that even the thing called new thought in America and England, whatever its aberrations and follies, is by intention on the side of God.

Of all ways of experience Mysticism is, however, the most secret, and its technology is, above all, most liable to misconception.

CONTENTS

vii

Contents

Contents

Contents

CHAPTER VII

Ways and modes of the Quest which ends in God—The paths
are many and the path is also one—It has also many names which
are reducible to the name of love—A path for each who under-
takes the Quest—The way of the Cross—The way of roses—Of
certain imprescriptible conditions—Of awakening to a sense of
the Divine—The path is within us—No man goes outside the
field of his own consciousness—The thesis of a lesser personality—
Of experience outside consciousness—The world that is within—
The preparation of love—The mystical aim defined—Mysteries
of Divine Love—Sanctity and its crown—The ascetic life—Its
merits and aberrations—The senses as natural sacraments—God
and personality—The nothingness of Molinos—Of false abnegation—The Children of the King—Self-conquest and self-
torture—The Path of Contemplation—Distinctions concerning
meditation—Contemplation and Love—Of images in the mind
—Of realisation in nakedness of mind—St. Thomas on intuitive-
ness—Modeless contemplation—Contemplation and Conformity—
Tabulations of mystical progress—The prayer formula—Eckehart
on the union—Capacity of will—Sanctification in love—Man
created for beatitude—The transmutation of love—Its Divine
work—Testimony of mystical writers on these subjects—Emanci-
pation from forms of thought—The void which is filled by God—
John the Scot on the soul's return to God.

Contents

CHAPTER VIII

CHAPTER IX

Contents

CHAPTER X

Of personality and its denudation—Of multiple personality—The true and only view—The distinction between personal and individual—Personality and capacity for union—Of the so-called personal and true self—The quest of individuality—The exploration of self—The self in God—Self-knowledge and knowledge of God—Sub-consciousness and transcendental self—The new and the old man—Our unity of self-knowing substance—The Ego as the vessel of reception—Western theology and the triad in man—The soul in Latin theology—The higher part of the soul—Of the· soul in relation to space and time—Difficulties of the theological view—Of psychic vehicles and the body of resurrection—The intermediate state—Of the soul as a spirit like God—The position of pure Mysticism on the soul in relation to space and time—The beginning and end in God—The intermediate worlds of experience—How all manifestation postulates space and time—Of successive vehicles—The desired end of being—An eirenicon between East and West—Advantages of this view—Whether time and space are illusions—A new light hereon—A word on trichotomy—The soul as the psychic body—Conclusion on personality.

CHAPTER XI

Our own self-knowledge as the one great fact of the universe —Of consciousness outside ourselves—Divine Consciousness—Definition of consciousness—The bond of union in consciousness—Of God entering or realised in human consciousness—Consciousness of the external order—Of the field beyond consciousness—The art of self-knowledge—Of contemplation on the self-knowing part —The witness of the inward world—The practice of the Presence of God—Some pitfalls of expression—The symbolical place of the Kingdom—The ultimate mystical process—Of separateness and union—Of sacramental union—The extension of consciousness—The emptying of mind—Isolation of the self-object—The reflex act—How the mystical process begins in consciousness—The opening of a new world—Psychical and mystical states—Inner life is a realisation of self in consciousness—Of higher self-suggestion

Contents

—The reflex act—The inward opening—Individual consciousness as a Divine centre—Testimony of man to himself and of the universe to man—Of man as the witness of all things—The Building of the House.

CHAPTER XII

Summary of the path which has been travelled—The records of the Quest in their application to life—False knowledge and knowledge of God—The interpretation of poverty of spirit—The direction of danger in asceticism—The question of conformity—Utility as a point of conduct—Natural and Divine Law—Renunciation and the Will of God—Distinction between resignation and conformity—The importance of attitude—Realisation of will in God—The reward problem—Errors of Quietism—The Voice within—Who goeth up to union with God ?—Will-renunciation and will-realisation—Böhme's witness—Marriage with the will of the universe—Redirection of purpose—The spirit in which to consider the mystical term—Variations in the way of attainment—A work of understanding—The Kingdom of Heaven—The Blessed Vision—Divine Union as a state of consciousness—Love and the body of desire—The quest in self-knowing being—The preoccupation of love—The Kingdom which subsists by love—That which precedes and comes after—Man and the thought of man—Growth in the likeness of God—Likeness and union—The conversion of reason—Brain and mind—Mystical experience as a state of *mens*—Mind as a sacramental channel—Mind as a Daughter of God—The alleged failure of the logical understanding—The Closed Palace—Intellectual Mysticism—*Via Dolorosa*—The Promised Land.

CHAPTER XIII

Our story of election—The world and a spirit in the world—The world as field and opportunity—As a gate of mystical life—As the place of our election—That which is ours—The way of joy—The condition of freedom—A way of union with Nature—Speech and silence in Nature—The world as pageant and symbolism—Our inward priesthood—Of miracles—A word on sanctity—The five wounds of Christian Mysticism—Contemplation and the casting out of images—A counsel on external

Contents

Contents

CHAPTER XVI

INTRODUCTION

THE relations between the Church and the world, between the age in which we live and the religion of Christ, are presented at this day in an enormous variety of aspects, not only by many who speak as exponents of official teaching bodies, with such authority as is resident in these, but by a great concourse of individual voices, being voices of all and any who are moved, in whatever manner, to take part in the one debate which is catholic to all ages and countries—that of the inter-communication between God, man and the universe. There is, furthermore, in another category, all that which is concerned with the history of religious thought, of religious movements in the past, of Christian origins and developments, or those of other great religions. There is, over and above these, the philosophy of religion, considered as a part of mental and metaphysical science. In each of these departments indifferently, the truly speaking voices are those which have a direct and awakening message to men and women, as they find themselves here and now, not only in the maze of great problems, but looking zealously for a guiding clue. So also in the work which I am taking here in hand, and through all its field of issues, that which will be of moment to us is that which for us has life, our specific and collective standing with the main subjects, all that they mean for us and in what manner—as the great practical question —we can proceed from thought to action in their respect.

Introduction

How keenly the broad fact is appreciated and what needs seem to be implied thereby, are points indicated by the general quickening respecting anything that belongs—integrally, approximately or remotely—to the experiment of the mystical life. The reason is close to our hands : this experiment represents by its hypothesis a method of investigation which offers an immediate answer to those problems of human affinity with God and the universe about which I have just spoken. There is no longer any question of simple faith in authority imposed from without, of the mere past and its records concerning Divine dealings with man : it is a matter of first-hand personal experience, and in what manner such experience may be secured, its claims being postulated at their face value for purposes of research, by those who are drawn to undertake it.

There was never a time and perhaps there was never a place in which the study of mystical literature was prosecuted with greater apparent interest, and—can I say ?— even zeal, than in England at this day—not to speak of the Continent or America. It is substantially catholic in its predilections, for one and all of the schools are embraced thereby, every age and its spokesmen, all modes and variations of thought on the chief aspects of the subject, and—passing beyond concerns particular to Christendom—the non-Christian religions that are dead and gone, with those that remain in evidence, the whole world over. But because in an official sense, and very often in one that is real, we are still typically Christian as a nation, the chief intellectual and literary, with all the devotional dealings are in Christian Mysticism. Many highways and byways of the past are explored on the quest of texts ; we seem within a calculable, perhaps even a short distance from the time when every record which deserves a name in memory will have been edited: even now the notable output stands for a very large circle of readers.

The first thing to observe concerning the bare literal fact is that it does not, except indeed sporadically, notify that a new department of philosophical, historical or literary exploration has been opened up. The worst possible summary of the position would be to conclude that the supply is in response to a demand of specific academical interest. Within its measures, the interest is practical; within its measures also, it is alive. It is native to a desire in the mind, to a preoccupation also in the heart; it is only of the quest after knowledge by raising the category of meaning attached to this word— as it is used in a popular sense; it has nothing to do with the mere improvement of understanding for the sake of understanding and improvement; or if this be a characteristic by chance in certain cases, they are not only in an utter minority but are so few that they do not enter into any serious reckoning. The motive is appreciable only as part of our solicitude for the soul within us, its maintenance and welfare; but this, again, brings us back to that question of inter-relation with which I made a beginning in these introductory words. I need not add that under such light the interest tends to assume an aspect of high seriousness; and yet it may be easy to exaggerate this aspect, though the concern, as I have intimated, exhibits some quality of life. It is valid, moreover—at least so far as it goes; it is part of our yearning to establish within categories of actual experience our origin outside time and our end beyond that which is manifest. But—after careful analysis—the concern is over-liable to emerge as an admixture, like our other motives and attractions, our tendencies and most of our aspirations in this vortex of the modern world. It postulates what I have called yearning, but the yearning is—for the better part—detached from faith ; above all it is anything rather than a witness of doctrinal belief or of integration in a specific system or school. I am speaking of the thing at large, not in the full diversity of its complexions. A considerable part of mystical book-production is ostensibly for the needs of that or this body of believers—as, for example and in a palmary sense, the members of the Latin Church ; but I have very grave doubts whether the bulk of readers belongs to that Church and whether the issue of valuable texts at the present rapid rate would be possible if their study were confined to the particular section—as indeed to any other. This may appear to be only a technical point, but it leads up to one of importance, namely, that we are in the presence of what is in a distinctive sense an eclectic interest. The message of those authoritative records to which I am here alluding is, among other things, a message of ascetic life ; but their study in the extra-Latin circles does not mean a disposition towards that life. It is, further, in relation, as an implied and unquestioned postulate, to a form of doctrinal Christianity which is of an exceedingly rigid type. Now, the fact that such works are read widely outside the Church of their origin does not signify that there is the slightest intention to seek reconciliation with that Church. The persons most concerned are not merely likely to have St. John of the Cross and the Blessed John of Avila side by side with L. C. de Saint-Martin, Engelbrecht and Antoinette de Bourignon, but the same shelves will not improbably contain the latest books on Vedantism, Sufic and Mohammedan Mysticism. It is a little difficult to characterise dispositions of this kind justly. We have seen that to term them a literary interest would be not less untrue than to speak of scholarship as the motive. They are really of the nature of quest, and the rich opportunities of the time enable this to be pursued in a number of directions almost concurrently, sometimes with intellectual benefit, sometimes to the increase of confusion. There is a restless activity towards certitude, a great desire to hear about the mystical work, path and term thereof; but any notions as to the direction and kind of certitude lie vaguely and indeterminately beyond the threshold of apprehension; while to be up and doing in the work itself remains somewhere between a purpose half-formed and a hope in dream. The last thing which most of us are prepared to change is the way of our daily life; and further, all our reading and thinking notwithstanding, there is often but a vestige of true conviction among us as to which is the better way of life and as to the right line of inception or procedure, if a need for change is recognised.

The interest is therefore likely to be pronounced upon harshly, as rooted in sentiment, in emotion—which it is frequently—as a deeper kind of curiosity—which it is also—as a new field of the philosophical *virtuoso*—which, however, it is rarely. It is even liable to be said that the adventures of the soul on its search after real experience in Divine Life attract people who have no design of prosecuting such a quest themselves, for the same reason that there is a steady demand for books of travel among those who have never travelled and may never do more than cross the Straits of Dover. In certain directions, and within defined limits, all these views are true, and to the full extent that they obtain we must beware of exaggerating the present vogue in respect of mystical life and literature. To their extent the fashion may and presumably will prove transitory ; it is one of the visitations and inspections of all realms of possibility at a period when the whole universe of life and thought has been thrown open for reconsideration from any and every standpoint, when no voice or its message is ruled out of the great court of inquiry on antecedent grounds, and when there is practically no tribunal whose decisions would be taken as final, but that least which speaks with arrogation of supreme authority.

It remains, however, that, over and above the characteristics which have been here enumerated, there is often a desire of the House of the Lord, and it is high, true and real, even if in a few cases only it can be said to eat up the heart. As such, it will remain with us because this is of the soul itself, an evidence of its " hunger and thirst," wherein is the spur of quest.

Now, a speculation interposes as to why the zeal emerges in these best cases as little more than an intellectual or theoretical concern. Is it simply that the practical side is overclouded by eclecticism, by picking and choosing on grounds of predilection rather than those of an expert, by paralysis arising from a multitude of irreconcilable counsellors, by labours of harmonising, by analyses and syntheses—as it seems to one, world without end ? Or is there some other cloud on the sanctuary of this great experiment ? Is it that the old witnesses, having conceived a certain end for their attainment, pursued the term by methods which, on the hypothesis at least, did somehow lead them rightly and might therefore lead us ; but, as it proves, they are not methods belonging to the age in which we live and move and have our being ? Are they interwoven with doctrine which we have ceased to accept, perhaps even provisionally ? Is it possible to reach the end by another path or mode, and by one which has begun possibly to open before us ? And is that alternative way of Divine Life and Union more practicable in our present state of normal thought and action ? If so, the old procedure may call to be regarded as exploded and recourse thereto will be compared—however invidiously—to the repetition of chemical experiments according to disused formulæ in text-books of two hundred years since. Latently or otherwise, these questions lie behind the mystical preoccupations of the period, and the fact that answers seem wanting, or fail in conviction, is perhaps chiefly accountable for the deficient or arrested purpose to which I have referred as obvious.

The primary design of this study is to consider the questions at large and to present an answer, including another and at least relatively more excellent way—because it can be a way for us. How difficult is the task before me may not be realised till the end, but it should be foreseen even from the beginning, if only because the exponents and disciples of the old great manner will assume out of hand that I am either proposing to find that short way to sanctity which I have condemned expressly in the preface or to invent a formula by which I conceive it possible to dispense therewith. The alternatives are not for my consideration at this stage, since he who reads will see ; but I state them to indicate one pair of opposites among the hostile conditions which beset such an inquiry.

In addition to the editing of texts, the law of supply

and demand has produced some beginnings of a new mystical literature, and I suppose that it will be accurate roughly to say that it falls for the time being into two chief divisions. There is that which seeks to restate the philosophy of life and mind from a mystical point of departure, or with an object in view which comes within one of the categories of Mysticism: some memorable and excellent books are included in this division. There is that which belongs to the department of compendium and summary, being largely a record of the past. The value in the first case, high as it reaches at the best, does not exceed the intellectual province of things, by which I mean that procedure from theory to practice is beyond its limits: it tells a man what he shall think rather than what he shall be. The exclusive concern of the second is with methods which obtained of old and results held to have been thereby secured, and we have just seen that the question is whether the compass of our modern need is here included. It seems to me almost beyond question that on both sides the appeal is not directly to the desire after spiritual life awakened within us, nor to ministry dealing with desire, though we can draw no certain line as to what may help towards awakening. Above all, if the question arises as to what shall a man do, here and now—here among things as they are, now in this twentieth century—in order that he may know God —which is the subject-matter of Mysticism—there is offered him, in the works which count as serious, either an open gate into paths of pure speculation or a counsel to reconstruct in his own person certain modes of life and faith which belong to another period; but this latter, in most cases, lies between the difficult and impossible. So long in particular as the consideration of Mysticism

Introduction

is confined within the limits of its history, of its records regarded as documents and their criticism, if at most it be a careful, summarised classification and panegyric of archaic ways of practice, a discourse upon Mysticism belongs—whatever its intention—either to historical or textual criticism, written from a special standpoint. I am proposing to take another course. The Way of Divine Union is either a way which can be followed in this present age of the world or to speak of it is actually that which we have agreed to set aside—a department of speculative, literary or archaic research. I have written in the belief that when it comes to be understood at first hand, and has been disencumbered of much that obscures it, this way—in the true and vital sense of the words—is practicable to a certain distance for every single-minded person who aspires zealously to enter therein and is prepared to fulfil certain broad or catholic conditions belonging to what is an experiment in life. If I put it forward as an easy path, even up to the point which I mean, this would be to fall within the category of those writers mentioned in my preface. To some it will be difficult at the beginning and to some easy, at least through the early stages. As there are natural hindrances to a work of this order so there are natural dispositions which are like dedication in advance. No hard-and-fast line can be therefore drawn. Beyond the point in question I have indicated already that it is the most difficult of all works. I believe that those are in-numerable who may dwell within the gate of the path and in the light which shines about it, to their great interior advantage. I believe that those who will travel it are a growing number, but most of them will pause there or here, though they will find—wherever they halt

—that they are in a land of the living. Those who will come to the goal are few indeed, because there is a change involved in the mode of self-knowledge, as we shall see in its proper place. The consideration of this subject will make evident in its own self-unfolding that if there be a new way possible it does not argue facility, or that he who runs can read, and much less that he can follow the quest of Divine Life except by the unreserved dedication of his whole being.

It will perhaps clear the issues if I add that the mystical experiment stands for my purpose on the warrants of the past respecting the facts of the experience, while in criticism of the experience and whatever is involved thereby I have followed points of departure proper to the purpose in view, without reference to guides or precedents. Many misconceptions of this epoch and some preceding generations may prove to be terminated once and for all, to say which implies that a satisfactory or any canon of criticism has not been established by old or current text-books, in whatsoever quarter produced. But I speak of theological quarters and things which depend from these. It cannot be affirmed that their recent records are memorials of the first importance, though there are good and informing works, of which two or three stand forth from the rest and are known— as they deserve—widely. I do not look to cover the whole ground, perhaps rather to have opened the path in part, by an indication of the first steps. If the cloud still remains on the sanctuary of a great experiment, I trust that the direction in which it shall be lifted may be nearer to those who seek.

I have attempted, therefore, a re-expression of mystical doctrine in the light of existing needs and to serve the

Introduction

most practical of all purposes as a manual of the mystical term and of the path by which it is attained, based on their understanding in the present state of human consciousness when it turns to the Divine Ends.

If personal vindication be required for having ventured to approach the Sanctuary, I submit that the life of the student is raised by continuous intellectual devotion to things that are holy and by their pursuit in sincerity and zeal. Herein, as it seems to me, is a valid apology for free speech in humility on the holy term. There are other and greater warrants, in respect of which I am not worthy to cast my garments on the path of those who go up into the Mountain. But I have seen with the eyes of the mind; I have heard with the mind's ears; and I know how that which has been testified by the great witnesses awakens a witness in the heart. In this manner I have seen Zion on the hill, and it shall be enough if I have delivered my message within those measures wherein the word has been given me. Therefore, by God's grace, having proceeded thus far, I have not waited for worthiness before I offered my findings in the search after the Great Mystery; and I know, if God blesses the gift in the light of Him, He will bless also the giver. Hereinafter follows a thesis in lowliness of mind for the place of a serving-brother in the Courts of the Holy Assembly. I know further that God fulfils Himself in many ways of books, and the reiteration of the high things is continued therefore incessantly. Having taken all Christian Mysticism for my province, I know also that the fire which " has come into the harp " has begun to cry out to God, as great unto great crieth, and I know, in fine, that God answers.

THE
WAY OF DIVINE UNION

CHAPTER I

THE TITLE OF THE QUEST

ALL the great subjects have their unhappy associations, as they have too frequently their unworthy and perverted side. But, if I may speak for once so obviously, it would be something worse than idle to renounce henceforward our confession to the rule of holy commandments, because they are dishonoured so continually by their breach rather than maintained in high reverence—as they are still assuredly—by dutiful and condign observance. So also the counsels of perfection, above the region of command, are not reduced in respect of their ultimate values if the denomination has been applied to substitutes, or if the real things have been current under names of convention. The Way of Divine Union— which is the crown of all the counsels—is the Way of the Mystical Quest, and the Mystical End is an old title for the attained Union. Now, the name of Mysticism and the denomination of Mystic have passed through various undesirable ordeals in their comparatively brief history ; yet they are terms which—in modern times—have been used to distinguish (1) the highest method and object of research which it has entered into the heart of man to conceive or follow, and (2) not only those disciples of the path who have embraced the method, but—speaking

ex hypothesi for the moment—those who have reached
its object. For this reason, as it is my intention to make
use of the words, it would be idle to consider in the first
place whether they should be abandoned preferably, nor
will it be needful to dwell at much length on the question
whether they can be replaced by other symbols of
language which would embody more efficiently that
which they have implied for the last two hundred years
or longer. That they are a perfect name and description
I am in no wise prepared to affirm. That in their conventional use they owe their chief efficiency to anything
but accretions superposed by custom I am prepared to
doubt. They suggest connotations in things like the
Instituted Mysteries[1]—more especially of the classical

---

[1] One of them is of modern origin : there is nothing in Greek or
Latin corresponding to our term " Mysticism." The root of all the words
seems to be μύω=*comprimo*=to keep close, dissemble, shut, cover;
μυστης=one who preserves silence for an allotted period—as, for example,
four years ; one who is learned in sacred things ; also the candidate who
is admitted, under pledges of secrecy, into the Sacred Mysteries. The
last idea is always connoted, but, although the line is not drawn closely, a
mysta was an adept rather than a neophyte. In Christian mystical
theology the word was never used, presumably on account of its relations
of such kind. It does not even occur in pseudo-Dionysius, though the
doctrine and practice of mystical theology were to be reserved in his
view, as we shall see in its place. In Latin, the substantive use of *mysticus*
as an equivalent of *mysta* is late. I have not met with it in mystical
writers till the end of the sixteenth century ; but *mystici dicunt* had
become familiar in the days of Antonius a Spiritu Sancto, who died on
January 12th, 1674. The terms *mystici, sancti mystici* occur in a letter
to the Sovereign Pontiff, dated December 13th, 1698, on the subject of
Quietism and the Mme Guyon embroilment. See Vincentius De-Vits'
Lexicon Totius Latinitatis, edition of 1887, which—s.v. *Mysticus=initiatus
sacrorum*—quotes *Inscr. in Corp. Inscr. Lat.*, IX, 3529. See also Stephanus:
Thesaurus Linguæ Latinæ, s.v. *Mysta=Sacra discens, mysteriorum peritus.*
We are not concerned with the use of the words in English, but I believe
that the substantive form " mystic " is of late introduction, possibly not
much anterior to *The Mystic and other Poems*, by Philip James Bailey,
1855. The *Universal Dictionary* of Barclay appeared about 1847, and
contains the plural " Mystics," with " Mystici " as an alternative, but not
the singular form, shewing, I think, that it was of recent use at that date.

2

world, and those of Greece above all—which are of great importance in symbolism and in the history of symbolism, but are adventitious for our present purpose rather than essential. What is much worse, they move in a cloud of illusory seeming because of the false mystics, the popular misuse of words, with all the unholy issues of occult pretence and delusion. But we have held to them so far because—as a fact—there is nothing better in the possible alternatives, and it comes about, therefore, that we must be content with what we have. Did I even know of something which might be held acceptable to replace either, I should hesitate to produce it now, on account of old consecrations arising from familiar use, the deficiencies and profanations notwithstanding.

The definitions of Mysticism are many, and as the subject can be approached or regarded from several points of view, a certain number among the modern instances may be allowed to pass muster within their particular limits, which—in each case—would be restrictions of the maker's consciousness. There is, however, scarcely one that will satisfy those who are acquainted, in the deeper sense, with the quest and end of which it is a title. This fact is not surprising in view of what has been indicated, namely, that the word is a modern word and that it does not comprehend the subject to which it is applied. It is obvious that neither the way nor the end of Divine Union is represented by a notion of secrecy. The latter is a counsel of conduct or a delineation of something that is inevitable. I know that there is a postulate of secrecy in this holy path of life, and for more than one reason. In the first place, it is strange, difficult and rarely followed ; furthermore, it is travelled alone ; and in the proper use of terms it is a path which is not a path, though it may be said that there is a place of entrance. Again, its business arises from peculiar postulates, or doctrines, and albeit in one sense no dogmatic system is secret *per se* there is another in which the high doctrines may always be called secret. They deal with subject-matters and experience that are beyond all common knowledge and can spell nothing to the ordinary concourse of men, though there is no condemnation of these in consequence and no distinction for this purpose between that which is common—as if it were for such reason unclean—and that which is exotic and hence outside the categories of popular convention. Finally, it is certain that after we have said everything, and have exhausted language, the path remains secret, because there is a saving fire in the heart and a saving fire in the head, the synonym of which is quickening, and those who have not that fire are without life and true understanding in respect of this subject. But when these things have been specified the root-deficiency remains—that concealment is a characteristic at best and neither this term nor its synonyms can shadow forth, much less embody, that which it is intended to convey by those who speak of Mysticism with any knowledge thereof. Hence the word does duty by way of substitution under every disadvantage.

Outside these considerations, a recurring difficulty arises from attempted speculative definitions on the part of persons who, standing on no certain ground, are misled by one or other of the fantastic issues which encompass the central concern. It signifies little whether their starting-point is in the etymology of the word Mysticism, or otherwise. In the one case definition goes astray through the region of so-called occult science, while in the other it ignores what is of real import in the term and its meaning.[1] The life and essence of the sub-

---

[1] A single instance must suffice and it shall be that afforded by A. L. Constant in his *Dictionnaire de Littérature Chrétienne*, firstly because the work is included by Migne in his encyclopædic theological series, and secondly because of the writer's later celebrity as an occult philosopher. In the course of a long article on the mystics, Constant betrays the most extraordinary confusion, foreshadowed eloquently enough by a pretence

ject escape in both cases. We have therefore on the one hand a word which is admittedly incommensurate and on the other an interpretation which too frequently carries it still further in extraneous or ridiculous directions. It may clear some of the issues to state that no born mystic ever characterised himself by this name in the old days, nor did he dream of his art and practice as embraced by the word Mysticism. That which was known and recognised was the branch of theology called mystical, and those who treated it have left us a clear understanding of the sense attached to the term. It is to their definitions and intimations that we must appeal. The distinction is of some importance and has not been recognised adequately, if indeed at all in the literature. I shall therefore offer certain citations in a roughly chronological order, it being understood that the antecedents of Christian Mysticism in non-Christian religious or philosophical systems are no part of my concern. There is a mystical theology in Plotinus[1] and it is of the highest importance, not only on warrants of its own but because of the influence which it exercised on Christian Mysticism ; there is otherwise the whole circle of Neo-Platonism ; and there is in fine eclectic Gnosticism ; but my

at definition contained in his opening words. " Mysticism is to piety that which poetry is to literature." The Mysticism of the Latin Church is said to depend from the dogma of original sin, while non-catholic Mysticism is the doctrine of secret societies, or the esotericism of natural law interpreted by human philosophy. There is also a Mysticism of modern philosophy which derives mainly from Swedenborg and an important part of which deals with correspondences or analogies. There is nothing worse than this in all the annals of the subject.

[1] The mystical work, says Plotinus, is " a flight of the alone to the alone." The soul passes from itself " as an image to the archetype " and so attains the end of its progression. The principle of Divine Union is that of " like with like." It is the state in which one sees no longer but " is the thing seen." According to another mode of symbolism, the soul is " filled with Deity," participates therein and is conjoined therewith. See the section " On the Good or the One," in Thomas Taylor's *Select Works of Plotinus*. Also Mead's edition, 1895.

research lies within the mystical consciousness of Christendom. It is enough, therefore, to recognise that there was a debt to the past, a derivation on many sides therefrom, as also from sects and systems amidst which mystical consciousness grew up.

I will speak first of the Mystical Theology which we owe to an unknown writer who assumed the name of Dionysius[1]—not because he is the first who could be mentioned but because of the high place that he occupies in the sacred tradition. His brief tract and some letters arising therefrom expound the doctrine and delineate the general heads of the practice by which the truth of that doctrine is, *ex hypothesi*, established in experience. There is—he tells us—a theology which is secret and mystical, another that is evident and known.[2] The first is symbolical and sacramental, the second philosophical and demonstrative, a more explicit definition being wanting in either case.[3] In the seventh century we have, however, the *Scholia* of St. Maximus on the works of Dionysius to supply the deficiency, up to a certain point, by affirming that the secret tradition of Scripture is explained in mystical theology, the transmission being

---

[1] I have used Migne's edition in the *Patrologiæ Cursus Completus: Patrologiæ Græcæ*, Tomus III: S. Dionysii Areopagitæ, *Opera Omnia Quæ Exstant*, 2 vols., edition of 1889.

[2] The second becomes known, that is to say, in virtue of ordinary methods of mental research: it is cognoscible by reason and is acquired. But of the other the most acceptable description would say that it is something infused.—See *Mystical Theology*, c. I, § 3. Therefore, many centuries later, Cardinal Bona defined mystical theology as an untaught wisdom, superior to all human wisdom, whereby the mind attains to a knowledge of God without discursive inquiry and partakes of Him without reasoning. By the hypothesis, it is a recompense attached to a certain inward way of life and is a knowledge at first hand, while ordinary theology offers an intellectual certitude, resulting from an ordered use of the logical faculty.

[3] The first—or Mystical Theology—is attained in a state of contemplation, but this is a state of ignorance, understood mystically—that is to say, as science raised to an ineffable degree (*op. cit.*, c. I, § 3).

by means of symbols.[1] It is informed with a certain
Divine efficacity which fortifies souls devoted to things
mystical and to contemplation, using symbolised enigmas
for this purpose and dissolving souls in Christ by the
revelation of Divine Mysteries in silence.

Next in the Dionysian succession, or towards the end
of the ninth century, are the luminous expositions, or
glosses, of John the Scot on the Mystical Theology of
St. Dionysius.[2] They tell us only that such theology
is termed closed or secret, because it remains hidden
and ineffable. It is *apophatica* or negative, seeking to
find God by divesting Him of all qualities and likeness
with things below, things medial, or things above. There
is also Georgius Pachymeres,[3] who wrote Greek paraphrases of Dionysius in the thirteenth or fourteenth
century and bears similar testimony to that of St.
Maximus, namely, that mystical theology shews forth
truth by means of figurative signs and does not make
itself and its subject plain to vulgar knowledge, which is
the office of affirmative theology.[4] Extending elsewhere

---

[1] The sense of this statement is not explained, but the attempt to
reach a conception of God by using the images of darkness instead of
light and by substituting negations for affirmations is, of course, a
symbolical device, and one line of criticism would object that to illustrate
mysteries by enigmas must leave them still enigmatic.—See Migne's *Codex*,
Vol. II, col. 415 *et seq.*

[2] See Migne's *Patrologiæ Cursus Completus : Patrologiæ Latinæ*, Tomus
CXXII : Joannis Scoti *Opera Quæ Supersunt Omnia*, 1865, col. 267
et seq.

[3] The paraphrases of Pachymeres are included in Migne's edition of
Dionysius, Vol. I.

[4] It would follow in logic that mystical theology was a storehouse of
secret doctrine, being that about which pseudo-Dionysius warned
Timothy to be careful lest it should come to be discerned by the unworthy. Pachymeres speaks as if this doctrine had been transmitted to
his own period. Such a traditional knowledge could have been concerned
only with inward meanings attached to the figurative signs. I shall mention this subject a little later in the text, but do not propose to discuss it.
Georgius Pachymeres was a Byzantine writer, who was born at Nicea in

7

the literal text of Dionysius, Pachymeres affirms that mystical theology is not of feeling, reasoning, activity, operation or fashion of mind, nor can it be explained by any principles or modes of ours. In a perfect suspension of thought, enlightened within itself, we know this theology to exceed that which mind can grasp. It is mystical because it is ineffable, and it is theology because it reveals concerning God that which is above all things.[1]

When the time came, later on in the centuries, for the Jesuit Corderius[2] to enter the chain of succession, and to do anything—for the most part—rather than elucidate Dionysian issues with his endless cloud of words, he goes much further and is much more expressive than his precursors, or indeed his source itself—on the particular question in hand. The discipline of mystical theology is not to be acquired by personal force or enterprise—that is to say, by intellectual effort—but is a work of Divine bounty, the inward motion and inspiration of God. It does not demand merely that simple light of mind which is sufficient for theology in other departments, but a peculiar grace and high prerogative of its own, which leads up to its own heights. God, who is its object, is embraced within mystical theology, so that it subsists

1241 and died about 1315. His paraphrase was published at Paris in 1561. At a period of some activity, working towards the reunion of the Greek and Latin Churches, he belonged to the opposing party.

[1] It was therefore an immediate revelation of God to the soul of the mystic, and that which was not to be revealed, and which constituted the store of doctrine, would be the methods of reaching the state. I have indicated already that Dionysius reserved these. The essential part of the practices would be obviously inward, but it is not inconceivable that there may have been an external side—e.g. the suspension of sense-life by entrancement, thus securing the subject from one source of intrusion. It should be observed that I mention a bare possibility and am not offering a hypothesis.

[2] Balthazar Corderius, a notable Greek scholar of his period, was born at Antwerp in 1592 and died in 1650. He was professor of theology at Vienna. In addition to other Greek fathers, he edited the Dionysian texts, by which he will be always remembered.

and is completed by intimate union with God—meaning that it is the science of experience attained in Him and is not of speculation or external dogma. In other kinds of theology the man who is inspired divinely appears as instructor in sacred things, but here "the doctor and rector of the Divine Oracles" is Divine Silence, or God Himself joined with deepest peace and stillness of the soul.[1] It is evident that between St. Maximus and Corderius there was a profound science of inward doctrine and experience growing up, of which the root was the Dionysian root, namely, that experience is the source of doctrine. We must go back upon the path that we have travelled to learn further concerning it.

Supposing, as a mere possibility which it might be perilous to entertain even tentatively, that the Dionysian writings were extant in the days of St. Augustine, it is certain that they were unknown to him, nor was the peculiar body of experience characterised as mystical theology more than implicit in his mind,[2] and then, I

---

[1] From the mystical standpoint, and taken within its own measures, it must be said that the definition is admirable. Corderius specifies also the nature of cognition, as it is understood in mystical theology; it is attained by intercourse (per copulationem) with God, all other cognition of things being abandoned—meaning for so long as the spiritual experience is sought and enjoyed. The annotations of Corderius follow the text of Dionysius in Migne's edition and are themselves followed by the paraphrase of Pachymeres.

[2] He speaks once in The City of God of "a holy conjunction with God," but it is in the sense of a state of grace, not certainly of the mystical union. He testifies to the way of the soul's freedom, but it is that of the ordinary Christian man, not the path of inward liberation. He describes the blessed state in the Eternal City, saying that he has beheld it intellectually; but it is the state of one who stands face to face with God—the Beatific Vision of Aquinas. And so external is his consideration that he discusses in all seriousness whether the saints shall continue to see God when the eyes of their risen spiritual bodies are shut and decides affirmatively, because of the eyes of the spirit.—See The City of God, Bk. X, c. 6; Bk. X, c. 23; Bk. XXXII, c. 29. St. Augustine died on August 28, 430, according to the Roman calendar.

9

think, as a mere vestige. He has been regarded as a witness, within certain limits, of mystical experience,[1] but I do not know in what sense, and of course it would be idle to look in his direction for any definition of the science. So late as the first half of the twelfth century, as much must be said of St. Bernard, who is also classed amongst mystics—mainly on certain evidences found in his treatise *De Consideratione* and in his sermons on *The Song of Solomon*. The truth is that mystical theology was only in the course of its development and at rather an early stage.[2] It is making some progress in Hugh of St. Victor,[3] the contemporary of St. Bernard, though it is held amidst the meshes of scholasticism, and it has reached no stage of definition either in him or his pupil and successor Richard of St. Victor—another master of contemplation.[4] It emerges with a fuller quality of light and clearness in St. Thomas Aquinas, one of whose distinctions concerns an important issue. He says: "That Knowledge which is called Mystical Theology

---

[1] He mentions the eye of the soul, as we have just seen, and, according to Vaughan, Hugh of St. Victor made this spiritual sense the "organ of his mysticism."—*Hours with the Mystics*, Vol. I, Bk. V, c. 2.

[2] At the same time, the Secret Mystical Tradition—if such there were—was passing out of mind.

[3] Hugh of St. Victor wrote a commentary on the Celestial Hierarchy of Dionysius and as it is not of undue dimensions it would have been well to include it in the comprehensive Codex of Migne, even at the risk of repetition when the time came—much later in the Migne series—to produce the whole works of the Victorine monk. I must not suggest that even the zealous reader should concern himself much with Hugh as a mystic, but there is an *Opusculum Aureum de Meditando* which is worthy of reference.

[4] In a supplement to his *Benjamin Major*, Lib. V, s.v. *Nonullæ Allegoriæ Tabernaculi Fœderis*, Richard of St. Victor gives us the benefit of his views on the mystical or hidden senses of Scripture. Between the historical and mystical sense there is a difference which is comparable to that between wood and gold. The prime place is occupied by the historical meaning. The mystical is tripartite and the ascending scale is (*a*) Tropological, (*b*) Allegorical, and (*c*) Anagogical. The Zoharic doctors did better when they discovered a sevenfold sense.

consists not in an operation of the intellect, but in an experimental act of love." St. Bonaventure, in whom mystical theology approaches a formal system, gives a succinct definition as follows : " Mystical theology is the drawing out of the soul in God through desire of love."[1] The two axiomatic statements belong one to another, shewing that there is an act on the part of man, an out-reaching of desire, and that it leads to a Divine Act, which is the drawing forth of the soul. Both are in agreement with Dionysian tradition, including its final development by Corderius, namely, that in so far as mystical theology comprehends a sum of doctrine, the source and evidence thereof are an interior state of the soul.

The secret world of relations between God and the soul was methodised exhaustively by Gerson, who defines mystical theology as " the experimental cognition of God by the comprehension of unitive love " ; and again as " the ensavoured "—i.e. realised or experienced— " conception, idea, or knowledge of God, while the supreme apex of affective power is truly united by love to Him."[2] This intellectual mystic was of the fourteenth

---

[1] The idea of love for God could never have been divided consciously from the idea of union with God, but it seems necessary, now that the word itself occurs for the first time in my text, to point out that neither in the Dionysian tract on Mystical Theology nor in the letters arising therefrom is there any of that insistence on Divine love which we find in other writings of the Areopagite. The exercises commended to Timotheus and the other recipients of communications are mystical contemplations in the undefined sense attaching to contemplations, and the final act is described as one of self-precipitation into the deeps of Divine Darkness, understood as a void in respect of images but the *plenum* of Godhead. The idea of love may have been regarded as too active and positive to connect with so inexpressible a state. I shall recur to this subject briefly in the next chapter.

[2] *De Mystica Theologia Speculativa*, 1748 (Tom. III, p. 384). Gerson says also that " it is the experimental and freely bestowed union or in-gathering of the humble in the mind of their heart with God."—*Ibid.*, Tom. IV, p. 341.

and fifteenth centuries; he was followed by Dionysius the Carthusian, sometimes called *Doctor extaticus*, though there was more than one claimant to the title, or—more correctly—it was imposed on more than one. He drew from the fountain of Dionysius Areopagiticus when he defined mystical theology as " a most ardent intuition of Divine Darkness."[1] It must be remembered that love is a dark state, till light comes in the union.

We are now on the threshold of a fruitful period, when names are illustrious and their number also is many. For St. John of the Cross, mystical theology is " the mysterious and supernatural knowledge of God," and " it is called contemplation by the spiritual,"[2] or " a loving waiting upon God." For Cardinal Bona, it is " the most secret discourse of the mind with God."[3] And as specimens of some later authorities, it is, according to Thomas a Jesu, " the experimental and free union or ingathering and exaltation of the humble in the mind of their heart with God."[4] According to Thomas a Vallgornera, " it is the most perfect and highest contemplation of God, the most fruitful and sweet love of Him in His intimate possession." But Philippus a Trinitate says that it is " a certain conception or realisation of God attained by union of the will in its cleaving to God."[5]

[1] *Opera*, Tom. XVI, p. 491.

[2] Quoted from *A Spiritual Canticle*, Stanza XXVII. We shall see that the word contemplation, as used by some mystics, calls to be understood in a particular sense, as indicated elsewhere by St. John of the Cross when he defines mystical theology as " infused contemplation, whereby God secretly instructs the soul in the perfection of love, without efforts on its own part beyond a loving attention to God."

[3] It was an experience therefore, as we see by the other testimonies, but was not its intellectual expression. Joannis Bonæ *Opera Omnia*, Antwerp, 1677. See *Via Compendii ad Deum*, cap. 3.

[4] Striking the keynote in chief of ascetical theology, Jacobus Alvarez says that its conditions are heroic abnegation and perfect mortification.

[5] So also Joannes a Jesu: " It is a certain most high experimental conception or cognition of God, whereby a peculiar and supreme action

The Title of the Quest

It follows from these citations, and would be exhibited yet more fully if they were extended further, that Dionysian Secret Doctrine—which was to be kept with anxious care from profane or unprepared persons—was a body of spiritual experience leading in realisation to a knowledge at first hand, which knowledge was designated ignorance as an illustration of the failure of language, but it was really an excess of science. In this dark-light it is idle to say that faith has not ceased—as it is understood commonly—and seeing that official theology is a body of doctrine based on faith, the denomination " mystical theology " is inapplicable in any literal sense. Therefore since the Latin of the schools was extended in every direction as the need of the schools occasioned, it is perhaps not a little surprising that no term was invented which would have been equivalent to our word " Mysticism." It was, I think, for want of this that *theologia mystica* continued to be used so long, though it seems to have applied so confusingly.[1] Whether the secret doctrine intimated by Dionysius was secret only because it dealt with inward experiences we do not know certainly ; but if it signified a peculiar and purposely hidden form of teaching and practice, subsisting side by

of the will with God is attained." Compare Antonius a Spiritu Sancto : " It is knowledge of God, but that knowledge consists essentially in contemplation of its object, not in an operation of will."—See Thomas a Vallgornera : *Quæst. Præmiali Theologiæ Mysticæ*, Art. 1 ; Philippus a Trinitate : *Discursus Præmiali*, Art. 1 ; Joannes a Jesu : *Scholia Orationis, Tractatus* XII, No. 2 ; Antonius a Spiritu Sancto : *Directorium Mysticum, Tractatus* I, Sectio 1, *Quid sit Theologia Mystica*. New edition, Paris, 1904.

[1] Scaramelli distinguishes between Experimental Mystical Theology and Doctrinal Mysticism. The one is a pure knowledge of God which the soul receives in the bright darkness of a certain very high contemplation, conjoined with an intimate experience of love, wherein it is lost to itself and transformed in God. The other consists in the criticism of mystical experiences and draws such conclusions as it can respecting their essential qualities and effects.

side with open and public teaching, the very interesting
question arises whether it was actually lost, or whether
it was preserved among a few and constituted a branch
of that secret tradition in Christian times the various
departments of which have been considered in some of
my previous books.[1] In the present place I put on record
the point only, because evidences or speculations on the
transmission of hidden knowledge are now beyond my
province.

The use of the term " mystical theology " passed over
to the non-catholic mystics, though it was employed
sparingly. I need give two examples only, independent
of date. It is specified by Robert Roach,[2] at the end of
the seventeenth century, as synonymous with Spiritual
Divinity. It is said to depend " more immediately on
the conduct and illumination of the Holy Spirit,"
operating on the soul (a) by the extirpation of evil and

---

[1] In that excellent work of compilation *A Manual of Mystical Theology*,
by the Rev. Arthur Devine, Passionist, this possibility is set aside at the
very beginning. "A person initiated into mysteries may be called a
mystic, and the science which treats of mysteries may be called mystical.
We must not suppose, from this acceptation of the word, that, when
'mystical' is applied to sacred science, there is in the Church of Jesus
Christ some occult science the secret of which is reserved to the initiated,
but that there is a science of the mysterious called mystical theology "
(p. 3). The reservation, if any, would be, however, a question of past
centuries and not of a secret doctrine subsisting at the present time.
Moreover, by an extraordinary want of insight regarding the *fons et origo*
of Mystical Theology, according to the chief deponents, this argument
misses the vital point of the mystical hypothesis, namely, that a knowledge, a doctrine, a theology is communicated by God in the mystical
states, and one which is deeper, more intimate than that which is attained
otherwise. There is no suggestion that it differs and the distinction may
mean only that it was a living realisation of truth, in place of a mental
comprehension; but we can well understand that it spelt danger to
official theology, and, while Dionysius was much too important to the
ecclesiastical system for it to be possible that he should be set aside as
a teacher of false doctrine, this distinction was tacitly ignored.

[2] See *The Imperial Standard of Messiah Triumphant*, p. 304.

(*b*) by leading to " Divine contemplation,[1] union and communion with God." Hereof are the power and the grace, but there is a practice involved also and a consequence, being " the rules, doctrines and experience of the most advanced spiritual Christians, both ancient and modern, in their process towards perfection." Roach adds that it is the same as to substance in writers of all ages. This is on one side, and on another the formula became among the few a denomination for cosmical systems, the fruit of personal revelations, like those of Jacob Böhme. Tracts on the eternal world, eternal Nature and her " seven essential forms," were included by Dr. John Pordage under the general name of *Theologia Mystica,* or Mystical Divinity.[2] As a rule, however, the post-Reformation schools in all their early stages were more concerned with the thing—as they understood it —than its name or definitions concerning it. But as time went on the variations of aspect began to call for new terminology, whether it was needed or not. The word " theosophy "—which is said to have originated in the school of Porphyry—stood with certain writers not only for theological science but for the practice of Divine union. In France, at the end of the eighteenth century, L. C. de Saint-Martin described mystical practice as " the way of reintegration ";[3] and about the same time M. Dutoit-Mambrini utilised " Mysticism " as a synonym

---

[1] Here most probably used in the sense of intellectual concentration on God and Divine Things.

[2] These also were a product of revelation, and Jane Lead testifies that Pordage was " caught up into the still eternity for several days together," writing subsequently of that which he saw and heard. She was a witness of his " wonderful transportations " of the spirit, " while his outward body lay in passive stillness in this visible orb." See the address " to the impartial and well-disposed reader," which forms Jane Lead's preface to *Theologia Mystica,* 1689.

[3] Saint-Martin derived the expression from his teacher Martines de Pasqually, whose *Traité de la Réintégration des Êtres* was published for the first time, at Paris, in 1899. It has, however, no concern with mystical practice.

of true quietism, though the word remained unrecog-
nised by the French Academy in 1814.[1] It was described
(*a*) as religion of the heart and of love, and (*b*) as life
inward, life concealed in God. Whether this is the first
use of the word Mysticism in French I am not prepared
to say; but unless within quite recent days catholic
writers in France have practically ignored it in favour of
la mystique, understood as the study of spirituality.[2] The
translation of Görres in 1854, the dictionary of Abbé
Migne in 1858, and the work of Ribet are notable cases
in point.[3] On the other hand, the independent philosophical mystic Récéjac uses the alternative word in
1897,[4] and I am inclined to speculate whether it was of
set purpose—to create a salutary distinction between
his comprehension of the subject and that of the opposite
school. The three other works which I have mentioned
are dedicated and over-dedicated to the wonder side—
the side of visions, locutions and auditions. *La Mystique*
indeed has been defined authoritatively as " the science
of the supernatural state of the human soul, manifested
in the body and in the order of things visible by effects
that are also supernatural."[5] Again, it is said that the

[1] See *La Philosophie Divine*. Par Keleph ben Nathan, i.e. Dutoit-
Mambrini, Tome II, p. 28. This work was published in 3 vols., 1793.

[2] So far back as 1732 the word *misticité* was invented or adopted as
a term of reproach and derision to characterise the so-called Quietism
of Madame Guyon. See the rare work entitled *Relation de l'Origine,
du Progrès et de la Condamnation du Quietisme*.

[3] *La Mystique Divine, Naturelle et Diabolique, par* Görres. *Ouvrage
traduit de l'Allemand par* M. Charles Sainte-Foi, 5 vols., 1854–55;
Dictionnaire de Mystique Chrétienne, 1851; *La Mystique Divine distinguée
des Contrefaçons Diaboliques et des Analogies Humaines, par* M. J. Ribet,
3 vols., 1883.

[4] *Essai sur les Fondements de la Connaissance Mystique, par* E. Récéjac,
1897. The author lays down that there must be recognised in Mysticism
a legitimate predominance of liberty over understanding and that the
substantive term Mystic must be applied only to those minds which have
sought the absolute outside dialectical ways.

[5] See the preface to *Dictionnaire de Mystique Chrétienne*.

question is one of evident, palpable facts, to be verified easily by the senses,[1] though it is admitted that the virtues of saints are to be admired above their prodigies.

To sum up at the risk of repetition, we know now that the formula " mystical theology " signified a life or practice which in a certain state of attainment infused into the soul a science or doctrine, being the knowledge of God in union. But seeing that no new truths or revelations concerning God were consequent upon the state, that which was reached—by the hypothesis—was simply a vital realisation of official doctrines. The " dilucid contemplation of the Trinity " adds nothing to our knowledge of the Trinity, so far as records are concerned.[2]

Having finished now with definitions of mystical theology, we must pause for a moment over those of the term Mysticism, but these are modern definitions. This is no day of masters, but we are made acquainted with certain aspects from which the subject is regarded by thinkers who have made it their study—as critics and students of literature, or as independent exponents. These are, I take it, the categories ; at least no one claims to speak with the authority which belongs to voices of the past bearing witness concerning the path from its furthermost points.

Let us note in the first instance how the subject stands now in the mind of the Latin Church. According to Devine, " Mysticism considered in its entirety forms a branch of theology, and understood in its general sense embraces all that part of the sacred science which expounds the principles and formulates the rules of

---

[1] *Ibid.* It follows that St. Catherine of Siena, St. Rose of Lima, Blessed Margaret Mary Alacoque, Maria d'Agreda and Jeanne Bénique Gojos, with a host of other ecstatics, are at the apex of mystical attainment for the purposes of the work in question ; and so they prove in its development.

[2] It would seem, therefore, that if " Mysticism " is confessedly a deficient term, " mystical theology " is scarcely less than a misnomer.

Christian perfection, or the supernatural life of the soul and its union with God."[1] As, however, he conceives that this statement may tend to an erroneous identification with ascetical theology, the writer adds — much after the mode of Scaramelli — that the mystical branch is divided into experimental, being the supernatural work of God in the soul, and doctrinal, being the sum of " facts and laws which accompany and regard these supernatural communications." In other words, it is the science of the path and term in Divine Union, and far as we may pursue researches I question whether we shall reach a more correct and axiomatic definition than I have attempted in these words.

Authorities might be multiplied indefinitely, but this will suffice, I think, for the Latin Church.[2] We may contrast, if we please, the alternatives of another useful compilation, that of Miss Evelyn Underhill, who says that Mysticism is the name given to an " organic process which involves the perfect consummation of the Love of God," or " it is the art of establishing conscious relation

---

[1] It is not a very good definition, because it ignores the Dionysian understanding of the term ; but it is just to add that no one in modern days seems to have realised its proper significance as a body of knowledge which, *ex hypothesi*, has arisen out of a body of practice.—*A Manual of Mystical Theology*, p. 5. It is certain that Christian mystical experience has never added one jot or tittle to the sum of Christian doctrine within the measures of the Latin Church. That which was imputed to be " the faith once delivered to the saints " would have been reduced or exceeded at the peril of any mystic. As it is, a certain extravagance of language brought trouble upon John the Scot and at a later period upon Eckehart.

[2] We may compare Dominic Schram, of the Benedictine Order— period 1668–1720—who says that Mysticism is a science proceeding, by means of things revealed, from God, through every grade of moral perfection, to an ever extending and ever deepening knowledge and love of God. It differs from scholastic theology because it is wholly practical and from moral theology because it is the practice of perfection. It is both science and wisdom.—*Institutiones Theologiæ Mysticæ ad usum Directorum Animarum*. Tomus I, § 1 : *Theologia Mystica Quid.*

with the Absolute." These affirmations are put forward as synonyms and one point of their agreement is that neither of the terms " consummation " and " relation " defines the nature of the union to which it refers.[1] When the first is used in respect of earthly nuptials it signifies something that is far from the mystical term, not by the nature of the act but because it is a shadow in realisation of that which the heart desires. The second may indicate kinship, or the kind of connection which subsists between the seer and the seen. It leads us, however, to another point of view, and one of marked interest because it is that of a rabbinical scholar who recognises the compatibility of Mysticism and Jewish theology.

Dr. J. Abelson defines Mysticism tentatively as " that phase of thought or feeling which tells us that God is a supreme, all-pervading, and all indwelling power in which all beings are one." We have here, within limits of a single formula, the doctrine (*a*) that God is transcendent—which is the idea implied by the word " supreme "; (*b*) is omnipresent—that is to say, " all-pervading "; and (*c*) is immanent—which is the idea implied by the term " all indwelling." The statement that all beings are one in His indwelling power is an equivalent of the old mystical doctrine that in Him we live, and move, and have our being. Dr. Abelson would probably allow that the latter is a much more exact form of the concept, as I feel that he is not using a familiar species of pantheistic terminology.[2] This be-

[1] See *An Introduction to Mysticism*, by Evelyn Underhill, 1911, p. 97. We may compare Eleanor C. Gregory's " Mysticism is the Science of a Hidden Life," which fails *qua* definition because it does not make clear that the " hidden life " is in God, though naturally this transpires from the context.—See *An Introduction to Christian Mysticism*, 1901.

[2] This is adopted continually by unaccredited mystical writers, but in the majority of cases owing to looseness of wording and inexactitude of thought.—See *Jewish Mysticism*, by J. Abelson, M.A., D.LIT., an article in *The Quest*, July, 1913. In a book under the same title, published a

comes evident indeed when the same writer says other-wise that " the mystic is conscious of God as an in-dwelling Father in his own soul, as an animant spirit of goodness in the world. His aim and purpose is to know this indwelling Father, to experience and realise this spirit of goodness, and by these means to unite himself to God in as close a bond as it is possible for any human being to effect." We have here exactly the kind of rela-tion of which Miss Underhill appears to speak—that of the Fatherhood of God and the sonship of all mankind. It may seem to define from outside rather than from within, but it is in particular consonance with the genius of Israel. There is, however, no question that the desire for the mystical union is for something much closer than any filial relation.[1] That is possibly the quality of remote consciousness which gives expression to the kind of rela-tion belonging to the life of the world—in so far as the world may be said to have any on the mystical subject of research. The realisation of its inadequacy impelled Christian Mysticism, by an imperious instinct, to sub-stitute the symbolism of nuptial alliance. Some Indian Mysticism has had the intention to go even further and has created, as we shall see, the Vedantic doctrine of identity, as if the nuptial union might be the *signum*

few months later, Dr. Abelson says that " the mystic knows God by contact of spirit with spirit; *cor ad cor loquitur*," p. 6. There is a more ambitious statement of the same position in an earlier work of this writer. " Mysticism, of whatever phase, must by its very nature be the most individualistic type of religion. The mystic believes in God not because he has been taught to believe in Him, whether by books or by men, but because he can experience God. . . . There is a contact between human spirit and Divine spirit."—*The Immanence of God in Rabbinical Literature*, 1912, pp. 340, 341.

[1] So also in Jewish theosophy of the Zoharic type there is the idea of an ineffable union to be consummated above, an union in the place of the highest and with the holiness of the world to come. Dr. Abelson recognises this and comments upon the importance assigned to love in the Zohar.

but that the *signatum* were behind and beyond. It has filled the world of thought with a great glory of paradox, but the instinct is a true instinct. The conclusion is that Dr. Abelson has given us some food for thought on the appeal and insufficiency of current valuations in respect of the whole subject.

Professor Rufus Jones says that "Mysticism is the type of religion which puts the emphasis on immediate awareness of relation with God, on direct and intimate consciousness of the Divine Presence."[1] Here the terms differ, though only in a slight degree, but the measure of conception is the same. It is still the idea of sonship and of a Father's presence. There is no question that the beginnings of experience are frequently of this order ; there is no question that such order is a notable characteristic of spiritual life in its more familiar grades ; and it is a definition therefore of these rather than of true Mysticism. The experience may proceed no further, yet is precious in its own degree. But a sense of the Presence is not the life of communion. And this leads me to say that not every one who dips into St. Thomas, *The Imitation*, Tauler, or *The Soul Contemplating God* and that Book of the Man from Frankfort which is called *Theologia Germanica*, has—for such reason—been enrolled in the great company, the choir of Christian mystics. So also there are many things which disclose a certain affinity with the term, though not actually belonging thereto. I wonder what would St. Thomas and what would Tauler, with the other admirable and illuminated doctors, think on their present thrones, "built beyond mortal thought, far in the unapparent," did we speak in their hearing of "the philosophy of things as they are and the science of life" under a broad denomination of Mysticism ? Yet it is of all truth that, in the proper understanding, these are in touch with the one subject which embraces all that is good and holy

[1] *Studies in Mystical Religion*, 1909.

in a world that is sealed with holiness and stayed up with graces of goodness.

A mystical book should be a Book of the End in God. The experience of approach to this end and the foretaste thereof, as it is possible to us here, have from their beginnings in Christian literature been qualified—as we have seen—by the term mystical. Their study in the modern world has been, however, more especially an intellectual pursuit, and consequent hereupon I believe that such experience has passed imperfectly enough into adumbration in literature. But even so it has carried on the saving intimations of that state in which it has been said that we walk no longer by faith only, but by sight also. It is understood here that faith is the great aid to vision ; but it presupposes that life which—in an old, comprehensive and ever-suggestive phrase—does come in fine to know concerning the doctrine. It is the glory of righteousness in this world and beyond ; it is the eternal rest in Buddha ; it is the knowledge of unity which, according to Krishna, is above wisdom ; it is the Sufic union of the lover and the beloved ; it is in a sense the Epiphany of Pythagoras, the vision from above, or alternatively the manifestation of the centre. It is the eternal repose and the essence, apart from mode, which all inward spirits have desired above all things. On one side of its realisation here, it is that which St. Thomas Aquinas terms a foretaste of the Beatific Vision. In its deeper states, it is an attainment of the Kingdom of Heaven ; it is Ruysbroeck's secret union of the soul with God. In the last resource, or final catholic reduction, it is an experience in consciousness of what it has not entered otherwise within the heart of man to conceive. It is because this, all this and more than all, is not of to-day only or yesterday, but *sicut erat in principio, et nunc et semper*, that Christianity has been always in the world, and looked at across the ages it seems to me that, *per omnia sæcula sæculorum,* it has grown from more to more.

When we dwell on it and would fain embrace it by apprehension, according to our various intellectual modes, we may be perhaps like the poet—that is, as one who should " sit and play with similes." We may be, in respect of it, like Sir Isaac Newton comparing himself to a child who gathers pebbles on the shores of a great ocean. If so, for these reasons and for others, it is right that we should call it what it is, a thing concealed and hidden, one also which passes very hardly, and then imperfectly, into expression. But if we have shared— ourselves—in any measures of the experience, having been strenuous followers of the path, we shall know much better—more intimately and directly—that it is secret, which is to say mystical, since it is neither given us to express nor convey—not even when it becomes our call to communicate. After all capacity of language that lies within us has been used and exhausted we shall have adumbrated and hinted only. It follows that the content is greater than the container in respect of the word Mysticism, as this is understood by us, and as all definitions of mystical theology prove. But to end these considerations in the sense of their beginning, a more commensurate word is wanting. So therefore, although I remember Thomas Vaughan and how he derided those who pinned, in his particular day, a specific and narrow name " to a science both ancient and infinite," we shall be content hereafter, as before, to be called Mystics and to speak of our science as Mysticism.

As against all lawful cause and reason, in a work on the Path and Term of Mysticism, it seems desirable to say one word in passing on the scheme of ascriptions passing under the names of occult science and philosophy, and on the thing called Magic, it must be explained that such need arises through mental confusions which have instituted, more especially during recent years, a multitude of false relations. Some distinction must be made in the first place between two departments of notions which are classed under the same denomination. There is, firstly, the popular idea of Magic, which regards it as a chain of occurrences postulated in the absence (*a*) of an adequate cause,[1] or (*b*) of any known cause at all. The second notion may be characterised broadly as a recognition of manifest effects the causes of which are hidden and unknown. The first view contains, by implication at least, a rough canon of criticism, namely, that works called magical are either trickery or lying inventions. As such, they are outside our province. The second is a vague generalisation and can only be made subject to reference when it is brought down within rigid limits, for example, if we understand Magic—hypothetically or otherwise—as a practice of dealing with spirits, producing effects by their intervention, with all that follows in a long series and arises from this idea. I affirm that the mystical path and term have no connection with operations of this kind, even if it can be supposed that they are veridic under any circumstances.

But if it be said that, in virtue of the word and its root-meaning, Magic means hidden wisdom, then I register as beyond controversy that it should never be used in this sense, owing to its abuses through the centuries.[2] Apparent justifications in philology count

[1] Conjuring is the apparent production of such phenomena, but in this case there is of course an adequate cause, resident in the skill of each artist.

[2] It is said for example that the Greek term μαγεία signifies *ars sapientiæ*, and Éliphas Lévi talked much in this strain, when he did not happen to be denouncing the occult sciences of which he claimed to have the key. The stock argument is, however, based on μάγος, held to be the equivalent of a Persian title signifying one who is wise. Subsequently the Greek word fell into corruption, and came to mean *prestidigitator*, sorcerer, etc. The question is not worth debating intrinsically, but unfortunately the Paracelsus atmosphere in which Jacob Böhme lived led him to discourse too frequently of a higher and a lower *Magia*, which

nothing in such a connection, because the wrested meaning has become ingrained in the general conscience. As a fact, the word Magic is never in these days regarded as an equivalent for wisdom, whether open or concealed, except by those who are working, of set purpose, to confuse the issues—as, for example, to introduce astral phenomena under the pretence that they are a part of Mysticism.

One distinction between psychism and Mysticism is that psychical experience is sought in the world of images, while that of true Mysticism is in the deep which " gives up no form." The psychic would exhaust this world and then imagine a new. The way in which he is dissatisfied with seeing and is not filled with hearing is that he seeks to vary the mode, to increase influx and output. But we must be disentangled from analogies of sense-impressions and experience before we can reach reality.

For those who are outside the threshold, some experiences which are the subject of Mysticism may seem a rare and wonderful kind of madness. But seeing that the mystic is not as such concerned with psychical de-

Edward Taylor explains to be " one of the unity, the other of the multiplicity, or of the astral powers." Neither seems to have had any connection with evocation of spirits, necromancy and so forth. Böhme supposed further that there were two Magi in man, one being the Spirit of God and the other reason, into which the spirit of evil insinuates itself with fatal facility. This kind of terminology is purely fantastic.—See *Jacob Behmen's Theosophick Philosophy Unfolded.* By Edward Taylor, 1691. The Teutonic Theosopher's successors and disciples spread the notion of a Higher Magia. Its influences are in the English semi-mystical literature of the Philadelphian School, in Saint-Martin, under a transforming mist; but they are, in a sense, unmasked by Mambrini. Saint-Martin speaks of a Divine Magic, but Mambrini, who had an almost exaggerated horror of animal magnetism, somnambulism and other phenomena of his period—notwithstanding the fantastic spirit which I have mentioned—never uses the term. The explanation is that in his times of clear sight, or when he was disembarrassed of the inner meaning of Scripture, he had true conceptions of the mystical end.

velopments or processes, of what kind soever, it is only in aberration from the path that he enters regions of mischance and loses mental balance. To all dwellers on the outskirts it may be added that the great experiences occur in a preoccupation of consciousness which is as far removed from normal modes of emotion and thought-processes as eyes which look on Heaven are different from those eyes that are dark for ever.

For the rest, concerning putative paths of power and distracted paths of research which are classified heterogeneously under the name of occult science, and how it can be shewn that these are no paths at all, I have said sufficient[1] in other works, and I need only refer to these. It is no part of my present design to dwell upon the secrets of the abyss or on the veiled doctrine of the second death. In the alleged masters of the evil path I believe as much and as little as in other inventions which have been brought out from the Pandora's box of modern occult speculations. But I know that there is a mystery of the will in separation, as there is a mystery of the will in union.

There are, however, comparatively few mental confusions and derangements which cannot be traced to some fact that is undisputed within its own measures. All those external manifestations of abnormal power which are among the chief concerns of occultism testify that the incorporation of man's self-knowing part in the flesh of his humanity is an accident of time and that he belongs to another order than the world of material manifestation. So also the mystical knowledge testifies that the spirit returns to God, from Whom it came forth originally. The mystery of experience in the annals of all sanctity is the proof of this fundamental axiom.

[1] In this connection I should like—a little against my usual sense of fitness—to refer my readers to an introduction prefixed to *The Book of Ceremonial Magic*, 1911. I believe that I have borne true testimony therein.

There is only one religion of humanity which corresponds to the truth of these things, and it is that which shews forth the practical process of our return to the home of the spirit.

I have mentioned elsewhere in this work the evidence of psychical research on certain questions of fact. When it is kept within its own measures such evidence is of vital import and value.[1] The chief danger lies in the false inferences which tend to be drawn from subjective experience of this order, while as an inquiry into the possible survival of this world in that which is beyond, the research is against reason, by the nature of things. Unhappily, for the increase of our difficulties, there is overmuch image-making even in the mystical life. The visions, the locutions, the auditions, and so forward, of real and imputed sanctity have done much to justify the notion, held too generally by sincere persons who do not realise the consequences, that occult and psychical activities may not be far removed from the mystical work. Apart from the marshalling of evidence and counter-evidence, we shall see as we proceed in our quest how these things stand as the poles asunder. We shall clear in this manner many spaces once filled with noise and confusion, when there will be so much the more room for God to come down and dwell in our hearts.

I have endeavoured in this chapter to give—for the first time—a true account of our titles on the basis of history. It could have been carried further, but the multiplication of authorities certifying to the same effect would only encumber the pages. That which is much

---

[1] To the mystic it is of course of no value whatever, of no import; his knowledge is from another source, and it comes by another path. He has no need of the soul's manifestations externally, by the way of what is called power, who has the higher certitudes of the soul within. But the evidence counts for those on the quest of evidence—or of the truth that the world of physics does not comprehend the all of possible human experience on this plane.

more important than any external question is the fact that certain citations, while serving our purpose in the present inquiry, are pregnant with meaning as to the real nature of the mystical work. I must not forestall the chief concern of my research, but the reader will do well to bear a few points in mind for future reference. According to St. Thomas, mystical knowledge is attained as the result of an experimental act, which according to Joannes a Jesu is one of the human will. But St. Bonaventura intimates that there is a corresponding Divine act, and Joannes defines the work as an interaction between the will of man and the Will of God. The ecstatic doctor is saying the same thing when he affirms that the soul is " drawn out in God." The intimations concerning this action and interaction have to be traced through the records of the whole chain of witnesses, for herein is the title in chief of our own quest. It will be found that the denomination " mystical " which qualifies the word " theology," as used by Dionysius and others, is further illustrated in the light of the experimental act. The theology is secret because it belongs to a direct knowledge infused or acquired as the result of a state which has put an end to the separation between subject and object. It is to the actual realisation of this state that all true mystical literature offers its testimony, but—as I have hinted in my preface— there is a cloud over the memorials, for which we must account also, so that the nature of the state does not emerge fully.

CHAPTER II

CONCERNING INEFFABLE EXPERIENCE

As the nature of the present inquiry differs from
other studies with which I am acquainted in the
same department of spiritual research, our first concern is to form as clear an apprehension of the end
attained by Christian mystics as the nature of the
circumstances will permit virtually, though of necessity
in general and unprecise terms. I have intimated
that, like other first-hand experience in consciousness,
mystical attainment has the usual ineffable characteristics and *qua* the experience itself is essentially incommunicable. That which remains for our estimation
is, therefore, its intellectual side, or whatsoever has
been affirmed concerning it by those who claim the
experience, and this I shall attempt, though it can be
at best but in a summary fashion, for the purpose of
certain chapters, tracing the testimonies through the
centuries and leaving things belonging to the sphere of
detail—if their treatment should prove necessary—
until a later stage. Supposing that there are variations
in the testimony, we may be able to distinguish certain
degrees in the experience; if there be anywhere radical
distinctions, we must seek a canon of criticism as regards
truth and values. We shall look to reach a first rule for
our guidance as to the status of several schools in Western
Mysticism; and at the close of our study we shall be
in a position to determine that which the experience,
taken on its own warrants, has reflected into the minds of

recipients, according to a common agreement, and that which it reflects into our own.

In stating that the experience is accepted on its own warrants, I am not designing to do more than postulate that there is a cumulative evidence of fact by which the inquiry is justified. It belongs to a much higher category than a personal conviction of my own, based on the consideration of years, though such a conviction counts as regards the genesis of the present research, which would not take place in its absence. *Mutatis mutandis*, in the matter of terms of description, modifications through particulars of mental environment, and so onward, the experience is everywhere in the world, across the ages and civilised nations. It may even be true to add that at this day, here " in the foremost files of time," its rumour awakens deeper echoes, hopes, longings and foresights more generally than ever. I also—if it be tolerable so to say—am pursuing no scholastic debate, for in the heart and the heart of hearts I can bear my testimony at need to the living presence of a witness.

It is assumed therefore that the mystical experience— and I am speaking here of that which is carried to its term, or so far as any witnesses have come back to testify —is veridic in its surface aspects and that it is not a mere pathological condition.[1] It is further not psychical

---

[1] Dean Inge affirms on the contrary that " it is more than doubtful whether the ecstasy, which the mystics valued as an anticipation of the beatific vision, is anything more than a proof of the wise maxim . . . that to strive to pass beyond reason is to fall outside it."—*Personal Idealism and Mysticism*, 1907, p. 13. It is not of my purpose to discuss here the comparative values of positions that differ radically. I note only that, according to St. Teresa, the state of ecstasy is beyond the state of union, and we shall see that in its proper understanding neither belongs to the Thomist mode of beatitude called the Vision, the condition which I have described otherwise as symbolically that of eye to eye. Rapture is the deepest state of which Christian Mysticism offers any record, and if—by possibility—it falls outside reason, in the sense of being beneath it, I must confess to some personal difficulty in understanding what purpose it

experience commonly so called, though it may be
undeniable that such adventures of the soul in a subjective world of images have served on occasion to open
those doors that lead to the inward life and its holy
places of consciousness. As regards the second of these
postulates, there is much that passes as Mysticism under
the ægis of the Latin Church which never emerges
beyond this penumbra of the threshold. We have seen
as much in a summary form already, when citing certain
text-books issued with authority in great theological
series, or bearing the *imprimatur* of one and another
examiner in high theological places ; such productions
have every title to rank among by-words of intellectual
research, and have served to distinguish *la mystique*,
with its connections, from the science of Mysticism.[1]

can serve any one to take Mysticism as his province. Pathology is an
empiricism and not a criterion.—See, however, Dr. Inge's *Studies of
English Mystics*, c. 1, on "Mysticism and Morbidity." After long study
of the records, I can find no ground (*a*) in philosophy, (*b*) in pathology,
or (*c*) in practical life for speaking of the state signified by mystical
attainment as delusion, or for distrust of the records which have been
left us thereupon, so far as points of fact are concerned. After what
manner we may be led to understand them on our own part is obviously
another question. So also the past aspects of interpretation are excepted
from the present recognition as regards the point of fact. About these
there is no criterion of certitude, because there is no common agreement.
St. Catherine of Siena and the visible stigmatics suggest pathological
conditions, though these are belied in the first case by her great political
aptitude ; but Ruysbroeck on the infinite sea, St. John on the summit of
Carmel, and the few who passed behind that veil which is called The
Cloud of Unknowing are beyond pathological categories, and deception
or self-deception would seem to have no part in them.

[1] The distinction between psychism and Mysticism will appear as
we proceed, and there is no call to anticipate. Psychism is the translation
of spiritual experiences and spiritual truths in the terms and phenomena
of sense—that is to say, by visions, locutions, auditions and tactions. It
is indispensable that a hard-and-fast line should be drawn round the
whole series, for, in the criticism of mystical experience, there could be
no more misleading distinction than that which the Roman Church
would make between the so-called astral experiences of modern psychics
and those, e.g., of St. Catherine of Siena, to whom Christ discoursed the

Neither the good nor the evil of these things is, however, on one side only. There are vacant formulæ and shibboleths, reveries and fantasies without end, in modern extra-Latin circles, which have come out of paths of experiment followed here and in America—notably under the guise of "new thought"—and which are like keys for opening doors into every kind of transcendental and inward folly. There is talk of "going through" in these days and there is talk of the "real experience," but one asks dubiously enough—What is the basis of it all? So remote from right thinking in the normal mind, so free from all seals of sanctity, it is difficult to believe that it represents anything but fantasy belonging to the flimsiest order. To say nothing of sanctity beyond citing the name, such pursuits are apart even from elementary devotion, and those who have graduated therein are no more entitled to a hearing on any matter of the spiritual life than the crowds who stand at the gates and look up to them for guidance.

These things are mentioned only for the purpose of setting them aside as no part of our concern—which is solely with the records of the past and that which follows from these. The true memorials of the mystical term fall under two classes, of which the first belongs to the experience itself, as delineated by those who went through it, while the second is the consideration thereon, set forth by them and by others. As such, it is a catholic and indeed a Latin research, or it will remain to be seen in a separate section whether non-catholic schools, actuated by motives and moving in intellectual regions which the Reformation had thrown open, have contributed anything to the subject. In the second class which I have mentioned there are those who have dealt with the records and have reduced mystical history

higher language of Vaticanism and whom He betrothed to Himself, using a psychic ring as the gage.

and literature into a more or less exact science, theologically understood.[1] They are not so very many and they have done an important work, but—except incidentally—they do not call for consideration in the present study, which is based on experience at first hand. We must seek on our own part to interpret the nature of the experience according to our highest lights, that which is involved therein and that which follows therefrom. We are undertaking in this manner a philosophical experiment, which demands precision and clearness in all that it is sought to formulate.

While the testimonies which have been left by those who have reached the mystical term are obviously our sole guides, we are faced by the initial difficulty, about which I have made a bare statement, apart from elucidation or commentary. It is held by many of the deponents and—I think—by all the scholiasts that the experience is ineffable, and this means—according to some modern criticism—that its reduction through the centuries into a long succession of memorials has provided a large literature but no certain guides. Indeed the question arises whether there are guides at all[2] and whether our

---

[1] The scholiasts and commentators must remain at their individual values, and there are naturally great distinctions. In their several grades they also are witnesses standing in the path of sanctity. *Theologia Mystica* of Dominic Schram, *Directorium Mysticum* of Antonius a Spiritu Sancto and the work of Scaramelli are invaluable text-books.

[2] Professor Wilhelm Windelband, writing in *The Quest* quarterly magazine for January, 1913, seems to answer in the negative, for he holds that Mysticism is possible as the "intuitive experience of the individual," but impossible as a scientific doctrine, at least in any positive respect, because the mystic can only seek expression in categories which have been rejected as insufficient. The late Professor James had affirmed some years previously that the "incommunicableness of the transport is the keynote of all Mysticism."—See *Varieties of Religious Experience*, ed. of 1913, p. 405. So also Sir Frederick Pollock, in *The Hibbert Journal*, October, 1913, agrees that mystical experience transcends dialectic, and that its logical definition is not therefore to be expected, though it need not be illusory because it escapes analysis.

proposed examination is not stultified at its very inception. In modern terminology, the alleged failure is due to limitations of the logical faculty. Of late years we have loaded this particular scapegoat with many burdens of the Israel of our nature, in addition to those which it may be entitled to bear lawfully, and it is desirable to relieve it when a valid opportunity offers. It is not to be pronounced guilty on this side of mystical experience. If we take this even in its most moderate aspect and describe it, with Professor Rufus Jones, as "immediate awareness and intimate consciousness" of God, it is obvious that such a condition of our inward nature can be named and may be thereby defined clearly in language of rational understanding, but the state which the words postulate cannot be itself communicated. He who tastes and sees that the Lord is sweet may bear witness to that sweetness but cannot thereby enable others to see or taste. You cannot impart an idea of the sky's blueness to a man born blind, nor can you convey a realisation of the event called nuptial intercourse to him who is an eunuch from birth.[1] You may set the heart

---

[1] The best illustration is one which I have given—overfrequently, if that indeed were possible—in my other writings, namely, the impossibility of imparting to Wordsworth's typical Peter Bell the conception that a "primrose by the river's brim" is more than a "yellow primrose." Compare the almost unknown but deeply spiritual writer Francis Rouse who, nearly three centuries ago, made use, as I have ascertained since, of my own analogy in the text above. "The true knowledge of the sweetnesse of God is gotten by tasting, and therefore taste first, and then see how sweet and gracious the Lord is. The taste of it will truly tell him that tasteth it, how sweet it is ; but he that knoweth this sweetnesse by tasting it cannot deliver over the full and perfect image of this sweetnesse to him that hath not tasted it."—*The Mysticall Marriage*, ed. of 1635, pp. 51, 52. We may compare Van Helmont, though he spoke only at a distance concerning the high quests. "There is another way of perceiving God in man's mind than that which is merely intellectual in the understanding, which, when it is felt, the mind loseth itself in the perception of a sweetness which is altogether incomprehensible and therefore inexpressible, and doth not proceed from man's

longing in either case, but you cannot satisfy the heart, and the persons specified are incompetent to pronounce an opinion upon the experiences here named. Two of these illustrations are matter-of-fact comparison drawn from things sensible and one of them is of the spiritual order, in part to establish their analogy and otherwise to indicate that states mystical are not only things of exotic sensation.[1] Their design is to place the mystical experience outside all canons of criticism on the part of those to whom it is an unknown region, while at the same time they indicate the true significance which attaches to the word ineffable in respect of mystical things. All first-hand experience is ineffable, and the statement applies to mental realisations as to those of a sensible order. The condition described by Pascal as " God known of the heart " is neither less nor more essentially undemonstrable to him who knows nothing of God than would be the heat and astringency of mustard to one who has never eaten it. The attainment of realised certitude in one of the two cases may be indefinitely more difficult than in the other, but the ground for challenging the alleged attained certitude must be sought elsewhere than in (*a*) difficulty, (*b*) rareness, or (*c*) impossibility of imparting it to the inexperienced. Where it is to be sought is not of my especial concern and, if anywhere, may be left to those who would find it. On the side of defence, the main appeal lies in the perpetuity, unanimity and extent of the evidence, and

own will, or from himself, but purely and alone from God, and surpasseth all understanding."—*Paradoxical Discourses*, Part II, c. 4.

[1] Compare the Rev. A. B. Sharpe, in *Mysticism : Its True Nature and Value*, c. III, 1910. " Sensation is incapable of being defined or proved ; the one thing that we know about it is that it occurs. Whatever the conditions may be and whether there is an adequate cause present or not, the one indubitable fact in sensation is the certainty of the experience." He proceeds to affirm that the case is the same with the mystic. The comparison misses its effect because it is expressed a little lamely, but the writer is seeking to say that which I have defined above.

in the character of the deponents thereto. This notwithstanding, it is and will remain unacceptable to persons who have no faculty for its conception or inward maintenance, and with them the hindrance must be left, as something to be expected antecedently. I suppose that if the vast majority of men were in a state of congenital blindness or sexual inhibition, any small percentage who had realisation after these manners might be held to demand examination for the diagnosis of their pathological condition.

I have now dealt with one side of the initial difficulty, and that which has been set for consideration may enable us at a later stage to discern what faculties of an inward kind are at work in transcendental experience, as also that the modes and ways—whatever their difficulties— are much nearer to comprehension than is thought by persons who do not realise with Khunrath that " simplicity is the seal of Nature and Art." But having found that the fact of its ineffability serves to place mystical experience in an universal category of experience and not in any isolated or rare position, there remains another side of the subject, which is the value of the records concerning it from a representative point of view. If the state of mystical attainment is not uncommon because it is ineffable, there is no question that it is very rare in occurrence and consequently transcends all general experience. There is no question that it must be proportionately difficult of intelligible delineation, however indirectly, in the formulæ of language. In addition to general *impedimenta* respecting powers of expression which constitute the age-long warfare of intellectual and literary life, there are particular *impedimenta* in respect of the subject. That which follows is a certain cryptonomy of the memorials, distinguished, however, from conscious obedience to the counsel *celare verbum*, characteristic of records belonging formally to the Secret Tradition in Christian Times.

Concerning Ineffable Experience

The reduction of the experiences into their lowest simplicity of terms and the attainment of their mean or harmony will afford in my opinion a way of escape from this difficulty as to matters of central fact. We shall find that one testimony is in reality given hereto and as to all that stands around it of detail and discussion, it is there—if anywhere—that we must look for errors, contradictions and sins against logical understanding; it is there too that we must locate the hindrances to which many memorials confess. In so far as the mystics testify to bare facts which have entered within their experience, they are at one with themselves and each other. The further that they enlarge thereon, the more liable they are to differ and to err. It follows that if we postulate the peculiar mode of attainment comprehended by innumerable delineations of the mystical term as a possibility of conscious life, we have guides respecting its nature; that at the least we are warranted in conceding a conditional place to their testimony for the old reason—*quod semper, quod ubique, quod ab omnibus;* and that this is the limit of reasonable expectation, as no one looks for unerring leadership in fields of criticism and debate. There is evidence among the masters themselves that ineffability was regarded as a hindrance to the communication of the experience *per se,* but not to the definition of its nature. Had it been otherwise, they would have differed from St. Paul, who entered the third heaven and experienced things that it was unlawful for man to read, not things which he could not utter. But they went also further and felt themselves competent to undertake elaborate intellectual discourses on that which was realised in their states of attainment, as well as on the conditions which led up to these. The result was often an attempted expression in directions where the better counsel might have been one of silence. Those who confess to mystical experiences in our own days go as far, or further, and fail more utterly. Having

certified to the insufficiency of rational understanding,
their reports, rumours and diagnoses of states, their
speculations as to what is involved thereby, doctrinally
and theosophically, are repeatedly an insult to the
logical faculty and create a very clear impression in the
critical mind that they are beneath, not above, that
faculty, as Dr. Inge would put it. If the old masters
fail to satisfy us, at least they do not offend, or their
offence is after another manner. It might be injudicious
to suggest that modern adventures in spiritual realms
are in a greater difficulty than some of the old travellings,
for as language becomes more plastic in our hands so it
appears weaker and is less representative in kind. The
explanation is rather that those who went upon the
quest in former days were comparatively of undivided
minds, but these are seldom dedicated to the task
amidst the fritterings of manifold interests and en-
thusiasms at the present time. There are also no masters
of sentences. The feeling of impotence to express
truth as it is realised seems to be more especially a
modern difficulty. Once it was unknown in the East,
and if in the days of great records the West felt it
occasionally, it was not in our own degree. One's
sympathy is with the modern experience, because it is
true at the heart, and all of us bear our witness. As
poets we fall short of our standards ; and the mystic in
literature is nowadays like the poet in literature, with a
living and awakened consciousness, everywhere passing
into expression and yet not more than approximating.[1]

[1] Compare Father Faber's " original dedication to *Sir Lancelot*, 1844."

> " The murmurs of my song
> In refluent waves were dying on my ear,
> The spoken music blending with the thrills
> Of that unuttered sweetness which remains
> A cherished refuse in the poet's soul,
> Still to distinguish him from all the hearts
> To which, by love constrained, he hath resigned
> So much of his interior self."

Concerning Ineffable Experience

But I think that—also like the poet—he can quicken those who are capable of quickening. To conclude therefore, confessions of failure—as in, e.g., *Theologia Germanica*—[1] are like the poet's confessions ; we must be content with that which mystics can tell us on the simple facts of experience and deal as we may with the rest, knowing that a voice answering within some of us concurs with the general voice of testimony.

Now, the nature of the mystical term has been indicated broadly by the definitions of the previous chapter, which were summarised in a single sentence when I described mystical theology as the science of the path and term in Divine Union.[2] The word " union " was used in its plenary sense and not in that of the authorities who say—as we have seen—that beyond the state which it indicates there is another that is called rapture.[3] It is obvious that, in the fulness of meaning belonging to the word itself, union—being union—has nothing conceivable beyond it, though within it there is perhaps conceivably a deep below the deep.[4] It should be understood, however, that the old

[1] It is said that the state of a man who follows the mystical life and light to the utmost of his power can never be declared aright, " for he who is not such a man can neither understand nor know it, and he who is, knoweth it indeed; but he cannot utter it, for it is unspeakable." *Theologia Germanica,* translated by Susanna Winkworth, c. xxi, ed. of 1874, p. 65.

[2] I have said elsewhere that Mysticism is the term of union by the path of love.

[3] The following distinction is made by a modern French writer, the Abbé Lamballe : Ecstasy is superior to union because (*a*) the external senses are more dead ; (*b*) the interior senses are more absorbed ; and (*c*) the mode of contemplation is more perfect. It seems certain that he is speaking of a deeper state of union, as he also should recognise, seeing that he says elsewhere, with much truth and precision, that " in the state of union there is an almost incalculable variety of shades of difference."—*Mystical Contemplation,* translated by W. H. Mitchell, M.A., 1913, pp. 181, 177.

[4] As a fact, some of the commentators on mystical states have been led to distinguish between ecstasy and rapture, as between two grades

masters were speaking of a state reached in this life
and not of an eternal mode of unearthly beatitude.
There is always a very careful distinction in this respect ;
and I suppose that when the late compiler Scaramelli
speculated whether God has been ever seen face to face
in this life, or without a veil, and when he left the
question undetermined, observing only that—if possible
—it was exceedingly rare, he went further—all his
caution notwithstanding—than would be suffered by
doctrinal teaching, and further also than most mystical
authorities would countenance.[1]

of the same interior mode.—See Antonius a Spiritu Sancto : *Directorium
Mysticum*, Tract. IV, Disp. I, Sect. XII, N. 95. The doctrine of ecstasy
came from the School of Alexandria and the nature of that experimental
act which it sought to explain was one of deification attained by love in
its most exalted degree of energy and purity. " By the property of love
the lover and beloved are identified ; by that of ecstasy, or supreme love,
man is identified with the absolute goodness, that is to say, with God
Himself."—See Vacherot, *Hist. Critique de l'École d'Alexandrie*, Tome
III, pp. 432 *et seq*. This doctrine and the practice to which it belongs
were connected with Empedocles, Pythagoras and Plato by means of
apocryphal writings produced in the Alexandrian Schools and known at
this day only through Arabian channels.—See the *History of Philosophical
and Religious Sects*, by Mo'hammed Al-Schahrestâni, who died in 1153.
The Arabic text was edited by the Rev. William Cureton, 2 vols., 1842,
1846, and Haarbrucker published a German translation at Halle, 1850,
1851.—There are strange things also in the apocryphal *Book of Theology*
ascribed to Aristotle, especially concerning the union of souls with the
Divine Word.—See St. Thomas Aquinas, *De Unitate Intellectus*, from
which it follows that he had seen the original Greek text. A Latin
translation, made from an Arabic version, appeared at Rome in 1519.

[1] The question is discussed also by F. Antonius a Spiritu Sancto, who
says that many doctors have decided that, in this life, no form of contemplation can produce a clear and intuitive sight of God. He adds,
however, on his own part : *Ego tamen existimo, dari posse in hac vita per
modum transitus quidditativam Dei visionem*, citing the case of Moses,
with whom God spoke mouth to mouth, and that of the prophet Elias,
who—according to the tradition of the writer's Carmelite Order—beheld
the Divine Essence *per modum transeuntis, non tamen per modum per-
manentis*, which is the privilege of the Blessed.—*Directorium Mysticum*,
ed. of 1904, pp. 333-335.

Concerning Ineffable Experience

I mention this matter because it seems to me that, at the beginning of our subject, a word ought to be said on that which, according to higher Christian eschatology, is reserved by God for those who love Him within the measures of such ordinary righteousness as *ex hypothesi*—and after purgatorial searchings—entitles the Christian to salvation. I am not of course intending to speak of any conventional glory and joy belonging to an " eternity of antheming," for these things have passed with protestantism. The term of redemption according to official doctrine of the one type which enters into consideration—I mean, that of the Latin Church—is the Beatific Vision, and had the poet whom I have quoted known, it offered him that " nearer insight into heaven " for which he was asking in one memorable verse.[1] This doctrine represents the highest conception of an everlasting bliss-state which has entered into the heart of Christendom at large concerning that which confessedly it has not entered into any human heart to conceive—apart from mystical experience. It is not the mystical doctrine of union ; on the other hand, it is assuredly that of rapture. It puts an end once and for all to the distinction between rapture and union— in favour of the former state—to which I have referred, or it reverses the order of succession.[2] In so far as it

[1] " O for a nearer insight into heaven,
  More knowledge of the glory and the joy
  Which there unto the happy souls is given,
  Their intercourse, their worship, their employ ;
  For it is past belief that Christ hath died
  Only that we unending psalms may sing ;
  That all the gain death's awful curtains hide
  Is this eternity of antheming."—T. Lynch.

[2] It is just to add that the mystical writers, more especially the makers of formal treatises which are of doctrine rather than experience, are for the most part opposed to the position which I have taken up, holding that the kind of union signified by a descent of God into the soul and a

41

represents—which it does at least occasionally—the local congregation of a great multitude that no man can number in a collective act of worship about a Great White Throne, so far the Vision is not a plenary symbol. It has much deeper intimations regarded as the beatitude of each individual soul in the state of eye to eye. The doctrine is in St. Thomas, and it reached an unexampled height of literary expression in the Paradise of Dante.

The panegyric of this authorised term of salvation is found everywhere in devotional books. Many of the greater mystics have written of the Blessed Vision in the terms of Divine Union by an intellectual confusion, the source of which is not very far to seek, for if such vision, by the hypothesis, produces an everlasting rapture of the soul, then the soul is in that state when it can be scarcely conceived as making conscious distinctions between subject and object. Yet intellectually the distinction remains. There are lesser writers of the mystical type by whom it is so described—unwittingly—as to accentuate that which obtains in the sense of difference or disparity, as—for example—Gerard of Zutphen. " Consider . . . how great a joy it is to look upon God for ever in very essence, to gaze with pure eyes of the heart upon the Most High and Undivided Trinity. . . . In this vision thou shalt see all things and know all that thou wilt ; by this thou shalt be filled with all good, all gladness and all joy ; in this blessed shalt thou be and shalt enjoy the Most Supreme Blessedness, which is God." This, as it is presented to my own mind, seems not less far from the mystical term, as the latter is understood in these pages, than is separation

sense of His immediate presence precedes Divine Vision. *Ad visionem beatificam prærequiritur, ut Deus illabatur in intellectum lumine gloriæ dispositum ac elevatum, ut sic ipsum in tueatur immediate præsentem, et voluntas ei per amorem fruitivum suaviter adhæreat.—Directorium Mysticum*, p. 8.

from union.[1] We have to make, however, the following important qualification, which may help to reconcile some mystics with themselves and one with another: While, on the one hand, there is the Blessed Vision and while there is otherwise the Divine Union, there are veridic analogies between them, because the eye which sees is the eye of entire consciousness; but if words hold their proper meaning undisturbed, the Vision is not the Union. The latter may, however, be a state beyond the Vision, so that they do not exclude one another: the Vision may be the final unification and transfiguration of all the images before they dissolve. According to Suso, it is the soul's repose in an ocean of infinite happiness.

The canon of distinction established in this chapter seems to me so important that I should have expected it to have been formulated previously. The word ineffable is otherwise of signal interest and importance in connection with the palmary secret of the mystical work. If that which has been called " the rapture of wedded love " exceeds verbal communication for those to whom the mystery of sex has never opened its doors, how much more is that love inexpressible that has taken its object into itself, or—*vice versa*—into which the self has been withdrawn by the object, so that there is a stillness of perfect union, in which " God is all in all." The substituted unions of human life dissolve here in the promulgation of a more excellent way. We reach in this manner a general rule for our guidance hereafter as to the kind of faculty which operates in

[1] It matters little that the same writer, speaking of the Spiritual City, its jewelled buildings and gates of pearl, its flowers, odours and abundance of delectable things, reminds us that he is speaking by way of a sensible image, " which was devised by saints to suit our understanding." The images of mind are based on sensible images, and according to true Mysticism both have to be put away.—*The Spiritual Ascent*, translated by J. P. Arthur, 1908, pp. 46, 47.

transcendental experience. The end must be like the beginning and the beginning must shew forth the end in that life which is called mystical. It is union in both cases, as this is the quest and the keynote. The subject is love, the path and term are love. The gift of the mystical spirit is an act of indrawing the Object conceived in the mind so that it is cherished in the heart and comes to be known, which is realised, therein, according to the sense of Pascal. It is a work towards the attainment of a state, and this is a state of being. The Object abides within us and is no longer held in an image. Here is also a canon of distinction between the true school of the mystics and a multitude of lyceums in the courts about its sanctuary which it has been customary to class with the sanctuary, but they are of another order, concerned with offices and observances, promulgations of cosmic systems, interpretations of sacred texts, and so forth, including the endless work in psychic picturing. These things are curiously interesting and not without aspects of importance in their own way, but they are not of the one end. From one of their vantage points it may happen that we open a door and find a path to the centre. We may open such a door from almost any point of life, but they belong of themselves to the world of intellectual travail and its great speculations.

CHAPTER III

EXTENT AND LIMITS OF ATTAINMENT IN CHRISTIAN MYSTICISM OF THE LATIN SCHOOLS

THE nature of the union being that also of the mystical term, I proceed in the next place to consider the witness of the chief masters of experience, to some extent in a chronological order, though I shall make a beginning with Dionysius, because he is the spring and fountain both of doctrine and procedure, and at least in one respect the root of the whole subject. There is no comparison between his testimony and that of the first Fathers of the Church, including St. Augustine. Let us remember at the outset, as regards all the deponents, that we look to find clearness and substantial unanimity as to that which was attained mystically, recognising that the state ultimate itself can be delineated by simple affirmations only—not otherwise or fully described. Attempts at description in detail and inferences from these may be important as approximations, but there is nothing to guarantee accuracy—more especially on theoretical and doctrinal points. Of these two departments one is the place of unity and the other of variation; the first must be taken or left, the second is a field of criticism.

Now, the basis of Dionysian theology may be summarised in its formal sense as an experiment in attempted realisation of Him Who is exalted beyond all essences and all notions, and the too brief tract on which we depend for our knowledge is therefore a formulated recollection

45

of that which was attained or communicated in the deep interior state, though on the surface it appears rather as an intellectual consideration. Behind the positive verbal formulæ lies the certitude of practical experience. If the unknown author could have been questioned at his period, he would have said that the written word of his discourse was a shadowy reflection at best of that which was made known in the experience. The form of instruction adopted is one of a master addressing some disciple, real or supposed, and he is called Timothy, to support—by a subsidiary fiction—the claim which veils himself. The counsel in chief concerning the path of realisation is a casting out of all images—whether of sense or mind. When, in the exercise of that faculty which is called mystical contemplation,[1] the soul has been delivered both from the material and intellectual worlds,[2] when it has ascended the heights of sanctity, it enters that which is termed the mysterious darkness of a holy ignorance, and is lost in Him Who can be neither seen nor understood. It is a plunge into the " mysterious brightness " of that " Divine Obscurity " which for us is a great Darkness. There God will manifest Himself " in His truth and unveiled." In this region language and thought fail, and hence mystical theology proceeds by the negative rather than the affirmative way, though absolute affirmation and negation are held alike unsuit-

---

[1] It should be noted at this point that contemplation—as understood normally—is the fixing of the whole mind upon a single object ; but this is not the understanding of Dionysius or his successors, because a mind-object is an image of the mind, and such images must be expelled, according to the counsel. But see Chapter VII for the consideration of this subject at length.

[2] The disciple of Dionysius is exhorted literally to " lay aside the senses and works of the understanding, all that is material and intellectual, the things which are, with those also which are not "—that is to say, the figments of the mind as well as intellectual truths—" and by a supernatural flight upward " to unite himself, as intimately as possible, " with Him Who is exalted above all essence and all notion."

able in respect of God. He is neither darkness nor light,
error nor truth ; He is not time or eternity, speech or
thought. He has no manner of being, and the graces
by which we are raised into goodness and divinity—
unquestionably, after our own kind—are not in the same
categories as the nature of this Supreme Being. Our
goodness and our divinity are but copies or images of
Him.[1] He is known in mystical experience after a
transcendent manner, but the hypothetical ground on
which this state is reached is that God does not subsist
nor is he known[2]—meaning by any search of the intellect.
Such an exploration lies within the rational pairs of
opposites—affirmation and denial, positive and negative
—and for the intellect God is undiscernible because the
Divine Being is not within such measures. The mystical
darkness of Dionysius and those who followed him is of
course a symbolism, and it is this in a high degree. It
is not the cloud of unknowing but the " Hid Divinitie " ;
it is not the desolation which follows the mystical rapture. The darkness is not darkness, but transluminous
obscurity. The blindness therein is an overexalted
seeing in the soul ; the mystical ignorance is a super-
keen precision of all knowledge. In a word, it is excess
of light and a realisation of that which is involved by
the notion of absolute transcendence. To attain therefore that state which is termed ignorance in this paradoxical sense, we must dare to set aside whatsoever can
be affirmed of God. Our mode of attaining knowledge
concerning other objects is a veil in its application by
analogy to Him. The testimony of His immanence in
Nature is true testimony, but it is only a path of the
transcendence when the witness of the veils has been
removed. That which casts light on all things else is an
occasion of distortion when it is reflected on Him. By

[1] See the second Dionysian letter to Caius depending from the
Mystical Theology.
[2] See the first letter to Caius.

a splendid extravagance of language, the path of His attainment—outside the natural theology which shines through woof and web of symbolism—is therefore one of sublime nescience, while He Who is the term of our research is nothing of that which is not, as He is nothing of that which is. He surpasses all our negations as well as all that we affirm.[1]

Such is the thesis concerning Divine Union according to Dionysius. It must be admitted—my own disclaimer notwithstanding—that it reads more after the manner of an intellectual exercise than of a work performed in love. As to this, I have intimated already that the word has no place, either in tract or letters. It is said only that the mystic in the deep state belongs neither to himself nor to others.[2] What is the nature of the union ? It takes place between " the most noble portion of the soul " and that which is termed Unknown, producing a knowledge that is above understanding. Those who deserve to see and to know God repose in that light of darkness wherein He is said to abide.[3] In respect of themselves they are not, but in Him they are truly, outside all communication to the mind by means of pictures. Dionysius affirms that if we perceive God in any state of concentration it is certain that this is an image only—a sacrament, a form assumed by the Divine. The inference may be that God realised as Something outside consciousness is God veiled : It is Jehovah in the burning bush, or a manifestation of that order. We can indeed formulate to ourselves the golden chain of all such perceptions, from the Blessed Vision in Heaven,

[1] The aspirant is " given up unconditionally " to the sovereign intent of being lost in God.

[2] Plotinus, in the third century, prescribed elevation from sensibles, liberation from all vice, abiding in that which is pure at the summit of intellect, ascent above science. To attain the end of the soul, being participation in Deity, and to remain in that state, all else with which she is encompassed must be cut off.—*On the Good or the One.*

[3] See the *Letter to Dorotheus.*

as represented by St. Thomas and by Dante, to that most clouded communication of all which takes place normally through the figurative delineations of sensible things.[1]

Many questions arise, and one of them is whether, on the assumption that all this is more than a very subtle debate, it is translatable in other terms of mystical experience, seeing that, however little it concurs on the surface with St. Thomas that " perfection consists in perfect charity," it does at any rate proceed from a common ground of ascetic Mysticism in postulating complete detachment from creatures for the purposes of the work in hand. There is, moreover, a further question, and this is whether the path of imputed or symbolised darkness and ignorance is not in its delineation part of an attempt to make capital out of the complete bankruptcy of mind in the face of the great problems.[2] If the mind be indeed bankrupt when so confronted, it may be good to make capital out of the fact, according to a law of paradox, rather than abandon the quest. We must even be content with what we have and go on somehow. As an old adage affirms, our need may be God's opportunity. For the rest, there is no question that we are bankrupt in respect of Divine things so long

---

[1] Those who are acquainted only with the path of simple faith and its sweet humanities will feel that the Deity of Dionysius is out of all relation with man. Yet in other texts he speaks of the fatherhood of God, the incarnation of the Eternal Word and the ministry of the Holy Spirit. A second class of persons, whose gifts are only from the normal source of intellectual light, will challenge the warrants of Dionysius for such a delineation of things Divine and may say that his mystic path suggests a path of atheism. There are yet others—and I do not think that they are to be counted among the elect—who may think that the pretended Areopagite is virtually concealing a commonplace in the language of acrid paradox. I have tried to indicate that his illustrations of the Divine state belong to a peculiar class of symbolism.

[2] It is certainly an attempt to express that which is ineffable by a play upon the alternatives of contradiction, or otherwise to convey an intimation although a contradiction is inevitable.

E

as we sit within the four walls of the senses, albeit material things are far more than a simple medium of exchange in the world of material vested interests. It seems to me therefore that this point calls for no further settlement.

A third and final question, however, remains, and this is whether people like Dionysius and his successors were not multiplying symbols instead of reducing them, when they laboured so much to exhibit this dark side of the shield of Divine things. We know that the state of consciousness in God must be the most remote of all experiences, outside any field of comparison. We gain nothing when we strive to speak of it in terms scarcely less desperate than those which might attempt paradoxically to explain how two straight lines may after all enclose a space. The chain of negatives may serve some indeterminate purpose in an experimental process for the emptying of mind, but as it implies of necessity the positive chain, I conceive that the images will remain, as one might say, on the threshold or latent, and confuse the workings by sudden interventions. Whether any realisation which may have been reached under the best circumstances would itself class as positive rather than negative, or as an undemonstrable *tertium quid*, lies beyond our jurisdiction, and as the solution of Dionysian problems will be found to lie in another direction, we shall do well to remember that the counsel offered to our consideration is one of nullity and stillness, the attainment of a void state, that it may be filled subsequently but not by our mind-activities. Whatever we add to this at the present stage will only cloud the issues. Above all, the term contemplation seems dangerous in this connection, because we have seen that it supposes an object, and all objects have to be put away. Otherwise we remain in the separation of subject and object. There is an instance in *The Cloud of Unknowing*, which deals with a work of contemplation and is constrained to find its object in the word God or Love. This involves either the presence of a mental image or of its reflection, its atmosphere. It is hard entirely to throw off these modes of the mind, but they carry their limitations with them, and so far as the term of research is concerned the text in question is like a path hanging out in space, leading no whither. It seems to follow that the negatives of definition in Divine things are not less dangerous than the positive, which notwithstanding it is well to remember in the obscure night of our inhibited days that God is Divine Darkness as well as Divine Light. Yet is this in respect only of our limitations and—as I think—of the sadness by which we are encompassed in our needs. Otherwise it can profit us nothing in a spiritual sense to join such a pair of cosmic opposites in the Divine Nature, or seek some way of escape between them. We have drawn no nearer to its mystery. I doubt if we should improve our position by adding—which is true equally—that God is indeed that *tertium quid* whereby they are harmonised. It is much the same with another symbolism.

We may approximate to a realisation of the ultimate mystical state by such expressions—now almost familiar in Mysticism—as the union of nothing with nothing, but the approximation is in virtue of an intellectual excursus only. There is no reason why one side of this additional pair of opposites should be more efficacious than the other. We might be able to approximate as effectively by saying that it is the union of all with all, or what is most probable we might find ourselves no nearer in the one than the other case. A certain harmony of both arises, however, from the fact that the old ascetic base is broken up by either, for its conventional terms are equivalent to a contrast of nothingness and the All. If we are nothing we have no part in God. Conversely, if we are anything and He is nothing, in the Dionysian sense, in Him we have still no part.

But when we have finished with the arid intellectual side there remains that which is behind it, namely, the state of mystical attainment wherein God is " known after a transcendent manner "—this is to say, not reflectively but realised at first hand, as, for example, by what Upton calls " the immediate feeling of God's self-revealing presence in our consciousness." This lies outside the symbolism of light and darkness. It follows —in reply to my initial question—that Dionysius is translatable in other terms of mystical experience and that he is saying after his own exotic manner that which is said by the whole cloud of witnesses.

It follows also and therefore that very early in the Christian centuries we find, under the Christian ægis, a deponent concerning the higher way of truth and life who is identical with the other testimonies, but is yet distinct because he is highly individual. Indeed his form of presentation is so new on the surface and so peculiar to itself that it has almost the token of revelation, looks almost like a new way to the Divine.[1] As we might expect, it is so far beyond the official field of sacraments and symbols that every doctrinal complexion of Christianity seems to have dissolved. The work delineated is one between the soul and God, as it is in *The Cloud of Unknowing* and a few other palmary texts. But if it be this and this only, is it not possible—once more—to present it after another manner, to sum up the whole doctrine of Dionysius in a few words as follows ? When the soul has been set apart and purified, when it has been sanctified by Divine Grace, when it has not so much entered upon the inward life as been taken over and included thereby, when the great population of images—the self-object included— has departed from its mystical city rather than been

---

[1] I do not intend to say that it is without root or precedent in any system whatever. Eastern analogies are numerous enough, and in the West there is sufficient likeness for Dionysius to awaken recurring memories of Plotinus.

expelled, and when the soul is therefore a place sacred
but vacant, she has made possible the realisation of God
in consciousness; and that which may follow is a response
of God to the soul in the work that is between the soul
and God.

Passing on now to the next point of our inquiry, we
have no need to go further than our great counsel of
caution, which is Vaughan's *Hours with the Mystics*, to
learn that the traces of the Areopagite are to be found
everywhere, or that in the writings of the mediæval
mystics—as indeed in those who are later—his words
are employed and " his opinions more or less fully transmitted." The truth is that the way of Dionysius, however it may be presented variously, is the way of all the
mystics. I do not think that it is needful—for a purpose
so simple as the present one—to make any prolonged study
of paraphrasts and commentators. Johannes Scotus
Erigena, who translated Dionysius into the scholastic
tongue, found great things in the Greek *Scholia* of St.
Maximus, and is said to have taken him into his very
heart. The work is concerned, however, with verbal
exposition and criticism, which offers little to our purpose. I note only that—in the mind of St. Maximus[1]—
we are united with the Unknown by the suspension of
all cognition: it is the most that we can derive from
him on the term of mystical experience, and it reiterates
with scarcely a variation of terms what is affirmed by
Dionysius himself. The Greek paraphrase of Georgius
Pachymeres was dedicated to Cyrus Athanasius, Patriarch
of Constantinople, and the tract on mystical theology
becomes in his process of expansion a work of considerable dimensions. It says that the light of this theology
is received in an absolute stillness of mind and is unattainable by mental processes.[2] It is therefore com-

[1] See Migne's edition of Dionysius, Vol. II, col. 422.
[2] Paraphrase of *Mystical Theology*, cap. I, folio 1015 in the Migne
edition, Vol. I.

municated divinely, and this intimation is really a keynote to the whole way of experience as it was understood among Latin mystics. They held that no man by
thinking could find out God and they accepted the dicta
of orthodox doctrine on the hypothesis that Divine Truth
was infused into the mind of the Church by the Holy
Spirit. The canon of the New Testament lay in front
of the paraphrast, and when he read in Dionysius that
God was not power, not truth, not wisdom, he remembered that incarnate Divinity had said, I am the truth—
and that the author of the *Epistle to the Hebrews* had
defined Christ as the power and wisdom of God. He
was thus in a difficulty on the question of texts and he
issued thence by the help of refinements, with the skill
of the schoolmen. He concurred therefore that God is
not truth or wisdom in respect of our human measures
of these qualities, but He is truth and wisdom essentially,
or in the absolute sense, in that which transcends all our
limitations utterly. In like manner, when his authority
denied that God is goodness or even Divinity, Georgius
Pachymeres explained that these other qualities are not
of the substance of God but of the glory by which He
is encompassed.[1] This is excellent as a *tour de force*,
which is to say that it is scarcely convincing. We have
seen that Dionysius himself, in his second letter to Caius,
has dealt with the difficulty after another manner—not
too convincing either. Perhaps in this instance the author
of the *Mystical Theology* had written more deeply than
he of the epistle had a mind to discern at the moment ;
but to go further would be to split hairs unduly over
what is after all language of symbolism. The paraphrase
of Pachymeres is interesting in several respects and
especially as an illustration of the ecclesiastical mind of
his period on the whole works of his author, including
the *Scholia* of St. Maximus. He has illuminating words
on spiritual ecstasies by which the living soul is entirely

[1] *Op. cit.*, Vol. I, col. 1058 *et seq.*

translated and reposes entirely in the Divine Object of her love, delivered from the self-presence. He therefore knew that the so-called contemplation of Dionysius is like the mystical term itself—in no wise apart from love but the quest of its ineffable mystery.

If we turn to the Jesuit Corderius, remembering that he is of the sixteenth century—and that I have given already one of his great illuminations—we may look for some adventures of the mind. To study him should fill us with admiration for the care-filled subtlety which has brought Dionysius into a perfect right line with later accredited theology, so that the Greek mystic seems almost as if he had entered the life of Christian literature to smooth the way for St. Thomas, the Angel of the Schools ; but it is within moderate limits only that this is a part of our concern. When Dionysius lays down that God is neither soul nor mind, Corderius explains that the term soul describes humanity by the principal part of man, while mind is angelical nature.[1] The Dionysian distinction is therefore merely between Creator and creature. So also God is not number, because He is of Himself that unity from which all numeration proceeds, though essentially He is above number. Now, Dionysius in the same chapter has categorically distinguished God not only from number but from unity.[2] Out of this dilemma the annotator issues by referring to the treatise of his author on Divine Names, where it is said that the Divine Unity is not part of a whole but the antecedent determination of all multitude and universality. Cor-

---

[1] *Op. cit.*, Vol. I, col. 1047 *et seq.*

[2] Precisely the same point is affirmed of the Zoharic Shekinah. The number 7 is the image of her who is the Mother below, while 50 is the image of her who is the Mother in the Supernal World. See *The Faithful Shepherd*, in *Sepher Ha Zohar*, Part III, fol. 108 b, and De Pauly's French translation, V, 274. But " the Shekinah is not contained in number." *Zohar*, Part II, fol. 164 b. French translation, IV, 108. See also my *Secret Doctrine in Israel*, pp. 128, 199.

derius on the mystical term considered in the Dionysian
sense is Corderius haunted by memories of a long line of
witnesses, from Ruysbroeck to Joannes de Jesu Maria and
Thomas de Jesu, so we hear of the purgative, illuminative
and unitive stages, and it is scarcely possible to extricate
anything that belongs to himself. But for him, as for
Pachymeres, whom he follows and extends, the work is
a work of love and an end in fruition of love. God
is apprehended by faith but is united by love to the
soul. The knowledge which mystical theology communicates is *per copulationem cum Deo*.[1] The Lover and
Beloved embrace in the Divine Darkness, and the inward
doctrine communicated to the soul therein is that
mystical theology which is understood of the heart in
rapture.

After Dionysius and his successors, whom I have taken
together, as among themselves they form a little school
of the elect, I must return as a matter of form to the
period which preceded Dionysius—understood with all
necessary reserves as the fifth century—and make a fresh
departure therefrom. When I speak of a matter of
form I am intending to intimate that ecclesiastical
writers belonging to early centuries of the Christian era
are scarcely witnesses to Mysticism, which to all intents
and purposes begins with the tract on Mystical Theology.
Outside it there are only vestiges, on which, however,
it seems desirable to say a few words—if only to shew
that the field has not been left unsurveyed. The doctrinal
thesis which characterises Christian Mysticism is established by Clement of Alexandria in words that are a
source of theology on the whole subject. " I know well
that He who has opened the door hitherto shut, will
afterwards reveal what is within ; and will shew what
we could not have known before, had we not entered

[1] *Op. cit.*, Vol. I, col. 1011 *et seq.* Other formulæ are *totus absorptus
in Deo, per amorem exstaticum, per amorem qui amantem in amatum
transfert,* etc.

in by Christ, through Whom alone God is beheld."[1]
The essential point of view could not be expressed more
clearly, and it belongs to the beginning of the third
century. That the Christ of St. Clement was understood as an indwelling power is made clear in another
place, where it is said that the man with whom the
Word dwells is " made like unto God " and even that
he " becomes God."[2] There is nothing to detain us in
Tertullian,[3] nor in Origen, though he was a great name
on what would be called, I suppose, the liberal side of
theology.[4] St. Gregory of Nyssa, in the fourth century,
affirms that the life of the soul is in God, and he is one
of the first writers who uses the symbolical formula
concerning spiritual marriage. It is said that this bond
of union is broken by the soul when defilement is admitted into the heart.[5] These things are pregnant as
simple intimations, but centuries had to elapse before
the seeds germinated in the mind of Christian sanctity ;
and as much must, I think, be said of the immortal
Bishop of Hippo.

It is perhaps only in virtue of special pleading that
St. Augustine has been classed with the mystics. He
was too much and too permanently conscious of the
" grossness and heaviness of the corruptible body " to

[1] See the *Exhortation to the Gentiles*, c. I, in *The Ante-Nicene Christian Library*, IV, 25.

[2] See *The Pedagogue*, Bk. III, c. I.

[3] Tertullian held that the soul has " a corporeal nature," meaning—
as I read him—a spiritual vehicle. She is not " made out of matter " but
is " endowed with a body." Like Plato, he identifies the spirit and the
soul, which is simple and indivisible. After death it remains in Hades till
the resurrection. Tertullian rejects disdainfully any notion that the
resurrection of the body is an allegory of entrance into a new or regenerate
life.

[4] Origen pictured the saints in the world to come as nourished on the
food of truth and wisdom and drinking from the cup of Divine Wisdom.
The likeness of God is restored to them. Contemplation is never mentioned.

[5] See the treatise *On Virginity*, c. 15.

57

be fully conscious in the region of the spirit and its freedom. He rose intellectually on the ladder of manifest things towards that "immutable truth which is very eternity." So also, and so intellectually, by a corresponding ascent, he passed in his own personality from the body through the "sensitive soul" to that "higher part of the soul" where reason sits in judgment on the senses and their testimony. Beyond this, beyond the "multitude of images and phantoms," he looked for the soul's "highest mode of conceiving and knowing" in that light which gives "knowledge of the immutable goodness." He sought in this manner to behold a vision of the Divine Being which our human mind can look upon only in fear and trembling, and he affirms that he did attain certain momentary glimpses of the Eternal Beauty, pictured, so to speak, in things that are visible; but the mind was blinded by that splendour; it fell backward; and there remained with him only the ravishing odour of heavenly food, the desire of which he was unable to satisfy and which indeed he had not as yet tasted.[1]

I do not know how this experience has come to be regarded by a few writers on Mysticism as one of communion with the Divine. For St. Augustine himself it was simply a confession of failure, because he had not yet accepted Christ Jesus as the Mediator between God and men, or indeed as other than a man of "admirable wisdom."[2] When he became a pillar of defence for the orthodox faith there is little to suggest his progress in conscious mystical union, but he bears witness to the apprehension characteristic of all holy men who are not mystics, to the joy in God, the intellectual knowledge of God, the peace of abiding in God and of God dwelling in us. *Semper ab illo fieri debemus inhærentes ei.*[3] He affirms that we live and are only in so far as we cleave to

[1] *Confessions of St. Augustine*, Bk. VII, chapter XVII.
[2] *Ibid.*, c. XVIII.   [3] *In Joan. Tractatus* XXIII, 5.

Him, but it is not a statement which classes Augustine as a mystic. He says elsewhere that man can attain a luminous impression of the Sovereign Good—*impressa notio ipsius Boni*,[1] but this indicates only that the Dionysian hidden night of Godhead was not present to his mind. He testified also that we cleave to God and are in Him—as one might say—suspended : *unde penderemus*.[2] He speaks further of a species of interior sense which impels us to seek God always : *interior nescio quæ conscientia quærundum Deum*.[3] But there is nothing here that exceeds the following of righteousness. So also distinctions like *spiritus noster cœlum est, caro terra*[4] are elementary mystical suggestions, but they are not the matter of the work. The affirmations that in Christ we may be made partakers of Divinity[5] and that if we love God we shall become God—as St. Athanasius had said in effect previously—are aspects of mystical doctrine,[6] but they are insufficient of themselves to place the Bishop of Hippo in the chain of mystical tradition. His greatness remains what it is—being that of a Christian apologist on the side of orthodox faith.

St. John Chrysostom belongs to the Augustinian period, and he makes a careful distinction as between the union of Christ with the soul and of Christ with the Father Almighty. The one is spiritual and is comparable to an agreement of mind, while the other is essential, being an oneness in respect of nature. There was also John Cassian, who speaks of " that unity which already exists between the Father and the Son, and the Son and the Father," which unity is " shed abroad in

---

[1] *De Trinitate*, VII. [2] *Ibid.*
[3] *Liber de Utilitate Credendi*, c. XVI. [4] *Sermo* LVII.
[5] *Enarratio in Ps*. CXXXVIII.

[6] So also are his words on the soul's attraction towards the Sovereign goodness in virtue of a kind of occult memory.—*De Trinitate*, X, III, 315. And again : " The human soul and rational mind do live, are blessed and enlightened only by the very substance of God."—*In Joan. Tractatus* XXIII, 5.

our hearts and minds," so that we are joined to God "by a lasting and inseparable affection." He is a witness therefore that love is the bond of union, and he seems to reflect St. Clement of Alexandria when he adds that, so united to God, "whatever we breathe, or think, or speak is God."[1] I suppose that if certain writers had been at the pains to notice Cassian, they would have been quick to class him as a pantheist on the authority of this one statement. In simple fact, he was neither pantheist nor mystic.

As next in succession, we may pause—but it shall be for a moment only—and listen to certain words which come from the chair of St. Peter when it is occupied by Gregory the Great.[2] In his day he was a master of doctrine, a writer of wonder-books in the form of Dialogues, a luminous moralist in great texts of homilies and a commentator who imparted a strange life of allegorical fantasy to gospel narratives. No mystic was he, yet he has left us certain lights in sentences there and here, scattered over his mighty memorials. In that which he called contemplation, vistas through great distances opened for him and may open now for us—at least in glimpses. It is possible, he tells us, for a human soul—"although enclosed in a mortal body"—to penetrate by contemplation not only "beyond all earthly bounds" but "to the very height of heaven."[3] This is an *aperçu* only, but it is intended to shew us that the experience of St. Paul in the third heaven is possible

[1] See the *Second Conference of Abbot Isaac.*

[2] There was also his contemporary St. John of Climacus, abbot of Mt. Sinai, who wrote *Scala Paradisi*, which contains many memorable sentences on the practice of the presence of God, which was the work of his whole life, and on that charity which enfolds the soul in the arms of the heavenly Father. His life and literary remains are included in the Greek Patrology of Migne, Vol. 88.

[3] *The Dialogues of Saint Gregory*, Bk. I. See Mr. Edmund G. Gardner's excellent annotated edition of the anonymous English translation of 1608, p. 2.

also to us, and I suppose that the recipient of experience
would see, as St. Paul saw, but whether with an eye
turned to an object within or to the pageant—as it
might be—of a certain third heaven, I do not know, for
he does not indeed say.

The science of official Christianity opened all its
departments to the great debate of scholasticism ;
there was the shining of an hundred intellectual lights,
stars of varying magnitude, and of him who is more
than a star—almost as a sun for splendour—St. Thomas,
the Angel of the Schools. I have said somewhere else
in my writings that he is comparable to one who has
taken a survey of some vast region, as if from a Pisgah
height, but that he does not come before us carrying
the distinct testimony of a man who has dwelt therein.
It seems to me that this notion is borne out by what he
tells us concerning direct vision of the Divine Essence—
visio per essentiam. It is communicated in principle to
believers by the faith of Christ, which gives to us the essence
and the substance of that which is true, after the manner
of a supernatural grace—as a seed that is sown in time within us but is to be developed in eternity. *Fides est habitus
mentis quo inchoatur vita eterna in nobis.*[1] That is a
great dictum, connecting faith with contemplation—as
the latter is understood mystically—and sufficient unto
the day is the part of life thereof for those who are
toiling to Zion by the road of the wayfaring man. But
we know that when the ground has been prepared by a
particular culture, the seed of eternal life germinates
here within us and that which grows up therefrom
recreates the whole nature. Beyond the Angel of the
Schools it is certain that we are called to travel, but we
may take on our journey his maxim—already quoted—
that perfection consists in perfect charity. It is attained
in the life of prayer and contemplation and in conformity
with the will of God. The implicit of these is humility,

[1] *Verit. Quæst.,* Art. XIV.

which is acquired by the denial of self and by extinction of the inordinate love of creatures. We may take also some of the intimations which came to him in his last moments, when the *Doctor Angelicus* was dissolved in the *Doctor inebriatus*, looking to be satiated in God and quoting the words of St. Augustine: "Then shall I live truly, when I shall be filled utterly with Thee alone."[1]

We are at the beginning of the scholastic period when we meet with a great galaxy of witnesses. Hugo of St. Victor tells us that to ascend unto God is to enter into oneself and to transcend oneself. Richard of St. Victor varies the words but bears the same witness— *ascendat per semetipsum super semetipsum.* The soul shall rise through itself and so pass outside itself.

For both it was a work of love, and as regards the satiation desired by St. Thomas Aquinas we may note that though it is possible by love to hold, even to encompass God, the soul in such loving is not by love satisfied. Richard of St. Victor's way to contemplation is purely a way of love, " wherein is the high peace of God that passeth man's wit,"[2] and is reached in a ravishment of mind.

Moving a little further through the Christian generations, let us hear what is spoken by Eckehart—and no one knew better or bore witness more clearly concerning God in His manifestations or the soul's nearness to God. No one realised more deeply that the Kingdom of Heaven is at hand for and in each of us. He expresses after the following manner the fundamental and terminal doctrine of the mystical end. The soul " may arrive at

---

[1] See *The Confessions*, Bk. X, c. 28.

[2] This is from *Benjamin Minor*, for which see *The Cell of Self-Knowledge*, as edited by E. G. Gardner, M.A., 1910. In the *Benjamin Major* there are great occasional lights, but it has not, I think, been translated. Richard held that in contemplation the soul passes upward from things visible to invisible things, or from those that are bodily to those that are spiritual. Unfortunately he is somewhat hindered by a fantastic spirit of symbolism. One of his great sayings is *Amor ubi est, ibi oculus.*

such an intimate union that God at last draws it to Himself altogether." This comes to me with suggestions of more than the Beatific Vision, more than the Divine Marriage, as of something hidden deeply within the Union. I can see from very far away how the Vision precedes Espousals—as we shall learn of these in the memorials—how their bond is indissoluble, and how therefore when Christ yields up the Kingdom to the Father, the King is not departing from the kingdom of the soul, but the soul is drawn as if into the consubstantial nature of the Blessed Trinity. Here is the absorption which I have mentioned elsewhere—as one speaking in fear and trembling ; and Eckehart adds concerning it : " There is no distinction left in the soul's consciousness between itself and God, though God still regards it as a creature." It is a merging of the many in the One, and the One contains the many without diminution of these. We shall know in that state how God shall be all in all. It is the day beyond the day when they sit down together in the House of the Father, and those who minister in the House serve the Supper of the Lord.

Eckehart reflects Dionysius in affirming that " when understanding and desiring end, then it is dark, and then God shineth." The condition is liberation in the Holy Ghost—or so at least I interpret, making a certain kind of harmony between several luminous distinctions. Eckehart has been accused of pantheism, but it seems—at least in part—owing to confusions of expression.[1] He says that a mirror reflects the sun and yet remains what it is—as though he were rebutting the charge.

---

[1] As, for example, when he says that " it is one and the same thing to know God and to be known by God." Another aspect of this notion is expressed by Dr. Rudolf Steiner, following Eckehart : " And the inner illumination is something that the soul must necessarily find when it sinks itself deep into the basis of its being." God is discoverable there because there is God.

After the same manner God is in the soul with His very nature and being and Godhead, and yet He is not the soul. The reflecting of the soul in God is God in God, and yet the mind is still that which it is. The verbal image-making is often disconcerting when symbol is contrasted with symbol, but here at least is an antithesis of pantheism. Again Eckehart says of God : " His being may not become our being, but it shall be our life." The alternative finds expression, however, in terms that are not less strong, as in the following typical example : " The eye through which I see God—that is the same eye through which God sees me. Mine eye and God's— that is one eye, one mode of knowing and one feeling."[1] So also in the distinction which he makes between the fathomless, unknowable Godhead and its self-realisation as God, it is said that Nature is a lower part of the Divine ; and again—almost as something that follows— in one of his twenty-eight propositions condemned by the Roman Inquisition he affirms that the Eternal Glory is manifested no less in the activity of that which is evil than in that which is good—meaning that all activity shews forth the Divine Glory, its own qualities not-withstanding. Yet he says elsewhere that God is not Nature but above it. Two things are obvious, one of which is general to the doctrinal question at issue and the other particular to our subject. In view of the verbal contrasts and antitheses which have been cited,[2]

---

[1] A recent translation of the Pfeiffer collection of Eckehart's writings, No. 99, appears to go further still. The question is how God may be apprehended without image and without semblance, but in particular whether this is possible for the soul, unless the soul be very God and God be very soul. Eckehart's answer is : " God must be very I, I very God, so consummately one that this He and this I are one *is*, in this *isness* working one work eternally."

[2] See *The Porch* for September, 1914, containing translations of Eckehart by C. de B. Evans. The literal rendering is more than *male sonans* as English, but the original meaning is reflected clearly. All such statements notwithstanding, the more one studies Eckehart the more

and of many others which remain, it would be nothing short of misstatement to term Eckehart a pantheist or indeed a pure theist, though I think personally that he leans in the latter direction somewhat more than the former.[1] Secondly, in the consideration of mystical experience to which he bears testimony it is quite indifferent whether he proves theist or pantheist, (*a*) because this is beyond the issues of experience, belonging to theological, theosophical, or metaphysical dialectics, and (*b*) because of that which I have intimated already and have marked for future development, namely, that in the perfect state of mystical union with God there can be only one mode of consciousness shared in common, and whether or not there is an ultimate distinction of nature between God and the soul, the experience of union can bear no witness to distinction, while the dialectical question is beyond decision on the basis of such experience.

We have seen as to the term of union that—according to Eckehart—God may draw the soul altogether to Himself and I have shewn how this statement has interpreted itself to my own mind. But as we are told elsewhere that the fruit of virtue in union " means an unclouded sight of the Divine Being with the eye of unity," and as —subject to the particular significance of the last three words—this teaching is expressed in the language appertaining to the Blessed Vision and not of the Blessed Union, it is certain that we must proceed yet further.

certain one is as to his doctrinal position, namely, that albeit " the soul is all things," according to one fashion of language, God, " wrought the soul " and concealed within her His Divine Treasure, being the Heavenly Kingdom. The relations are therefore those of Creator and creature. See the Sermon on the Kingdom of God, translated as above from *Meister Eckehart und seiner Jünger*, by F. Jostes, 1895.

[1] This is illustrated, I think, by the axiom : " God and I are one in the act of knowing." So also when Eckehart says : " Even though we turn away from God, yet God can never turn away from us "—there is a very real distinction implied.

Now, it is said in one of Eckehart's sermons [1] that "likeness is ever rooted in separateness," and the remark applies equally to sight or the state of eye to eye ; but at the end of all the spiritual travelling the soul finds, according to our witness, that " she herself is that which she had sought in vain for so long." [2] And again : " She and God are but one bliss and one kingdom." In the archetype " the soul is God, and there she enjoys and orders all things as God. . . . The soul and the Godhead are one. . . . She has found that the Kingdom of God is she herself." [3]

Hereof is the Divine Union, according to Eckehart. Whatever our opinions may be as to doctrinal and philosophical positions, in Mysticism he is and will remain great among the great names ; but the time came when he was not, for God took him—or perchance the Roman Inquisition.

The next witness is Tauler, and he also is great, there and here in the records, though I have never felt that he is in the same category with his predecessor and master, whom he reflects continually, faithfully and almost in a literal way. It is substantially the master speaking when Tauler testifies that " if man is in reality to become one with God, then all energies and powers, even of the inner man, must die and become silent. The will must turn away even from the good, and become void in

[1] It is that on the kingdom of God already quoted. Part of this sermon has also been rendered into English by Helen Rand in *The Seeker* for August, 1914.

[2] This discovery is the reward which comes to the soul after it has suffered " the lowest death on her way to Divinity "—that is to say, after she has died not only to her own works but has consented even to the loss of God. Compare the teachings of Quietism in the eighteenth century.

[3] According to Eckehart and Ruysbroeck, this prototype is Divine Understanding, or " the Person of the Son " in the Holy Trinity. Now, according to St. John, this Son is the Word by Whom all things were made. He is for Eckehart " the exemplar of all creatures."

respect of will." And again : " All that the spirit knows, can, loves, possesses is shipwrecked in the inexhaustible abyss of the Divinity. God so ravishes the spirit above its own capacity that it is, so to speak, clothed with the form and image of God.[1] Self-knowledge is exchanged for another knowledge, self-love for a love infinitely more perfect."[2] *In vastissimum Divinitatis pelagus navigare,* says Ruysbroeck, with another quality of meaning, but —as might be expected—Tauler's formulæ do not always consist with one another.

The doctrinal side of the question is always with us, and arises generally from terms used by the mystics when they attempt to formulate their experience at its highest. There is an important passage of Suso in the 33rd chapter of his *Book of Eternal Wisdom.* It affirms (*a*) that the soul " remains a creature in God " in the state of union—meaning in God consciously, for in Him we live and move and have our being; (*b*) that in the abyss of Divinity the soul does not think whether it is a creature or not—the reason being that personal consciousness is not reflecting back on the self, even as now we lose—at least momently—the realisation of the self-sense when we are wrapped in the contemplation of an object of rare beauty and wonder.[3] This is how I understand Suso,

[1] According to Latin theology, the human soul is the form of the body which it assumes, and according to Eckehart, God is the form of the soul.

[2] " Whensoever a man is raised into this condition of ecstasy by a singular favour of God, he sets free the highest part of himself from the yoke of the world and time, so that he experiences, within a certain measure, the blessedness of eternity."—*Institutiones,* c. XXX. In the Sermon preached on the fifteenth Sunday after Trinity, Tauler says that the soul dwelt eternally in the Divine Abyss prior to its creation—a reference to Eckehart's prototype, understood as a Divine Idea.

[3] It is lost most especially and above all other instances of the manifest order in the love between man and woman, when this has been raised into Tolstoi's state of ideality or poetry. I suppose that it is the nearest instance offered in normal human experience to a realisation in pure loving intelligence of the suspended reflex act. It shews that there is

and the indication is of real metaphysical importance, as we shall see fully later on. The whole question itself lies really to the credit of scholasticism, and it must not be supposed that I am doing more than interpreting Suso, who may not have realised all that is implied in his statement. In another place he reflects Dionysius, when delineating the state of ineffable union with the Christ-Spirit. He says that " the place of the Son's pure Godhead is in the form-pregnant light of the Divine Unity—a light which may be termed in its unnameable-ness a nothingness ; in its inward concentration, an essential stillness ; in its indwelling outflow, a divine nature ; in its peculiar property, a self-comprehending light. . . . In the modeless darkness of this light all multiplicity ceases ; the spirit loses itself as self, and comes to an end as regards its own activity. Ever to lose oneself in this is everlasting bliss."[1] I should add that the transit of the soul into the abyss of Divinity is affirmed elsewhere to carry it beyond time and space. It is dissolved in God by a loving intuition.[2]

According to Ruysbroeck, the union is " repose in God above all resemblance." He says also " repose in God, above the self, in unity,"[3] which, I suppose, is a reference to the self understood as at first in separation, since it is obvious that capacity for such union is therein

a region of human love which awaits exploration and has as yet not entered into the heart of man to conceive.

[1] *The Life of Blessed Henry Suso by Himself.* Edition of Dean Inge, 1913, pp. 240, 241.

[2] If there be any distinction of meaning attachable to distinction in terms, it is beyond research how a soul which is " dissolved in God " can remain " a creature in God." But in the one case Suso is making a short contribution to theological dialectics and in the other to records of experience in the imagery of sensible things.

[3] *Ibi jam saturi sumus et abundamus, et cum Deo supra nosipsos æterna plenitudo sumus. . . . Semper ergo supra nosipsos quidem cum Deo in unitate saturi, at in nobisipsis, ubi justitiam amamus et vivendo colimus, famelici sumus.—De Vera Contemplatione Opus, cap. XVI.*

and can be else nowhere. Ruysbroeck mentions further "repose in God by love,"[1] but love is the condition of repose, and otherwise it is not given to anyone to find rest for his spiritual feet from the call of questing.

I have made elsewhere my contribution in brief to the panegyric of Jan van Ruysbroeck.[2] If his be not the greatest name in Christian Mysticism—as a writer of memorials in attainment—I should bracket it with that of Eckehart and that of St. John of the Cross, but I have a feeling that he stands first on the ladder of ascent to the Supernals. He has drawn from heights almost inaccessible, and up from hardly sounded wells of being, such rumours of eternal things and states of the soul therein as have never passed otherwise into language in the Christian world—not even in *The Fiery Soliloquy of the Soul with God*,[3] not even in Jacob Böhme, though his is another voice which I should have mentioned a few lines earlier, were it not that he seems to me a man of strange and wild experience in pictured vision rather than of that experience at the centre which is apart from pictures. I admit that in his case it is a difficult distinction, and I need not press the point, which is for the few who understand that a cosmical philosophy received by the way of personal revelation does not answer to the real needs of the soul, and that the inner

[1] *Ibid.*, cap. XXVI. See also *De Septem Custodiis Libellus*, cap. XII. Many other references could be cited.

[2] *The Secret Tradition in Freemasonry*, Vol. II, pp. 293, 294—and in other places.

[3] Master Gerlac Petersen, of Deventer in Flanders, was born in 1378 and was therefore contemporary with St. Thomas à Kempis. He was a Canon Regular of the Order of St. Augustine. He connects with the Dionysian tradition, affirming that "it is in the power of the deiform spouse to strip herself naked of all forms and images and look into the very Truth and Superessence of all beings throughout all creation." This is the quest of Divine Presence as the noumenon behind phenomena, and that which Gerlac calls otherwise the attainment of liberty or beatitude. There are deep things in this little book of "the deiform soul," and it ought to be re-edited.

sense of the Jewish and Christian Scriptures is a thing
which stands apart, a byway of the soul's research. When
the voice that sounds from very far away speaks to the
soul amid silence, it discloses other secrets.

Into Ruysbroeck's most inward glass of vision Dionysius
had reflected—we know not surely how. The Flemish
mystic enumerates four modes of love—that which begins
in precept, that of elevation of spirit, that of the Sons of
God, and that in fine which is of union with God in love.
The fourth is a state of emptiness in bare love and in
Divine Light.[1] It is therefore an imageless state, and
this is how it connects remotely—but, in my thinking,
not uncertainly—with the epoch-making tract on Mystical Theology. Ruysbroeck speaks also of our eternal
archetype, wherein we are one with God,[2] and this is
otherwise the wisdom of God Who has put on the nature
of us all. The Divine Union of the soul with God is
therefore in Christ, which is the paramount implicit of
Christian Mysticism and will call for consideration at
length at a later stage. Ruysbroeck elaborates the
analogies between the activity and repose of the soul in
God and the activity and repose in the Divine Nature
Itself. The co-ordination of these two states is most
important. That which it is sought to enforce and that
which must be enforced otherwise is the necessity of
willing correspondence between them, so that our attainment in the working life without may be no less great

---

[1] *De Vera Contemplatione*, cap. XIV. See also cap. XXIII, *et seq.*,
and *De Septem Gradibus Amoris Libellus Optimus, passim.* The seven
steps or stages described in the last treatise are (1) Good will; (2) Voluntary Poverty; (3) Chastity; (4) Humility; (5) Desire for the Honour
of God; (6) Dilucid contemplation, the three characteristics of which
are insight, purity of spirit and nakedness of mind; (7) Most Sublime
Contemplation, and this also is in identity with the fourth mode of
Ruysbroeck's alternative classification—the state above all knowledge,
realisation of the infinite abyss of God within us.

[2] See *ante*, s.v. Eckehart and Tauler, pp. 66, 67. The question of
this archetype or prototype will be considered further in Chapter X.

and holy than that of the life within.[1] It is more impossible than difficult to draw clear distinctions, but perhaps the most profound dicta on the union are contained in the following passage, which I have reduced slightly in rendering. There is the fruition of souls in God, and there is the fruition of all souls who are one with God in love—meaning their conscious intercourse. It is a still, glorious and essential oneness, beyond the differentiation of persons, who are united in fruitful love, as in a calm and glorious unity. It is fathomless rest and joy, the crown and recompense of love made perfect in eternity. Hereof is the communion of saints expounded for the first time through a true medium of language by one who had realised the meaning which belongs to the formula. I do not think that there is anywhere in mystical literature so catholic and perfect an intimation of that communion and of the life everlasting on its holy human side.[2] It is the co-consciousness of the redeemed in God. There is, however, a single glorious sentence of the same mystic which seems to stand at once for the sacred path and term. " We go forth from ourselves to flow into God and again flow back into ourselves."[3] So is individual being maintained

---

[1] They must be in a state of unity, and this is what we should understand by mystical resurrection, being the attainment of Divine Life in all parts and works of the personality. It is the sense of the apocryphal saying attributed to Christ about the coming of the Kingdom when " that which is without shall be as that which is within." The later non-catholic mystics had vestiges of intuition on the subject, but this was scarcely possible under the ascetic rule of the Latin mystics.

[2] Ruysbroeck gives a variant description as follows, but I am summarising again. We draw within ourselves all spiritual and corporeal faculties. We uplift ourselves towards that Supreme Thing Which we struggle to attain. There we meet with the unity of all loving spirits in the source of Divine Grace. There all loving spirits form a spiritual unity. In them God lives by His grace, communicating it to each according to the dignity of each.—*De Vera Contemplatione*, cap. XXVI.

[3] *De Vera Contemplatione*, cap. XXVII. Compare *De Ornatu Spiritualium Nuptiarium*, Liber II, cap. LXXIX, towards the end, and

in the Supernals. And it happens also that here is an antithesis of pantheism—Gerson's accusation notwithstanding. This is illustrated further when Ruysbroeck says elsewhere that " love makes us like unto God and makes us one with Him in love, not that we can become God, or His equals in grace, wisdom, knowledge, in love itself, or in anything that is peculiar to His nature."[1] It is in the light of this statement that we must dwell on two other memorable words: (*a*) " Those who are enlightened by Divine Grace find within themselves, above reason, the Kingdom of God and God in His Kingdom " ;[2] (*b*) " In the simplicity of love there is found no difference between Lover and Beloved."[3] This is the last word on the Great Mystery of Love in the eternal, as it is the last word and ineffable secret of love on earth. It is by reason of this that the Eastern mystic knows in his heart and says with gracious lips : " Thou art that," while the *Sepher Ha Zohar* affirms (*a*) that God sent man into this world for no other purpose than to learn that Jehovah is Elohim,[4] and (*b*) that God and His Shekinah are one.[5]

My final extracts shall be from *The Book of the Twelve Béguines*,[6] which seems—short and simple though it be—in some respects scarcely less important than the *Adornment* and perhaps something more clear, because it is more concise. It affirms that " the closed heaven

Maeterlinck's translation—*L'Ornement des Noces Spirituelles*, where the corresponding chapter is numbered LXXVII.

[1] Compare *De Vera Contemplatione*, cap. XIV ; also cap. XXI.

[2] *Ibid.*, cap. XVII. [3] *Ibid.*, cap. XXV.

[4] See my *Secret Doctrine in Israel*, pp. 191, 213, 231, 255.

[5] *Ibid.*, chapter XVI, *passim*.

[6] I believe that no titles were prefixed to his works by Ruysbroeck, and Surius has included this tract in *De Vera Contemplatione*, of which it forms the first sixteen chapters. The French translator R. Chamonal follows the arrangement of Surius, though he translates from the Flemish text, to which we owe the alternative. There is an English rendering of *The Book of the Twelve Béguines* by John Francis, 1913.

opens " for the inward man who is recollected in himself, is free, empty of earthly things and " turned with a full heart towards the Eternal Goodness."[1] There are four stages, and in the first a light descends from the face of Divine Charity, while the Spirit of the Saviour speaks in the loving heart.[2] The second is one of abiding in God's presence unveiled.[3] The soul receives light and counsel from the Father in a state of uplifted thought, apart from images.[4] Ruysbroeck adds that the light is not God but is itself an intermediary. It causes the soul to behold the face of the Father, meaning the substance or nature of God, in a simple gaze, beyond reason and without preparatory considerations.

It seems obvious that the face of God seen through a vehicle—whether this is called light or by any other name or names representing sensible things—is itself an image. This illustrates the fact that under the best circumstances some contradiction of symbolism is always involved when it is attempted to translate an ineffable experience into words. Moreover, the notion concerning " imageless ideas " involves a question which we shall have to consider carefully at a later stage. It is not a logical point—as of, e.g., contradiction in terms—but one of intellectual precision and the nature of the psychological field which, by the hypothesis, subsists apart from objects realised in the mind. Meanwhile, it may be noted that Ruysbroeck ends his thesis on the

---

[1] *The Book of the Twelve Béguines*, cap. X. Here is the rendering of Surius : *Dum se bonus quispiam et internæ vitæ deditus, in seipsum intrô recipit, vacans et absolutus ac expeditus à quibuscunque rebus terrenis, et cor habens superius reverenter apertum erga æternam bonitatem Dei, hic jam occultum patet cælum*, etc.

[2] *Ibid. Spiritus Domini eidem amanti patientique cordi loquitur.*—Surius.

[3] *Ii revelata sive detecta facie in Dei præsentia coram assistunt.*—Surius. Chamonal has misunderstood this passage and makes the text contradict itself. A correct rendering from the Flemish is given by John Francis.

[4] *Supra imagines, supra rationem et absque ratione.*—Surius.

second stage of experience by a qualification, when he adds: "The soul becomes conscious that it sees God, so far as man can do in this mortal state"—which is one of images, substitutes and intermediaries without end.[1]

The third stage is rendered *speculatio* by Surius and is said to be like seeing in a mirror[2]—a form of symbolism which leaves us where we should look to be—still in a world of reflections. The illustration nearest to my hand is in Tennyson's *Lady of Shalott*, who was bound by a spell to see things of the world beyond her island through the reflection of a mirror only. But Lancelot at last came riding by, with all his harness and knightly panoply, at the image of whom she could brook the glass no longer and risked the doom of her spell to look directly. Hereof is the validity of mirrors. But the fourth stage is an elevated and illuminated exercise in love for the most sweet will of God.

Ruysbroeck calls these stages of contemplation, but it does not appear in any that the mystic has reached the end of his travelling. The alchemists said of one another that a major difficulty about the memorials of adepts was to know at what stage of the process a particular text started and—on occasion—where it came to an end. In the records of mystics there is no question about the point of departure, but much debate is possible as to the grade attained. Apparent divergences in testimonies have arisen in this manner, lending a surface-warrant to some current opinions on formulations of incommunicable experience and their validity. The manifold tabulations of witnesses like Eckehart, Ruysbroeck and others of the Latin school, though each of them is easy to follow in its own way, tend to confuse the issues. As to the term itself in Ruysbroeck there is no confusion, however. In one form of symbolism it is "the fixed gaze of the

---

[1] *Ibid.*, cap. XI. *Quatenus eum in hac mortalis vitæ conditione cernere licet.*—Surius.

[2] *Speculatio dicitur, quasi quædam in speculo intuitio.*—Cap. XII.

spirit " in " the secret manifestation of God " for ever ; and this is the Blessed Vision.[1] But beyond this—as I deem it—there is the still beatitude of rapture in those souls of whom it is said: *Manentque intus in perenni fruitione, et supra dona omnia unum sunt cum Deo.*[2]

That anonymous English text which is called *The Cloud of Unknowing* shall serve as our next witness, and it may be said at the outset that its compass lies wholly within the measures of Dionysian symbolism. It is a text of the first importance, both in the essence and accidents : essentially, because of what it indicates and also because of its limitations ; accidentally, when considered as a jewel of mystical literature produced—we know not by whom nor how—in the country which has contributed least to the high history of Mysticism, whether in life or in literature. I shall speak of it somewhat fully.[3]

It should be explained in the first place that the term " cloud of unknowing " signifies that state in which the mystical work is accomplished, according to this text. It applies indifferently to the path and term of quest,

---

[1] *De Ornatu Spiritualium Nuptiarum*, Lib. III, cap. 3.

[2] *Regnum Deum Amantium*, cap. XLIII.

[3] There are two editions, which differ conspicuously in their claims. That which was edited in 1871 by the Rev. Henry Collins, under the title of *The Divine Cloud*, was made from a corrupt text, of which fact the editor was perhaps unaware. His intention was " not to reproduce an antique, but to give a beautiful spiritual work to the present generation." That which was edited in 1912, under its proper title—*The Cloud of Unknowing*—was intended, " not for the student of Middle English, nor for the specialist in mediæval literature ; but for the general reader and lover of mysticism." It was produced from one of the six MSS. in the British Museum, compared with four others, and is therefore excellent. The textual part was the work of Mr. David Inward, while the editing was that of Miss Evelyn Underhill, who has added a good introduction. Perhaps some day there will be room for a definitive edition for specialists in mystical literature. The present one is modernised. Some readers of the new edition miss the Ven. Augustin Baker's prefatory remarks and notes in that which preceded it.

for the progress is likened to a cloud of unknowing,[1] while " the feeling or seeing of God " takes place in a cloud of darkness.[2] The darkness is a Dionysian " lack of knowing " and a forgetting of that which is known.[3] It is not fantasy or false imagination,[4] nor is it a question of attainment by " travail in the wits."[5] One principle is that the natural understanding cannot lead to a knowledge of spiritual things but " failing to understand may."[6] It is actually that work and state in which man was at the beginning and wherein he would have remained but for " the sin of man."[7] The condition in chief is love,[8] in virtue of the postulate that God is comprehensible thereby.[9] It is love apart from condition[10] and outside thinking[11]—an intimate love " pressed in a cleanness of spirit on the cloud of unknowing "[12] and suspended with longing desire therein. The state itself is a state of will and the will " feels a naked intent unto God."[13] Given this and the plenary postulate of love, the work is the shortest and lightest imaginable[14]—a moment of the will.[15] The Divine comprehension attained is a miracle of love, going on for ever, in an experience that is endless bliss.[16] That which is attained is a kind of union, a state of being united to God in spirit,[17] by dwelling in the highest and most sovereign point of the spirit.[18] This notwithstanding, there is always a cloud of unknowing between the soul and God.[19] There is no clear seeing by

---

[1] See p. 72 of Miss Underhill's text, from which all my references will be drawn.   [2] *Ibid.*, p. 73.   [3] *Ibid.*, p. 84.

[4] *Ibid.*, p. 82.   [5] *Ibid.*   [6] *Ibid.*, p. 297.

[7] *Ibid.*, p. 77.   [8] *Ibid.*, p. 71.

[9] *Ibid.*, p. 76.   [10] *Ibid.*, p. 87.

[11] *Ibid.*, p. 89. Compare Richard Rolle: The soul that knows the mystery of love " with a great cry ascends to his Love."—*The Fire of Love*, Miss Frances M. Comper's edition, 1914, p. 161.

[12] *The Cloud of Unknowing*, p. 121.   [13] *Ibid.*, p. 72.

[14] *Ibid.*, pp. 72, 75.   [15] *Ibid.*, p. 75.   [16] *Ibid.*, p. 77.

[17] *Ibid.*, p. 160.   [18] *Ibid.*, p. 191.   [19] *Ibid.*, pp. 132, 294.

the light of understanding,[1] no true experience in the sweetness of love.[2] Such feeling and knowing as there is granted of God is not of Himself as He is, nor as we shall know Him hereafter, but as He vouchsafes to be known and felt by a meek soul in the body.[3] Sometimes a beam of ghostly light pierces the cloud and reveals a vestige of " God's privity," whereof man cannot speak.[4] The union, such as it is, requires " soothfastness and deepness of spirit,"[5] and as the work must be continued through life so it needs health of body as well as of soul.[6] The distinction remains throughout between God and His creature, all union notwithstanding.[7] The work is described otherwise as a " labour in the nowhere and the nought,"[8] with a naked desire of will to possess God in His naked being, the man being above himself and under God.[9] But that which is nought to the outer man is all to the man within, and the soul is really blinded, not by intensity of darkness but by excess of light.[10] Among the earlier experiences are visions of that which is thought to be paradise or even heaven.[11] So also in the peace and the rest the soul thinks that it sees God.[12] But to see, hear or feel anything indicates deception and that which is called obscurely a working against the course of Nature.[13]

The text as a whole is comparable to the far-off report of an experience.[14] It is not even a discourse

[1] *Ibid.*, pp. 104, 129. [2] *Ibid.*, p. 129. [3] *Ibid.*, p. 120.
[4] *Ibid.*, p. 164. [5] *Ibid.*, p. 221. [6] *Ibid.*, p. 203.
[7] *Ibid.*, p. 287. [8] *Ibid.*, p. 290.
[9] *Ibid.*, p. 286. See also p. 150. [10] *Ibid.*, p. 291.
[11] *Ibid.*, p. 294. [12] *Ibid.*
[13] *Ibid.*, p. 296. We have seen that Dionysius bears similar testimony.
[14] It may be read in connection with Hilton's *Scale of Perfection*, which belongs approximately to the same period of English mystical literature. Walter Hilton describes the true union as following on illumination of grace. It is knowledge, comprehension, and—as he says in another place —it is light of knowledge. He affirms further that in such grace the soul beholds God, attaining Divine knowledge at first hand. There is a day

concerning the term in union : it is an inkling and a vestige. So far as it proceeds, I call it true testimony, but assuredly the cloud encloses it. God is thought to be understood as Christ, and the soul in the darkness is said to have the love of the Spouse but not the knowledge. The abiding in the cloud of unknowing is in analogy with that mystical state called death in another form of symbolism. This also is a condition of inward suspension in its completeness. In these days there is a disposition of unwary people to experiment in the attainment of this and other experiences by methods of concentration apart from spiritual training. If there be any meaning in the term sanctity and in the living of the life, the danger signals loom redly over ways like these, supposing that they were pursued consistently ; but the initial failures are commonly an adequate check on the zeal of the moment, or the concentrations—if continued—are changed in respect of the object and distributed to no personal detriment, if to little purpose, in the exploration of symbols, or devices of such kind.

St. Ignatius of Loyola, who after the unknown author of *The Cloud of Unknowing* may stand as our next witness in the order of time, was a man of vision, but one who was stayed about continually by objective graces of seership, and there were moments when he was not exactly wearied or satiated, but when he was humiliated and dismayed at the assumed weakness which required such hills of vision to protect his personal and inward Jerusalem. The fact indicates that he knew—intellectually at least—of a region where beyond these images and " voices there is peace." It does more perhaps than all the formulated *Exercises* to place him in the chain of mystics, for in most of the patent respects he belongs to another school of experience—

and' night symbolism in Bk. II, chapters 5 to 8, but it owes nothing to Dionysian symbolical formulæ.

that of the stigmatics within the measures of the Christ-Life formula and that of the psychical brides within the formula of the mystical marriage. It has been pointed out by a recent writer that the practice of the *Exercises* was a work of incessant self-suggestion.[1] This is true of all mystical practices, but those of Ignatius reduced the art to a science: yet it was essentially a science of images. Auto-suggestion is of the way of the soul to God, but so long as there are images, the soul is in the Divine Cloud and not at the formless centre. For the rest, *The Spiritual Exercises* [2] of St. Ignatius do not seem to be a fountain of light, in the mystical sense of these words, but they are good practice and in a deeper understanding they may become a great practice. If we take his Third Truth: " I am destined for God " [3]—apart from most of his disquisitions and considerations thereupon, we have the subject of our daily life set before us. There is also a ground of salvation in the recognition of man's greatness and its evidence of his end in God.[4] Most important of all is an intimation that the Blessed Vision merges into the Divine Union, as I have suggested further back in these records. It is said that " the soul sees God, and this sight—in a manner—transforms it into God Himself,"[5] according to the words of St. John.[6] It is a ravishment

[1] Compare William James who describes the *Spiritual Exercises*, much too inadequately, as " a graduated series of efforts to imagine holy scenes "—a sort of picture-palace of the mind—and adds : " The acme of this kind of discipline would be a semi-hallucinatory mono-ideism."—*Varieties of Religious Experience*, 24th impression, pp. 406 to 407.

[2] The editions are innumerable, but I will mention only *Exercitia Spiritualia*, Antwerp, 1732. There is an English translation—*Manresa* —adapted for general use.

[3] See the *Spiritual Exercises for Four Weeks* : First Week.

[4] " I am not made for a mortal man ; I am not made for myself ; I am not made for an angel. . . . I am too great for a creature, however noble, to be my end."—*Development of the Principle of the Exercises*.

[5] *Exercises on the Blessed Life of Jesus Christ in Heaven* : Second Point.   [6] St. John : I, III, 2.

for ever, and this is the "beatitude of will." The "blessed forget themselves, to be lost in God." The love is so ecstatic that "the soul goes out of itself and passes entirely into God, to be consummated in unity with Him."[1] Here is a state which is beyond all that is signified by the word "vision," whether the author of the *Exercises* realised it or not.

There is nothing else in the literal teachings of the work which is of the least consequence in respect of path or term, and I am afraid that if it were read at the present day by persons trained in metaphysical speculation, some parts of it would excite their derision, nor indeed quite unjustly, outside all questions of orthodox Latin doctrine. The attempt to conceive eternity as ages continued henceforward is one case in point; and of course there are all the conventions of popular theology in endless arid tabulations. Having said this, I must add that if the plan of the *Exercises* were raised from their particular sphere of motive and applied to the practice of the hidden life in God, I can think of no greater aid to realisation for persons in search of a method and in need of precise formulæ.

The little book which is known among us under the title of *Theologia Germanica* but is, unquestionably, the same text that is called otherwise *The Book of the Man from Frankfurt*,[2] was issued, so to speak, with the *imprimatur* of Martin Luther and has long been of great repute with persons of the protestant persuasion who are disposed mystically. If I think that it has been a

[1] Compare Godinez: *Prax. Theologiæ Mysticæ*, Lib. VI, c. 6. "In the finding of Thee I have found also myself, and in Thy loss my self is lost."

[2] This is the title ascribed to the text by Dr. Rudolf Steiner in his study of mystics referred to the Renaissance epoch. A preface to the ancient Wurtzburg codex states that the author was "a warden in the House of the Teutonic Order in Frankfort." *Theologia Germanica* is much too sweeping a title. We should hardly be justified in issuing *The Cloud of Unknowing* as *Theologia Anglicana*.

little over-estimated, this is merely a personal view and stands at its value. It is not a protestant text or a post-Reformation text, and as I do not know that its orthodoxy is under any serious question—though there is some language which would be called incautious [1]—it is a matter for regret that it has not been edited with prudence in a Latin-Catholic interest. In that department of religious life the forewords once ascribed to Luther have been sufficient to account for the taboo which obtains respecting it. There is not very much to our purpose, but I must give a brief analysis on account of its vogue.

The Union is attainable on earth [2] and is a perfect integration in the eternal Will of God. The inward man stands immovable therein, and the soul receives commands, counsels and teaching, becoming a partaker apparently of the Divine Nature, by entering into the mind of God. The beginning of this state is in holy practices and ordinances, [3] but the end no man can declare, for the experience is beyond expression. [4] The doctrine of the state is that Christ is the Way and the Door, and that we must go in and out through Him. [5] There is nothing new in all this, except in so far as the stress laid on the idea of ineffability is a little more express than it is in some of the testimonies.

In St. John of the Cross and St. Teresa, whose external work was cast to some extent together, and who had many opportunities for comparing their inward experience, we have two important and indeed palmary concurrent witnesses of the attained union. At the

---

[1] The state of liberation in which fear of hell and hope of heaven have been replaced by " pure submission to the Eternal Goodness " would of course recall Quietism to the minds of those who condemned it.
[2] That is to say, after the manner of foretaste.—*Theologia Germanica*, translated by Susanna Winkworth, Chapter VIII. See also Chapter XXIV. [3] *Ibid.*, Chapter XXVI.
[4] *Ibid.*, Chapter XXI. Again it is said : " But what the end is knoweth no man to declare."—Chapter. XXIII. [5] *Ibid.*, Chapter LII.

same time there were never more distinct deponents testifying to the same term. St. John of the Cross tells us that the state of Divine Union consists in a total transformation of will into the will of God, operated in such a manner that every movement of the human is invariably that of the will of God only.[1] It is of threefold nature, being an union of understanding, volition and memory.[2] There are also three stages of progression—transitory, abiding and perfect. Owing to some defect in expression, the evidence is not quite in harmony with itself at all points. It seems to be suggested in one place that these stages are consequent on a habit of mind in this life and are reached here. This is intelligible and consistent. But elsewhere it is said (*a*) that union can be perfect only in the life to come, (*b*) that an abiding sense of it is impossible to the faculties of the soul as now insphered, but (*c*) that there is a passing sense of it, (*d*) some anticipation of the sweetness to come, though in a manner wholly ineffable.[3] Probably St. John of the Cross is in agreement with St. Bernard when he states that the rapture of highest experience seldom endures above one quarter of an hour. It is reached apparently in the third stage of progression, being that called perfect; but how the transitory, within a space measured by minutes, can be called abiding, or the imperfect termed perfection,[4] must be interpreted as we best can.

The transformation of the will is an operation of the love principle; the one is the state and the other the

---

[1] *The Ascent of Mount Carmel*, Book I, c. 11. See also Book III, c. 15 for " the active detachment of the will, with a view to its perfect establishment " in the virtue of the love of God.

[2] See Book II, c. V—and the work generally.

[3] This is intimated in *A Spiritual Canticle*, Stanza I, par. 15, developed in Stanza XXXVIII, par. 3, and carried into fuller expression in Stanza XXXIX, par. 7.

[4] In another place, when speaking of perfect tranquillity, there is added—" so far as it is possible in this life."—*The Dark Night of the Soul*,

bond of union. The greater the soul's love, so does it enter the deeper into God,[1] becoming a partaker of Himself—that is to say, of the Divine Nature. It is reached in " dark contemplation," the attained knowledge of God being clothed in none of the images or sensible representations used otherwise by the mind.[2] To accentuate this Dionysian view, it is said elsewhere that in ecstasy God begins to communicate Himself no longer through the channels of sense but in pure spirit— that is, not in successive reflections but in an act of pure contemplation, to which neither the exterior nor interior senses of our lower nature can ascend.[3]

St. Teresa, who speaks of stages and states more especially in the terms of prayer,[4] as others speak of contemplation, is in agreement with St. John of the Cross that there is an union of three faculties—classed as will, understanding and memory.[5] She makes a very

Book II, cap. XXIV, par. 3. See also *The Ascent of Mount Carmel*, Book II, c. 5, for a distinction between the " perfect and abiding union," which seems to be " a habit " of this life, and " actual union " hereafter. . Compare what is added immediately : " There is not and cannot be in this life any abiding union."

[1] *The Living Flame of Love*, translated by David Lewis, Stanza I, par. 15.

[2] " It is called night, because contemplation is dim ; and that is the reason why it is called also mystical theology, that is, the secret or hidden wisdom of God, where, without the sound of words, or the intervention of any bodily or spiritual sense . . ., God teaches the soul . . . in a most secret and hidden way."—*A Spiritual Canticle*, Stanza XXXIX, par. 15.

[3] *The Dark Night of the Soul*, translated by David Lewis, Book I, c. 9, par. 11.

[4] They are (1) mental prayer, (2) prayer of recollection or quietude, (3) prayer of union, and (4) prayer of rapture or ecstasy.—*The Life of St. Teresa of Jesus, written by Herself*. Translated by David Lewis. Edition of 1911. See Chapters XI–XIX. It is to be understood that the life of the Presence is the life of Prayer.

[5] In his Bampton Lectures on *Christian Mysticism* Dean Inge considers that this classification proves Saint Teresa's acquaintance with scholastic philosophy.

subtle distinction as to the will of God. After conformity, surrender, abeyance, transformation of the human in Divine Will, God restores her will to the soul, nor this only, for He gives her His own as well. It is St. Teresa also who tells us that there is a term beyond the Union, being that which is called indifferently rapture,[1] transport or flight of the spirit, for these three are one. She has said elsewhere that in the Prayer of Union the spirit is united utterly to God, with a peaceful and supreme content of the will and " a feeling of repose." In this state the soul " cannot decide with certainty what it enjoys."[2] Her power is absorbed in contemplation, activity ceases, the presence of God is realised, and she rests certain subsequently that she has entered into the Divine Being. Not satisfied with having united the soul to Himself, God begins to caress her, revealing His secrets. She is deprived of her exterior senses, lest they should distract, and this produces what is called rapture.[3] It is explained that in union we remain on our own ground, but rapture is irresistible.[4] The intimations call to be collected from different places of record, and, as in St. John of the Cross, there does not seem to be full verbal agreement throughout. It is not indeed to be expected.

St. Teresa's House of the Soul is a House of Prayer, wherein the seventh floor is a heaven and a place of

[1] There are many places of reference to ecstasy and rapture. See among others *The Life*, Chapter XX. The experience was often accompanied by bodily levitation.

[2] *The Way of Perfection*, Chapter XXXI, par. 8. Compare my reference to Suso, p. 67, and my distinctions on mystical experience, s.v. Eckehart and his alleged pantheism, pp. 63-66.

[3] *Ibid.*, Chapter XXXII, par. 11.

[4] *The Life*, Chapter XX, par. 3. The *Dabistan* also appears to recognise a state beyond union, being a dwelling in Deity and an indwelling of Deity in the soul, the sense of personality having dissolved. The state is called rest, but it will be seen that it is formulated in the terms of that union which is said to precede it. Compare the Sufic aphorism : " I am the soul of my Beloved."—Tholuck : *S. Sufismus*, 1821.

marriage.[1] Christ lives in the soul and there is a clear knowledge of the Holy Trinity.[2] Heaven, mystical marriage, realisation in the mystery of God—one would say that these signify the perfect beatitude of the soul, the repose beyond the union, the state that is called rapture. But if such is the testimony found in *The Interior Castle*, *The Way of Perfection* seems to convey a different message. The rapture described therein is a quick, sharp shock, as of the power of the Lord manifested.[3] It is accompanied by great fear, strange detachment, a pain that we ourselves can neither inflict nor remove. There are loneliness of spirit, desire, bitterness and extremity of need—some of these befalling one and some of them another soul. In the highest state of the rapture, the soul does not see, hear or perceive. There is pain on returning subsequently to normal life; but the fruits abide in the soul, which does everything for the glory of the Lord, and according to His will.

This is comparable to St. John of the Cross, who affirms (*a*) that union of the soul and God is the highest and noblest estate attainable in this life;[4] (*b*) that it does not consist in spiritual refreshments but in the living death of the cross, experienced sensually and spiritually, outwardly and inwardly;[5] (*c*) that it is attained when man has been brought to nothing, when his humility is perfect.

---

[1] It lies beyond all that is understood by the Prayer of Union. See *The Interior Castle*. I have used the French translation called *Le Château de l'Âme* in Arnaud d'Andilly's *Œuvres de Sainte Thérèse*, Vol. II, 1855.

[2] *Ibid.*, c. I, § 3.

[3] See also *The Life*, c. XX, par. 10 *et seq*. The suffering is at the same time full of sweetness—par. 20. "I would not barter it for all the graces"—par. 21. But in itself there is a great grace—par. 22.

[4] *A Spiritual Canticle*, Stanza I, par. 15, and Stanza XXXVIII, par. 3. Above it, in the world to come, there is "the union of glory."

[5] Compare the "wounds of love," which inflame the will, and "the secret touches of love, which, like a fiery arrow, pierce and penetrate the soul, and burn it with the fire of love."—*Ibid.*, Stanza I, par. 23.

The Way of Divine Union

We have now finished with the great witnesses and can deal briefly with those whom it is desirable to cite among the remaining deponents. It may be thought that I should have classed St. Francis de Sales in the more important category, and I know that there are many respects in which he is both lovable and illuminating ; but we must each speak as we find. It seems to me that if he is not in the Court of the Temple instead of the Holy Place, he is at least in the Holy Place rather than the Holy of Holies.[1] I will ask to be forgiven beforehand if the more blessed and perfect essence has perhaps escaped me. In his—to me—unconvincing *Mystical Explanation of the Canticle of Canticles*, it is said that the " perfect resignation of the soul into and unto God " is the end of mental prayer[2]—for, like St. Teresa, he adopts the Prayer formula—and the highest degree of spirituality, which is the close " union of the soul with God by devotion."[3] Now, devotion is a word of the path, but is inadequate for the state of attainment, and I am reminded irresistibly of the saint's *Philothea*,[4] which is so very good for the ordinary believer, who is to be kept in the right way by the practice of piety and to be fenced up against common temptations, but is rather

---

[1] He recognises, and none more clearly, that " the secret of perfection is the secret of love." The soul's progress is for him a progress in love, and is without end, like love. See *L'Esprit de Saint François de Sales* . . . *Nouvelle Édition*, 1747.

[2] The thesis is that in Solomon's *Song of Songs* the intention of the wise king was to produce a devout memorial on the subject of mental prayer. " He supposes the spouse, that is, the devout soul, to be already married to her Divine Beloved, and represents their holy and chaste married loves, practised by mental prayer "—understood as the consideration of Divine Things.—See the Saint's preface to his *Mystical Explanation* in the late Canon Mackey's translation, 1908. It seems necessary to say, with great reverence, that the thesis is not less than ridiculous.

[3] *Ibid.*, p. 40.

[4] The alternative title is *An Introduction to a Devout Life*. There are many English editions. What I believe to have been the first English translation was " approved " by ecclesiastical authority in 1847.

as a desert for the mystic. The *Commentary*, however, uses another manner of formula in a later place—distinguishing, with several earlier writers, between active and passive unions, in each of which there are held to be various degrees. The highest attainable in this life is intellectual passive union, and God is contemplated therein apart from perceptible images, by the aid of an intellectual supernatural light darted into the soul.[1] " Herein—though God be not seen as He is—yet is it clearly seen that He is and is also incomprehensible."

No inconsiderable proportion of books that pass as mystical, or the authors of which have the repute of mystics, are exhortatory, explanatory, or spiritual treatises of an elementary kind. I have mentioned one of them under the name of St. Francis de Sales. *De Ascensione Mentis ad Deum*,[2] by Cardinal Bellarmine, is a second case in point, though it claims to erect a ladder by which man can " ascend as high as to God Almighty," beginning with the consideration of man himself. Its notion concerning the end does not reach further than the ingathering of those who attain redemption into that " land of the living " where they shall be enlightened with the brightness of the Divine Presence. They will not comprehend God, but will behold the Divine Face without a veil. It is promised, however, that the kind of seeing shall truly satisfy.

The truth is that the age of recorded experience at first hand has given place to one of commentary and

---

[1] Compare *The Cloud of the Unknowing*, c. XXVI : " Then will He sometimes peradventure send out a beam of ghostly light, piercing this cloud of unknowing that is betwixt thee and Him ; and shew thee some of His privity."

[2] I have used the edition of 1615 published at *Colonia Agrippina*, but there is also an English translation of 1703 by H. Hall, addressed to protestant readers and omitting certain passages relating to saints, angels and so forth, as a concession to prejudice. I do not think that, either in the original or the rendering, it has any message or appeal to mystics.

explication. In England there is the Venerable Augustin Baker, who drew, as he tells us, from more than forty treatises for the production of *Sancta Sophia*—an excellent and indeed noble compendium in which the sanctity and genius of the writer count for much. I do not know that there is a better guide to the witnesses or a more accurate harmony of their evidence ; many beautiful and moving passages informed by a blessed spirit might be quoted and would adorn these pages, but it would be reproducing and not adding to our array of testimonies respecting that which Baker calls so truly " the secrets of Divine Love."[1]

Scaramelli is also one of the great compilers, and from his elaborate treatises there are at least two passages with which I will close the memorials of the present section. The state of Divine Union is defined to be " an experimental love of God, so intimate and close that the soul loses itself utterly in Him "—including all feeling and consciousness of itself and its acts. But it is not a fusion or transformation as to substance, nor is it a transmutation of essence in the being of God.[2] Here is the first point, and the second tells us that perfect Union constitutes a wound of love—on account apparently of its transitory nature in this life. The separation which follows is an agony, as if death itself must supervene.[3]

---

[1] *Sancta Sophia* is a digest of several collections of Augustin Baker which themselves remain in manuscript. It was the work of Father Serenus Cressy, also a Benedictine monk, and was published in 1657 at Douay. Baker himself died in 1641. Abbot Sweeney's edition of 1905 under the title of Holy Wisdom is excellent in every way.

[2] Compare Cardinal Bona, who says : *Stat Dominus innixus scalæ, ut animam amoris igne candentem sibi intimé uniat, et indissolubili charitatis nexu secum conglutinet.—De Psalmis Gradualibus*, cap. 15.

[3] We have seen that St. Teresa is an authority for this view, and it may be added that, according to St. John of the Cross, the union with God on earth is not only attained on the cross but is part of our life-crucifixion in the path of sanctity. Mr. D. H. S. Nicholson has published a very brief analysis of Scaramelli under the title of *A Handbook of*

Christian Mysticism of the Latin Schools

A consensus or harmony of the chief witnesses as to the term attained by them under the ægis of Latin Christianity has been ingarnered in this section, and as I believe for the first time, apart from the consideration of ways and means and processes. It will assist us to see where we are in the research which follows. The memorials meanwhile have told us that all the work is an experimental act of love ; that this is the bond of union between the soul and the Divine ; that faith, contemplation, prayer are within love itself or its fruits ; that self is the path by which we journey to that which is above self, being the state in which our life is God's own life ; that the mystical work is one of the will in God, an incorporation and total transformation of human in Divine will by virtue of the love principle. It begins with an intention to do the will of God, not because we know it but in order that we may learn in the doing. This also is part of the great experiment. That which is not disclosed although it is implied everywhere is the nature of the passage from the state of the soul in separation to that of the soul in union, but it has been made plain—in bare outline—on my own part in the previous sections. It is said truly by Böhme that the will is the *mysterium magnum* and thereby the soul may become what Madame Guyon calls an instrument of God. The reason is that will under impulsion from the love principle inspires the human subject with the Divine object of desire, and this is a work in the self by which the soul reaches at last the state of self-knowledge in God and God is its knowledge of self.

Mystical Theology, 1913. The original was written in Italian—*Il Direttorio Mistico*—and appeared at Venice in 1754. It is one of the largest compilations on pure Mysticism. There is a good Latin translation.

CHAPTER IV

DERIVATIONS AND REFLECTIONS OF THE MYSTICAL TERM IN POST-REFORMATION SCHOOLS

In my consideration of the chief witnesses, our subject of research has been brought to the first quarter of the seventeenth century—compilations not included—or something like two hundred years after the attempted purgation of the Church by Martin Luther. There, remains over a later testimony within the Latin Church which was held by that institution to be not of it. I should scarcely have detached this owing merely to a charge of heresy, but it connotes—as I think—unquestionably the introduction of a certain new spirit, if not of new elements; and although there was no sense in which the little group of mystics concerned can be said to have drawn from sects or schools of protestantism, it is better that a distinction should be made—while guarding against its exaggeration and against confusion as to its real nature.[1]

There were also the non-Catholic schools which connect with Mysticism and are considerable after their own manner. They are more important for their variations from the doctrine, practice and experience of the Latin Church on its mystical side than for that which they had to offer on their own part in any or all

[1] There is a reasonable question whether what I have called the new spirit manifested in Quietism was not consequent upon a new spirit abroad in the world of religion, though not less counter thereto than to the self-protecting interests of the Latin Church; but I should need a special section for its consideration—and for this I find no warrant.

of these classes. I should add that there are great names connected with them and that I am not seeking to reduce their message or its influence. That which it is essential to affirm is the fact of a complete, an almost absolute difference. The concern is God and the soul ; the Way is Christ. Man is designed for God and does after some manner enter into communion with Him. But the central truth is overlaid with endless accretions of dream-hypotheses, with cosmic schemes and strange Scriptural exegesis, as we shall see immediately, so that it scarcely emerges as the term in view, but rather as a notion underlying a wide region of fantasy. And for the rest the *mise-en-scène* has an aspect of utter newness. It is not that the cloister has been shaken off : it is forgotten. It is not that the ascetic life is under sentence : it remains as to first principles, but it has been transformed. It is not that another formula has replaced the symbolism of crucified life : this has come into greater vogue and has reached its term in a far more elaborate development. It is not that the formula of the mystical marriage has passed out of mystical consciousness : one of its most curious texts is the work of a militant protestant in Cromwellian England. It is not that there is open hostility to Mysticism of the Latin type : to all intents and purposes that type is non-existent for the later witnesses. I have searched their records for indications that they were tolerably acquainted with the lives or literature of those who preceded them, but with next to no result. I question whether these precursors would have stood for anything acceptable, and this for the reason given—that no two groups or schools could well have been more distinct.

Latin Mysticism was a monastic growth and a gospel of ascetic life presented in a particular form. In Germany of the fourteenth century there was an attempt to proclaim it before the world at large ; but to all intents and purposes it remained under the same ægis, carried the same titles and inculcated the same rule of thought and conduct. Every deponent whom I have cited in the previous chapter was of monastery, convent or hermitage, and I have not made an arbitrary selection, for other witnesses there were none. The instructor of Tauler is said indeed to have been a layman, Nicholas of Basle, one of the Friends of God,[1] to whom the Holy Inquisition procured the crown of martyrdom.[2] But he left nothing behind him, or it has remained in that house of reservation which gives up no secrets. I do not suggest that the German movement subsided without effect. There is no question that it sowed certain seeds, and they did not fall utterly upon waste ground. Whether they led up to the Reformation, whether they helped merely to make it possible, or whether they were first-fruits of that which was working to cast off a grievous yoke are other questions and not of my concern here. The fact which emerges is that the need of Mysticism had to declare itself without as well as within the pale of Latin Christianity, and the declaration came. It had practically no witnesses to any of the Latin types; it might have never heard of Dionysius; and it filled

---

[1] Their records shew that they recognised and sought to rectify the evils within the church, and in this sense they represented that anti-papal spirit which preceded the Reformation of which Gabriele Rossetti wrote. They were not intentional innovators working within the field of doctrine. They were believers in a personal devil, in multitudes of devils, in purgatory, hell and paradise, where Tauler—according to his legend—remained for five days after his death. Above or beyond paradise was " the blissful company of the blessed in eternity," a place of " unspeakable joys." See Susanna Winkworth's preface to *Theologia Germanica*. The Friends of God are not to be classed among mystics in any general way.

[2] Rulman Merswin was also a layman, but he exchanged the life of a merchant for that of contemplation and an asceticism comparable to the self-tortures of Suso. Vaughan gives a good account of his work called *The Nine Rocks*. It is (1) a book of visions, (2) an account of the evil state of Christendom, and (3) a delineation at the end of the soul's progress towards a higher life and return to God.

the mystical mind with a whole world of new images. In these respects it was not less unlike the German Mysticism of the fourteenth century. It was not a work on the part of men who were under the rule of " counsels of perfection " ; they were men in the world ; they were married for the most part ; and if their doctrine, practice and experience are to be counted as mystical, it was novelty as such and owed little to the mystical past—even when it borrowed unawares. Men and women, the prime movers have been classed indifferently as mystics, and we have either to justify or to reject their inclusion.

A clear line of demarcation in the history of our subject belongs to the late sixteenth century, which saw the development of a cosmic philosophy, being of the nature of revelation and as such not unconnected with a doctrine of inward life. The latter remained, however, within defined limits and was mainly in the psychic realm, though it had undoubtedly a deeper side. Whether it owed much, little or anything to the movement of the fourteenth century, as opening a gate of possibility, is a question that seems likely to remain unanswered for want of materials. Were it otherwise I feel that the judgment would be in the form of a decisive negative, save in so far as that movement first began to transfer the sphere of mystical thought from the cloister to the hearth of the layman. What we do know, however, is that the Reformation threw open the Holy Scriptures to the study of the Christian world at large. The old rubbish-heap of crass, vulgarian thought and noxious emotion which protestantism has gathered about chained Bibles is at this day less or more scattered to the four winds, though sporadic dust of it is blown into our eyes occasionally. I am not therefore proclaiming a liberation of texts in words of zeal. Had the houses of learning procured and utilised more chains than they did, it might not be our part to lament so bitterly and vainly the loss of so many priceless works. But there can be no question that Luther's German Bible marked the beginning of a new era in the intellectual world, though it is for the last of all reasons that protestanism would acclaim or recognise. The right of private judgment exercised on texts is of course inalienable, and to this prerogative we owe the *magnum et infirmatum chaos* of irresponsible critical opinion, as well as those expositions which are authorised by knowledge and insight. Out of it there came, among other things, what I must call—somewhat loosely—the mystical interpretation of Scripture. At the period with which we shall be dealing the long succession of commentators, from Pope Gregory to Cornelius a Lapide, was not less effectively chained than that example of the Bible in Luther's monastery which caused the restless monk to believe—granted there was God in His Heaven—that there was yet something wrong with the religious world in the midst of which he was dwelling. They were chained and inhibited—tacitly, almost unknowingly— by the neglect following revolt against that authority which maintained its official centre at Rome. The exegesis of the two Testaments had to be remade in the likeness of reform ; and when the need for Mysticism began—as I have said—to assert itself in the new schools of thought, there arose a mystical interpretation of Scripture. It sought, all unconscious, for the most part, of such an analogy, to do for the Christian world what Zoharic theosophy had done—and in the persons of its commentators had barely finished with doing—for the world of Israel. It found intimations in the texts of the two Testaments that they—or part of them—were written within and without ; and the first thing which happened was the direction of Jacob Böhme's wonderful glass of vision to the meanings that lay, *ex hypothesi*, behind the written word of each. Jacob Böhme is the source and well-spring of most protestant theosophy down to the end of the eighteenth century—when the closing was taken in all grades of Mysticism—much as the French Magus Éliphas Lévi is the well-spring of modern occultism. The particular qualities of the Teuton's own arcane philosophy, his own cosmogenesis, his own Way to Christ are reflected through his various successors, approximately or remotely. The kinship—by him unrealised—of his Scriptural interpretations with those of Jewish Kabalism brought the Christian students of the latter—sometimes quite unawares—into the line of succession from the Teutonic theosopher—e.g. the Kentish "philosopher by fire," Robertus de Fluctibus, and even Thomas Vaughan.[1] If the growth of non-Catholic Mysticism in Germany, France and England cannot be termed a development of Böhme's doctrine, it represents at least a perpetuation of his strange influence. That which was indirect in Engelbrecht, Poiret, Dutens, Marsay and Antoinette de Bourignon was obvious and permeating in Jane Lead, Pordage, William Law and Saint-Martin. All are linked into the chain at one point or another. The sleep of the mystical tradition at the close of the eighteenth century brought it to a term, and thereafter came the hollow substitution of occult science in its revival.

[1] We must beware of exaggerating or pressing analogies of this kind. The distinction, for example, between Böhme and Robert Fludd was that the first was a man of psychic and the second of intellectual vision. The one beheld his revelation of the cosmos in the inward state; the other excogitated a scheme. The one was more especially a seer and the other a man of learning. Still the analogies exist and I am glad that the Rev. J. B. Craven in his excellent study of *Doctor Robert Fludd* has proved himself alive to the fact, though he does not enlarge thereon. The fact is otherwise of no particular importance to my subject, and I question whether any mystic will be at the pains of verifying it in the forgotten folios of Fludd. The position of Vaughan in the sequence is after a similar kind. It signifies little whether either of them had come across a single line of Böhme's theosophy, though it is known that Vaughan had, for he refers in his *Cœlum Terræ* to the *Discourse of the Three Principles*.

Cosmical philosophy evolved in psychical or even mystical states is no part of our concern, and I have mentioned it only to indicate one important and recurring point of distinction between the new and the old schools, it being understood that the basis is always a hidden sense of Scripture, which differs in each case from the remaining examples, as the systems themselves differ. But while there were macrocosmic revelations as a result of seership, there rose up also a new understanding of the microcosm, or of the work of man upon and within himself. It is in this sense exclusively that the post-Reformation schools may appeal to us, and when I have given their intimations concerning the term of the soul in God there will be only two other points of view from which I must recur to some of them.

For Jacob Böhme, the lineal way into eternal life is a discovery to be made in man, whose work is to seek and call upon the Holy Spirit within himself, for " it is there that God dwelleth in His Heaven and taketh in the soul's will with its desire." [1] The work is an union of the soul's will with the spirit of Christ in the inward ground, the last words being valuable, as indicating that the root is intention rather than conduct. [2] The creature is not God but remains under God eternally, [3] Whose light blazes through it. [4] I must not say that there is no sense of the mystical term, as this

[1] See Considerations upon Isaias Stiefel's *Threefold State of Man*, par. 116. This is also the doctrine of Franz von Baader, who speaks of the perfect inhabitation of the Divine Spirit in the spiritual man—a state which he terms " the end and the Sabbath."

[2] Of course in the sense that intention produces conduct, and in so far as the one leads to the other. Gichtel says that God is not in us unless and until we are surrendered to Him without reservation of any kind. But this surrender is an active work of the will. The doctrine concerning it is part of the life of grace in the soul.

[3] We have seen that this is also the testimony of Eckehart.

[4] *The Holy Week, or Prayer Book.*

was understood by the Catholic witnesses; but it is so overlaid with the singularities of Böhme's individual system that it is almost lost. Yet he was a certain light of the world in his age, a saving prophet of the worth and consequence of daily life.

Some other points may be collected as follows: (1) All spiritual knowledge is of that which God knows in us.[1] (2) God Himself is the Being of all beings, and we are as gods in Him: it will be observed that this is a question of comparison or analogy.[2] (3) God dwells in the regenerated man substantially, by means of the resigned will: this contains a most important implicit.[3] (4) To walk in God's love is to have an open gate into the Deity: but this is another way of saying what all have said—that love is the path of union.[4] (5) The will is the *Mysterium Magnum*.[5]

Towards the end of the seventeenth century there arose in England a direct successor—with a difference —of Jacob Böhme in the person of Dr. John Pordage, also a cosmological seer, who entered into hidden mysteries of Deity by the path of vision, like him who had preceded. The *Theologia Mystica* of Pordage supposes various worlds contained within an archetypal world and interpenetrated one by another. "Thus the Eternal World passeth through all the worlds which it

[1] See Böhme's *First Apology*, Part II.
[2] *The Threefold Life*, Part VI.
[3] *The Forty Questions*. Two things follow: (1) That resignation is an open door to the mystery of the New Birth; (2) That God abides within us as a transforming will which we have sought and taken into our hearts, and as part of the work of love.
[4] *Aurora*, Part XIII. The work of love is a work of the will within us.
[5] *The Small Six Points*. The Presence within us manifests as will; the quest is that of God's will; this quest does lead into true knowledge; the knowledge is realisation; and in its deep stages we enter into what Joseph Glanvil called the intentness of Divine Will. By intimations like this we see that Jacob Böhme is the deep unto deep uttering voice and the height unto height shewing knowledge.

comprehends within its circumference, for else God, Who fills this world and dwells in it, could not be omniscient, omnipotent and omnipresent God." This is not convincing exactly, either as vision, as theosophy conceived intellectually, or even ordinary debate ; and although in the main Pordage drew from Böhme—at least in the sense that they saw through similar glasses, however sparsely the later theosophist confesses to the fact itself—I do not pretend that he reproduces the Teuton literally.[1] While Böhme is incomparably greater, Dr. Pordage is much clearer, could we take him at his own valuation ; but were it possible—as it scarcely is—to tolerate the cosmic revelations, his external psychic history, auditions, locutions and unvolitional dealings with devils are beyond human patience.[2]

What is obvious in the case of Böhme is a good deal more than obvious in that of his successor. Both beheld a great pageant of cosmic images ; and it might be of considerable interest to aspirants—if any—after seership of this class, had Pordage left an account of the practices which induced his interior states : but this is wanting. He contributes little to our subject and is scarcely a mystic in the sense attached to the word throughout the present work.[3] When he says in *Theologia Mystica* :

[1] In the *Treatise of Eternal Nature with Her Seven Essential Forms*, Pordage says that " the highly illuminated Böhme " explains the bringing forth of elemental fire by the Eternal Will of God. P. 117. See also pp. 120, 122, 127. Böhme's terminology is used freely and some conceptions are almost identical with his.

[2] Dr. John Pordage was born about 1620 and died in London, 1698. He was in Holy Orders and had a living at Bradfield, from which he was ejected. The circumstances, being alleged ghostly visitants and supernatural communications, will be found in *Celebrated Trials*, 6 vols., 1825. He wrote *Innocency Appearing* in his own defence.

[3] In his discourse of the Most Holy Place or the still eternity, he affirms that the glory of the Deity is there beheld nakedly, " eye to eye and face to face," but it is entered apparently in this life, or was at least by him who narrates its wonders and the inexpressible joys therein.— *Theologia Mystica*, p. 55 (second pagination). Its proper inhabitants are,

" I now proceed to open the Mystery of the Holy
Trinity," he may not have been wanting in reverence,
or even in personal humility, but the mode of expression
—like the undertaking itself—may well seem stultifying,
and as to the discourse which follows, happily it is
beyond our province.

Thomas Bromley is much more to our purpose,
being a man of interpretation, not a man of vision—
in the sense of pictures and images. He had also some
conception of the mystical term, but he belongs more
especially to the consideration of my seventh chapter.
His explanation of the journey of the Twelve Tribes
of Israel on the quest of the Promised Land would be
a curious subject of study in connection with certain
sections of the Zohar and with the *Traité de la Réintégration des Êtres* of Martines de Pasqually. Between
the three there is at least one point of union in their
exercise of arbitrary skill to educe meanings from the
body general of the Scriptural text which had never

however, neither angels nor human souls but perfect simple spirits
belonging to another hierarchy and one in " communion with the
Blessed Trinity."—*Ibid.*, pp. 75 and 89. There was also Edward Hooker,
a bosom friend of Pordage, who wrote an effusive and tiresome introduction to *Theologia Mystica*. Though evidently a great light in the
Philadelphian circle of election, there is only one passage of his reverie
which bears quotation. He affirms that revelation of the Blessed Spirit
of God comes (*a*) by Vision, wherein heavenly ideas are presented to
the inward senses of man : this is the lowest degree ; (*b*) by Illumination, when the spirit of the mind is illuminated by a ray from the
Holy Spirit and thus purely apprehends the very sense of that Blessed
Spirit, without any " presentation of external objects " ; (*c*) by Trans-
portation or Translation, when the spirit of the mind is in very truth
and reality rapt and caught up, transcendentally and divinely, into the
very principle itself, there to introspect and comprehend the wonders
of the Ever-Adorable, Holy and Blessed Triune Deity ; (*d*) by the coming
down of the Holy Spirit into the essence of the soul, there to complete
the work of regeneration, opening the glories of the New Jerusalem,
coming from God out of Heaven into the soul's centre. This is the
Day of Pentecost. The account has high claims.

entered into the heart of its writers. Bromley reminds us of Dionysius when he speaks of the annihilation of all thought and of withdrawing from fantasy into the silent mind. He calls irregular imagination the false prophet— a statement which applies equally to the images of sensible things and those of the mind.[1]

A very curious and informing study is the deeper side of spiritual feeling which lies within and about the period of the Philadelphian Society—towards the end of the seventeenth century. Its chief light was either Pordage himself or Jane Lead, his co-heiress in a particular world of Divine Vision. Behind them in the near past shone a silver light from the Cambridge Platonists, full of sweet thought and enthroned reasonableness. I have spoken of the Philadelphian school and its concerns in another memorial,[2] of its testimony to a Secret Church, its expectation of a Christ to come and its ideas of a risen life. There is a sense in which the witnesses testified to the mystical end as the report of it comes to us through the Latin chain of succession, but it is clouded once again by the extrinsic spiritualities just cited and by many others belonging to a confused wealth of image-making. When Jane Lead says to her little circle of perfervid disciples: " Learn to live God, and God shall live thee," we know that she is one of us, notwithstanding the entertainments of a thousand and one aberrations. When she says that those who would know the proximity and immediacy of the Kingdom must not look outside but in the Book

[1] He expounds regeneration as follows: *Its beginning* is change of soul when the will is swayed God and heavenward. *Its progress* is growth and motion of soul from the image of the earthly towards that of the heavenly. *Its end* is the perfect and complete likeness of God in our humanity, or attainment in Christ. *In its fulness* it is that transforming, quickening work of God's Spirit by which the likeness is created.—*The Way to the Sabbath of Rest.*

[2] See my Introduction to *Some Characteristics of the Interior Church*, by Lopukhin, p. 33 *et seq.*

of Life within them, we know that the path of true Mysticism has either been travelled by her or that she has stood at the gates and looked down it. When she testifies that this kingdom shall spread "within and throughout the soul's issues to deify it, so that it may abide in the unalterable substance of a Godhead nature," we know in fine that she is with us and in a sense of us, though her language is not ours exactly. But when we come within the reverberation of seven apocalyptic thunders, when we are present at the breaking of seals, when we hear of the soul "seated as a high principality before Jehovah's throne," we know that we have been brought unawares into a world which is not ours and that we have no real part therein.[1] There is much cognate witnessing all round about the period, onward from the moving intimations of George Fox. Bramwell and Langdon and Hester Anne Rogers, Thomas Tryon, Hartley and certain obscure writers on Seraphic Love speak words of power and occasional words of grace, which are thoughts of mystics and would shine in any anthology, but to ingarner them here and now would not serve a purpose.

There is one more name in connection with the Böhme succession in England, and in citing that of William Law I should begin by saying that from my personal standpoint his position seems to have been exaggerated. It is barely possible indeed that he is more fully entitled to remembrance as the author of *A Serious Call* than he is as a mystic. In the treatise on *Christian Regeneration* he says, re-expressing once again the doctrine which seems everywhere, through all records and all tabulations of mystical experience : "This and this only is the true kingdom of God opened in the soul, when stripped of all selfishness, it has only one love and one will in it, when it has no motion or desire but what

[1] See *The Revelation of Revelations*, by Jane Lead, in Pratt's reprint of 1804, pp. 91, 23 *et seq.*, 32 *et seq.*

branches from the love of God and resigns itself wholly
to the will of God."[1] There are excellent and beautiful
things in *The Spirit of Love* and *The Spirit of Prayer*,
and it seems to me that, within his own measures, Law
is always luminous even when he is a little or more
than a little tiresome. What I miss in him is a vital
consciousness of the mystical end, and what I regret is
his polemical method. Yet he had a true sense of the
Christ Mystical dwelling in the regenerate soul " as
certainly as he lived in and governed that body and soul
which He took from the Virgin Mary."

If we turn now to France of the eighteenth century,
some of us may remember that the protestant pastor
Jean de l'Abadie, being on his bed of death, wrote a
spiritual testament, "praying God, my origin and
ocean, that he will take me into Himself and engulf me
eternally in the Divine Abyss of His Being." That is a
mystical aspiration, and what therefore is his testimony
otherwise ? The few who at this day are acquainted
with *L'Art de se Connaître Soi-même* will—if they are
concerned with the quest—not only have a kindly
feeling towards the work and its author for the pleasant
spirit which pervades it, but because it was the *vade
mecum* of L. C. de Saint-Martin in his early days,
and he confesses to its influence in the formation of
his spirit and mind. It is by no means a mystical work,
but it moves in the kind of atmosphere which is like
an outer court of the subject on its non-Catholic side.
It does not draw from mystics and indeed betrays no
acquaintance with the chain of witnesses.[2] I can say

---

[1] See *The Grounds and Reasons of Christian Regeneration.* Works.
Vol. V, edition of 1893, p. 179.

[2] However, Miss Una Birch says that Jean de l'Abadie—or Labadie
—had " studied and loved " both Hugh of St. Victor and St. Bernard.
There is a good account of him in her *Anna Van Schurmann, Artist, Scholar,
Saint*, but with *L'Art de se Connaître Soi-même* she seems unacquainted,
though she names several of his writings.

only that de l'Abadie's art of self-knowledge does not differ in its essence from lesser spiritual directories of the Latin Church. I shall recur to it in the seventh chapter, when considering the ascetic spirit as a guide through the paths to their term.

Contemporary with Saint-Martin was Dutoit-Mambrini, tinged by a spirit of fantasy and yet shewing here and there a marked degree of consciousness respecting the mystical term, especially respecting faith as our guide on the path of union. He says indeed that " in this life the ineffable union is in faith."[1] And concerning it there is one notable distinction—that " in faith we do not see Christ but possess Him,"[2] as if by some interior realisation. Dutoit-Mambrini speaks also in the Dionysian manner of obscure faith—" not that it and its objects are other than most clear in themselves, but because faith darkens reason by an indefinitely higher splendour."[3] This faith is Christ dwelling in the personality,[4] or possessing it, as has been said previously. When faith is changed into sight, then is the Blessed Vision.[5] But it is apparently not so changed on earth: we must have put off " the gross body."

It will be understood that during all this period the Catholic Church continued to produce its minor witnesses, and albeit there are no great names, there are certain interesting texts. There were also some curious devotional and spiritual works which have now passed out of general knowledge, though I think that they are collected eagerly on the rare occasions when they are obtainable.[6]

---

[1] *La Philosophie Divine, par* Keleph Ben Nathan, 3 vols., 1793. Vol. II, p. 230.

[2] *Ibid.*, p. 232.   [3] *Ibid.*, Vol. I, p. 71.

[4] *Ibid.*, Vol. II, p. 227.   [5] *Ibid.*, pp. 227, 228.

[6] *Le Directoire Spirituel pour ceux qui n'en ont point* reached a fourth edition in 1699, and is a rare and interesting book. It gives counsels on prayer, more especially to people in the world. It recognises that to do the will of God in all things is a mode of continual prayer, and to

The Way of Divine Union

When the mighty voices of the past had become little but a muffled echo, when most books of devotion had ceased to signify in any mystical sense, there arose suddenly a distinct note, which was that of Quietism, represented in the first instance, and mainly, by the Spanish Jesuit, Michael Molinos, who was acclaimed at the beginning of his teaching as might have been another Ruysbroeck, another St. John of the Cross. Now, Quietism was a product of the period and at the root it does not differ from universal principles of the

substitute formal exercises out of their season counts for sin rather than virtue, because it interferes with necessary practical work. It is said also, on the authority of St. Augustine, that "a Christian prays unceasingly when the Love of God rules all his life, when his heart is filled with God's love, when he has one desire only—which is to please God." A new spirit of mystical life and devotion could have been educed from this view; but it often happens that the deep implicits of theses escape the makers of theses.

After the Quietist period there was *L'Année Affective*, written by R. P. Avrillon, a Minorite. It is a treatise on the Love of God, and the author has tasked himself rather hardly by his enumeration of fifty-two qualities of Divine Love, distributed over the weeks of the year. But the book itself is much better than its arrangement, and it is not surprising that it became a popular handbook of devotion, of which four editions are registered between 1706 and 1727. It is another commentary on *The Song of Solomon* and its major divisions are those of the Purgative, Illuminative and Unitive Life. Two kinds of Divine Union are distinguished, being (a) that which is common to all just persons and (b) that which God grants to the most perfect, who are His intimate friends. Grace and charity are conditions of the one, but great progress in Divine Love is title-in-chief of the other. The first is the contract made when love dawns in the soul; the second is its crown and consummation.

The Latin understanding of the word conversion is illustrated in some of its developments by the anonymous *Entretiens avec Jésus Christ dans le Très Saint Sacrement de l'Autel*, a new edition of which appeared at Paris in 1736. "Conversion entire and perfect" is really deliverance from sins, not only those which are "mortal," by the hypothesis, on account of their gravity, but those which are called venial—assuming that they are committed deliberately. The practice towards conversion is by prayer, but the deliverance is by grace operating from

Mystical Term in Post-Reformation Schools

mystical life.[1] It stood for the repose of the soul in God as the resting-point of all that ardour of activity which takes the soul to the centre.

Molinos, Guyon, Fénelon: my last words notwithstanding, I question whether the deep had shewn them its inmost secrets or the height its final treasures of attainment; but posterity has largely revoked the judgment pronounced against them by the tribunal seated at Rome, and not because posterity was concerned with the defence of Quietism, but because it had come to see that the charges preferred would obtain with similar force in the case of many canonised mystics, for the same teaching abounds throughout mystical literature. I have explained elsewhere the mistake in chief of Molinos, which was in respect of prudence, not in respect of doctrine. Canon Lynn also has noted it when he says that to class " meditation, confession and outward penances " as " necessary only for beginners in the spiritual life," was a thing which " struck hard at cherished practices of the day."[2] The actual position seems to be put a little too strongly, but it is set out in a broad sense. We are not concerned with the debate and the judgment matters nothing. If we search

without and is performed by the Lord Christ as One Who is entirely distinct from any Divine Presence in the soul. There is no word on the sudden change in the heart, no word as to a working from within.

One of the rarest collections is the Advent Sermons of R. P. F. Guillaume Martin, a Capuchin preacher, under the title of *Les Marques des Enfants Predestinéz, Citoyens de la Cœleste Hierusalem*. It belongs to the year 1613. But I have found nothing to any mystical purpose. It is said that God dwells in the souls of the predestined (p. 276), being those elected to the joy of His Jerusalem. Their election is in the sense of St. Bernard, Sermon 79 on Canticles. God receives the predestined, after the warfare of His world, with great joy (p. 626).

[1] Out of this fact has arisen an old debate whether it originated with Molinos or with some other writer on the higher aspects of spiritual life—e.g. Desmerêts de Saint-Sorlaise.

[2] See the preface to *Extracts from the Spiritual Guide*, edited by Canon R. Y. Lynn, from the translation of 1688.

Molinos himself, we shall find that with him, as with all mystics, the soul on the path is drawn out of sensible things, images and persuasions of the intellect, and passes on wings of love to the exploration of its own centre, " where is the Image of God." It is an exploration in obscure faith, in a secret place of the darkness, and the light which comes to the soul, " aided by the Divine Gifts," is one of " simple apprehension." In other words, it is " a recollection in pure and universal faith " and the gate of entrance therein is " the holy humanity of Christ," which leads through cross and passion to silence and quiet in the presence of the Lord. The peace of this silence is reached in no sensible delights, in no spiritual consolation, but rather in renunciation of these and in the familiar self-martyrdoms of ascetic life. Perfect contemplation is attained in perfect annihilation,[1] and it is by way of nothingness that the soul must come to lose itself in God. This bars the door to all that is not God, and when annihilated the soul is transformed. " The Divine Spouse speaks in the heart of His bride and teaches her High and Divine Wisdom."

The nothingness of Molinos is to be distinguished from that of Dionysius, who did not overload the attaining soul and mind with the opprobrium which characterises the lowermost grooves of ascetic terminology. The counsels to abhor self with a mortal hatred, to vanquish the seven-headed beast and monster of self-love are stupefying when we have to remember that, according to the same witness, the self of the soul is a temple and that this temple has a sanctuary " where God keeps His throne and communicates Himself with incredible intensity and delicious affluence." It is not, however, the abominations of language, but

---

[1] This is actually and literally like a transcript from St. John of the Cross, whom I have quoted as saying that the union is attained " when man has been brought to nothing."—See *ante*, p. 85.

the false pretences of the system which lead one to divine rebellion. Molinos *et hoc genus omne* knew perfectly well that there is but one vessel of election and if it requires purification it is good to get to the work, but unmeasured vituperation is not a cleansing fire.[1]

The testimony of Madame Guyon, even when she is at her best and highest, being full of what used to be called sensibility, has a disposition to vary with her emotions and would be difficult—were it worth while—to harmonise. The term of union is said in one place to be a state of infinite freedom. Alternatively, the soul acts no longer, having become an instrument of God. This is to be conciliated as we can, having regard to the logical difficulties respecting an infinitely free instrument. But the exercise would not be worth while, for in *Spiritual Torrents* we learn that the soul herself exists no longer—as a free instrument or otherwise. It is easy to see what the devout lady is trying to express there and here, namely, that liberation is in union itself, that the soul acts in God and God operates in the soul.[2] She reaches after it otherwise, though the result must have been *male sonans* in the ears of the Anti-Quietist party. "Others enjoy the sun: those who are in union have become one with the sun."[3] She says also that "the soul flows into God, so that she loses herself,"[4]

---

[1] This was the view of St. François de Sales, though it is expressed differently. He has luminous counsels on benignity and patience towards oneself. The charity which imposes these virtues in dealing with the faults of others counsels their exercise towards ourselves.—*L'Esprit*, Part XVIII, c. 13. Compare Juan de Avila, writing to Juan de Dios : "Know that the man who of all others is most recommended to thy care is thyself. For it will profit thee but little, though thou shouldst draw all the world out of the mud, if the while thou thyself remainest therein." There is, of course, a sharp distinction.

[2] She sees, however, that the soul realises life in God and that God works in the soul.—*Spiritual Torrents*, translated by Miss A. W. Marston. Second edition, pp. 105, 106.

[3] *Ibid.*, p. 145. [4] *Ibid.*, p. 148.

but does not add—with Ruysbroeck—that subsequently
the soul returns or flows back into herself, bearing the
Divine within her into manifest life. "All her movements are of God, by Whom she is guided infallibly."
It is affirmed that the state is permanent.

I suppose that, if drawn out of all her forty volumes—
including the commentary on Genesis, for she also
interpreted Scripture—the real contributions of Madame
Guyon to mystical science would fill but a few pages.
Let me add that some of them would be priceless, and
I have said enough of a writer who has left much to
distinguish her in spirit, though not in doctrine, from
the Latin mystics who preceded her, but who does
not differ from any of them as to the nature of the term
in God. She also, like Molinos, erred in respect of
prudence when she counselled her followers not to be
concerned for their salvation. Some things that are
true in themselves have an air of falsehood on the
surface as stated, and the text should not be delivered
apart from the inward context, or it may prove to the
simple a stumbling-block and to many of the conten-
tious foolishness, because they are not qualified to see
what lies behind it. In conclusion as to Madame Guyon
and her Quietism, she has left us at least one memorable
record of personal experience. "When I had lost all
created supports, and even divine ones, I then found
myself happily necessitated to fall into the pure divine
. . . through all which seemed to remove me further
from it. In losing all the gifts . . . I found the Giver."[1]

I have loved Louis Claude de Saint-Martin from
the beginning of my fellowship in knowledge of his
life and writings ; and knowing also that he is a man of
light in the spirit, I could wish to shew forth his brightness in these pages ; but I should be travelling in the
first place over too familiar ground, and in the second
I should have to illustrate at considerable length his

[1] *La Vie de Madame Guyon, écrite par elle-même.* Part I, c. XXVIII.

distinctions from the earlier masters; but for this there is no space. A few words must suffice. He followed the inward way, but—as I have said—he sought " the Divine by the active path of works," which path was a way of reintegration, and the gate of it was " a second birth." The end of all was understood as a return into unity,[1] but on his actual application of these words and the state which they signified he says nothing. Yet in another place he may be held to give up the whole mystery of his meaning—as if unawares. " The only initiation which I preach and seek with all the ardour of my soul is that by which we may enter into the heart of God and make God's heart enter into us, there to form an indissoluble marriage, which will make us the friend, brother and Spouse of our Divine Redeemer."[2] The author of *Le Nouvel Homme* stands therefore integrated in the unity of Christian witnesses.

Saint-Martin himself closed the canon of Christian Mysticism, " trailing clouds of glory " into the dead night of the early nineteenth century. We are indebted to him for the memorable dictum that the uttermost deep gives up no form,[3] and I accept this as true not only of the Divine Nature but of our inmost selves. We must seek in our own deep beneath all images: there, as it may be, is the bond of union.

The general conclusion of this section is that if the post-Reformation schools are to be called mystical it is

[1] *Traité des Bénédictions, Œuvres Posthumes*, II, 168.
[2] *Correspondance*, Lettre CX.
[3] It will be found in Letter XXIV of the Correspondence which passed between himself and Baron Kirchberger, who had asked whether there were " visible manifestations which come from the centre." Saint-Martin replied that, in his opinion, the deep centre " produces no physical form." I suppose that Saint-Martin would have made the same answer if the question had been one of mental images. The mystical theology of Dionysius depends from this, for on the hypothesis that forms of the mind are produced from the Divine Centre, they would be the path for attaining that centre.

in a sense which is largely distinct from the one term of experiment, or, in other words, from the Mysticism of the Latin Church. Therein is true Mysticism— apart from cosmological hypotheses and debates on the sense of Holy Writ. It is true that according to St. Maximus the secret tradition of Scripture is explained by means of mystical theology, but the meaning is that the Word of God is expounded in knowledge of God infused by the mystical life. The subject of reference is not therefore an exegetical system of the formal kind. The latter stands at its value, and as there are many systems which agree only in excluding one another, while we have no canon of criticism which will enable us to adjudicate between them, the value is one only of inward personal impression, an interpretation to the self of the thinker, and that which it may profit to him. The vast and varied results of cosmological seership are in the same category. Unfortunately—and even unto this day—every reader behind the sense of texts believes himself to have reached the secret mind of the writer, and every dreamer of cosmic dreams thinks that the universe has opened before him like a parted veil and has shewn that which is within to him only. Both, however, have read themselves out of court. Apart from these debates, perhaps the best that can be said for most non-Catholic mystics is that they move in a realm of moral and spiritual intimation which encompasses the mystical sanctuary, but that sanctuary was entered by very few.

CHAPTER V

CONCERNING UNION AND IDENTITY

THE twin-sisters Emanationism and Pantheism are old systematic attempts to deal with the mystery of manifestation. The latter in particular is so protean in its aspects and so difficult of escape that it is to be found lurking continually in reflections of utterly diverse thinkers—for the most part outside any conscious intention—who are seeking to deal at first hand with problems of life and mind. It seems almost as if it were a natural form of thought, or something so near to the truth of things that the intuitions of speculation are always assuming its vestures. Emanationism is regarded usually as a typical characteristic of Jewish Kabalism and Pantheism of Indian philosophy, represented more especially by Vedantic teaching. While they have never offered a solution as excogitated systems, and while their appearance in the field means—at the present day more even than in the past—a declaration of active warfare, there is no element of better satisfaction to be found in the idea of creation by a *fiat* of omnipotence, which—under the ægis of the Hebrew canonical Scriptures—has ruled in all orthodox Christendom. We shall see in the course of our contemplation that there is a higher pantheism, because God is our source and goal. We shall see that the term of our desire is for God to be all in all. We shall see not alone that the Vision is He, as a great poet has said, but that He is the mode of our fulfilment. This formulation belongs, however, to the term of things, not to their beginning, and it is as much the doctrine of union as that of identity. Moreover, it does not exclude emanationism as an hypothesis of origin, nor that of creative act. In this manner it leaves the great schools of debate a free field for their intellectual exercise, and this for the best of reasons—because the Mystical Quest is concerned with a goal to be reached, and with nothing else. But seeing that in the next chapter something must be said briefly of Eastern Mysticism, a consideration of identity and union seems necessary at this point to clear the issues. Let it be remembered throughout that we are not—except incidentally—debating questions of philosophy but experience and that we are not therefore concerned—primarily at least—with philosophical and doctrinal postulates, nor with conclusions which follow from these. Such questions are in fact extraneous and dialectical for the most part, though some need for their examination may arise on moral or practical grounds.

As regards emanationism—if I may speak for a moment within the limits of verbal symbolism—it seems to me beyond controversy that the Christ of Nazareth, than whom no one in this world ever stood more apart from formal dogmatism, has transmitted to our memory for ever in the Lord's Prayer a most simple teaching of emanation. The kinship which it institutes between God and man is that of Father and Child, and its implicit is that the human soul has come into being by a mode of generation, as the child enters into this world through the office of natural parentage. Those who deny this—and, to be frank, they are the makers at large of all official theology—are really accusing their Teacher of creating a false analogy, and they substitute on their own part the relation of Master and Servant in the teeth of the spirit of the Gospel. From the correspondence instituted by Christ it follows that the soul is conceived in the Divine Nature as well as brought forth therefrom, even as the living body of the infant is brought forth from the human mother. The analogy therefore postulates a principle of motherhood in God as well as a paternal principle. I am not concerned with the essential value of these things, but with the question of rational consistency in a comparison originating with the highest warrant in Christendom. I believe on my own part that the symbolism shews forth a truth which obtains through all hierarchies of individual intelligence, but I am not otherwise an emanationist, and not certainly in any conventional sense of the term. Moreover, the analogy is approximate and not literal, much less comprehensive, as containing the whole truth. Christ has put it into our hands, and we must deal with it as we can best. It illustrates the mystery of our coming forth, but on the other hand the end conceived by true Mysticism seems to have no place therein, because the human child does not return into the nature of the Father and Mother, but separates more and more from these. The symbolism of pantheistic hypotheses has also no place in that of the Lord's Prayer, because there is no identity between the child and its parents, nor in respect of the mystical end can that go back to God which is very God already.[1]

We have seen that on the basis of an ineffable experience in mystical life and practice no contribution can be expected to the age-long debate of the schools which I have described—somewhat roughly and imperfectly—under the denominations of theism and pantheism, of thinkers who maintain that there is an essential identity between God and the human soul and those who regard

[1] If it be said that the comparative position of Creator and creature, according to the *fiat* hypothesis, offers sufficient correspondence with the position of Father and son for the purposes of simple analogy, we must remember that elsewhere in the Gospels Christ teaches the attainable sonship and union of all humanity on the basis of His own Sonship and His own union, but the relation of the Divine Father and the Divine Son is not that of Creator and creature.

the latter as the product of a creative act. Mystical experience is out of court when it postulates or infers identity, having no criterion of judgment, while it is in the same position if and whenever it happens to deny identity. The explanation must be sought in the nature of the experience itself, which is a vivid realisation of the presence of God in the consciousness and of the consciousness in God, through a change in the mode of self-knowledge. It is otherwise an union of Divine and human consciousness, or the state of consciousness in God. Whensoever that state is attained it implies a sense of identity and is accurately oneness, so long as the experience endures, but it provides no guarantee as to unity of essence or substance, nor—on the other hand—any evidence against it. The comparative value of both views must therefore be determined on considerations outside the state—that is to say, on intellectual grounds. We have found that the western witnesses are disposed to affirm theism, or the distinction as to substance between Creator and creature. Hence they make use of the term union to define mystical relation between the soul and God. They use also the word vision in the sense of Divine Attainment.[1] The theory of union cannot rest on any thesis of identity when it is postulated in the mind. Union is between things that have been separated somewhere and at some time. Identity is not union : those who say so, if any, are talking against the sense of words. These facts notwithstanding, the language of

---

[1] According to Suso, the spirit of man in union " retains its own nature as a spirit, while it enjoys the co-eternal, co-omnipotent, indwelling and outflowing Persons "—that is to say, of the Most Blessed Trinity—" and high above the clouds and bustle of things below contemplates with fixed gaze the Divine marvellousness." At the same time, " in this merging of itself in God," although " the spirit passes away " in a certain sense and manner, it does not lose itself entirely by immergence in God. " It receives indeed some attributes of the Godhead, but it does not become God by nature."—*The Life of Blessed Henry Suso*, English Translation, ed. 1913, pp. 242, 245.

identity—as we have seen—is liable to be used unwittingly by western mystics, though it contravenes
their own postulate that union is a state to be reached,
not a state *ab origine*, to which realisation at the end of a
life of quest can add nothing and from which neglect
or a reverse quest can in no wise withdraw anything.
The use of such language is readily intelligible in view of
what has been just said as to the nature of mystical
experience, while the intellectual denial of identity which
tends to be found in the context may be as much a consequence of *a priori* doctrinal belief as of thought at first
hand on the subject.

With this subject we ourselves are concerned only in
so far as it affects the human soul, and the rational
understanding of things as conceived on our own part.[1]
In respect of the alternative point, the eastern hypothesis
of identity affirms that the spirit of man is always and
essentially one with God, but that we are at present—
or normally speaking—in a state of illusion by which we
are prevented from knowing it. Such a position is inevitable for the hypothesis, but a paradox is involved,
though it is apt to escape notice. The thesis implies that
God in His manifestation as putative individual spirit is
not normally conscious of Himself. The idea of super-
consciousness is, of course, excluded by the terms, since
the greater must include the lesser. As regards ourselves,
after every allowance for the depths and heights and
distance of all potentialities within us, we can never in
actuality be that which we do not know ourselves to be,[2]

[1] I am anxious that this point should be clear in the reader's mind.
As a mystic, I care nothing for the debates of the schools on *fiat* hypotheses, pantheism and emanationism, assured that they will go on ever-
lastingly to the especial profit of no one. Mystical experience testifies to
life in God and the union, and it is experience, not dialectics. I am
thankful that it throws no light on the latter, and it is matter of supreme
indifference which of the theses is true—if indeed any.

[2] It must be remembered that there are two aspects of consciousness
which may be characterised, on the surface at least, as the inward and

because in the word being, as here used, the question of consciousness is involved. Our normal conscious part does not know itself one with God, while if there be any region within us—as some modern speculations allege—that is outside normal consciousness, and is otherwise equipped in respect of Divine Science, we can predicate nothing concerning it, neither separateness nor identity, and assuredly—all the dreams notwithstanding—not even existence itself. Speculations like these are generically distinct from the implicit of the mystical work, which postulates on the basis of experience the possibility of union with God by a change in the mode of consciousness. There is furthermore a *reductio ad absurdum* in what may be called a moral sense, as I have already hinted.

The state of union—which is the subject-matter of Mysticism—presupposes, as we have seen, a state of non-union or separation, together with a capacity for union as a condition to be reached and hence a motive for action. The eastern doctrine of identity between the spirit of man and God, but in a state of non-realisation owing to cosmic delusion, offers no motive for action which can be called vital, and is to be set aside—if for this reason only. We are in a condition of unescapable union ; nothing can alter the fact, and as to realisation—we may prefer to experiment therein at a later period, or in the next hypothetical incarnation. When reprisals are threatened by metaphysics of this kind in an earth-life to come, it should be noted that they will be delusion in

outward modes. The first is called self-knowledge and the second is knowledge of that which is outside ourselves. The secret of both is contained in the word becoming, because we can grow in both. There is something else that they share in common, that the manner of knowledge is objective in both cases. Both, however, tend towards subjectivity, but normally without attaining it—things external by becoming part of us in their knowledge and things within by self-development in our own subject.

like manner.[1] Of course, any hypothetical enjoyment
which may carry the hypothetical penalty is equally
Mâyâ, but it suits us perhaps at the moment to be
deceived in this manner. On the other hand, the
Christian union with God, founded on a doctrine of
theism—whatever intellectual value may appertain to
the latter—offers all that identity could furnish when the
path of liberation has led to the consciousness of union
and in addition the saving motive of a goal to be won as
a reasonable and sufficing ground for action. The pearl
of great price is hidden in a very secret treasure-house,
and the way of its discovery demands the whole man.
The culminating point of life overshadows and possesses
the life itself of a seeker, and the awakening of consciousness to experience in the term proposed is not a work of
to-day and to-morrow but of all manifest existence.

Speaking now of the path which leads to experience, I
want to say with due deference but also with a particular
and serious persistence, that when we " go into ourselves,"
according to the accepted terminology, in search of that
which is within, it is in all simplicity into ourselves that
we go—not outside ourselves, not in quest of an extrane-

[1] In an exposition of the *Vedic Dharma*, Professor Sudhakar, M.A.,
speculates on what follows from the doctrine that " God is all and all
is God," affirming that " no question of merit, demerit, sorrow and
suffering, virtue and vice, self and not self, here and there, now and
then, can claim our attention." I should add that the arduous way
of escape which is the concern-in-chief of much eastern philosophy
might be reduced to an intellectual assent as conferring liberation in
full, because fundamentally there can be no distinction between activity
and idleness, quest and non-quest. He who is on the search is there
already at the goal and he who is in sense-illusion is not separated by a
hair's-breadth. The same writer reminds us of Hegel's scornful comparison when he termed absolute oneness " the night in which all cows
are black."—See *The Vedic Magazine*, Vol. VIII, No. I. There is another
point liable to escape attention. If all spirits are of one substance with
God, all are of simple nature, and there is no lower or higher in respect
of anything which is marked by illusory individuality. The eastern
doctrine of hierarchies falls with this postulate.

ous personality, not of any object beyond us, but into our own subject ; and if it be true, as the testimonies affirm, that we find all things within, it is for the simple reason that it is we in whom they are—being there to the extent of our realisation. In so far as they are outside ourselves they are to us unprofitable, or, in other words, non-subsistent. This is why merely external matters— things beyond our concerns and callings—are without life for us. Here is the true understanding of the poet's words : " All that interests a man is man." I put aside in this connection the false-seeming ties and those which distract from the term, as the place of their consideration is not here and now. This is the key of human love as well as of Divine Love, and it is an intimation of the path to their marriage.

The immanence without in the universe is like the immanence in the soul of man. They are one Divine Presence, but its objective realisation, compared with that of the God Who abides within us, is like a journey through some great distance. We shall see at the proper time that the powers of the world about us communicate graces and glories through all the channels of our being, but we receive in proportion as we unveil the Presence within us, as a centre which communicates indissolubly with whatsoever is divine in the universe. There is no other way of the quest, and so, as I may have occasion to say with the poet full often in these pages : " That is best which lies the nearest."

The imagery of going and coming is, however, illusory on both sides of the alternative. There is no going to God, if God be within ; there is no coming of God to us, if God be within : it is entirely a question of realisation, and this is a work of consciousness. Now, the implicit of realisation is love. How do we seek the kingdom of God ? It is not by a journey through the blue distance. The search is love. The depths and heights of the knowledge of God are depths and heights

of love. As regards love, it seems to me that a definition
of it has not been found, because it is an absolute state
in attainment and is therefore ineffable, or outside the
circle of expression.[1] We can approximate only. In

[1] The union being a love-state is therefore also ineffable, and an
intellectual survey of its conditions is beyond all things speculative.
I think that what follows offers some curious points by way of debate
and I give it at any value which it may have for any reader as an aid to
reflection, but attaching to it no importance on my own part.

The state of indissoluble union is not that of A becoming B, nor of
its alternative. For the purpose of this consideration A and B are posited
as in separation ; but if on account—for example—of love they must
attain that mode which we agree to call union—not that we are satisfied
with the expression—this is not reached by one becoming the other, as
if B should absorb A, and as if A ceased consequently as such, or conversely. We approach more nearly to a notion of the descried term by
postulating that both become C, being the undefined condition represented by union. The question which arises for our consideration is
whether union in its realisation can attain that indissoluble state which
is synonymous with oneness. It may appear that union is rather in
virtue of a bond—as, for example, in mechanism, when a joint is made
to unite two pipes, which remain two pipes, distinguishable clearly
as such. It is the joint that is called an union. This is comparable
to the conventional state of earthly marriage, as by law established, or
by the Christian Sacrament as this is received commonly. It may be a
light yoke or a burden. It serves a recognised purpose, but the bond is
the union and—except in so far as that " union " is love itself—the
personalities may be and usually are in mystical separation, not in union
or oneness.

Let us take, however, the streams D and E, which have a point of
union at F and become G, wherein they are one river henceforward.
Here is a plausible illustration of love-union, but it is not adequate,
because the streams D and E remain, while in the postulated condition
of love's consummation A and B do not remain as such, our symbolism
not including an implicit of antecedence in time. We may think the
mixture of two gases which are changed into a third gas very nearly
perfect, or good at least as we shall find. H and I are both essential for
the production of J, yet the analogy fails in love, for the notion of
vivifying love does not tolerate after separation as a thing possible ;
but the gas J can be separated at any moment into its constituents. It
is in the mode of temporal union, not of oneness. At the same time it
does not so resolve by a working from within, but only by interferences
from without. Now, this is always possible hypothetically in human

the human order of things it would be worse than in-commensurate to say that it is contained in the idea of attraction or in that of ordinary desire. These things lie within it. If we adopt a much loftier symbolism and describe love as the sum of the necessity of union, a question again arises whether this contains the state, and I think that it carries also some seals of insufficiency, though it reaches out in a true direction. Love is self-emptying, self-effacing, self-outpouring in an uttermost love on earth, but not in the state of Divine Union. As we know it, therefore, here is union but not oneness, even in the best love-state of our present life.

Let it be affirmed in the next place that whatsoever within us is cap-able of attaining Divine Union reaches towards its Divine object. This desire or outreaching is a mode of love—desire being always for that which is not so far possessed or realised. Let us say further that the Object is reached, and that there is a knowledge of Divine Presence inwardly. This may conceivably come about (a) as a realisation of God within us immanently, (b) as an abiding in God, or (c) because—qua consciousness—we are actually the God immanent. If K, which we call our knowing and self-knowing part, is visited by L, which is God in the state of being within us, we may say that the result is M, or that mystical experience which, according to the annals of sanctity, is occasional but never con-tinuous in this life. Transitory union is attained but not oneness.

We are in exactly the same position if K, which is our consciousness, goes forth to abide in God, understood here as N, the result of which is O, but again it is transitory, and what we need is permanence, or there is no oneness. On the other hand, if K—which is our consciousness—is, subject to realisation, P, or actually the God immanent, and if realisation is Q, being a state of God-consciousness, then also we need it in permanence, or there is no oneness. Note that in this case immanence is a variant description of K, being our consciousness.

But there is also R, representing all other forms of consciousness called individual, and all—subject to realisation—are S, which is the catholic mode of Q, the state of God-consciousness. T is its realisation, and this produces V, which is the oneness of all individual consciousness, so called, in the God-consciousness, typified by S. We may say that this is synonymous with W, which is the communion of saints. In this case, the term immanence is descriptive of all manifest consciousness. But as there is a state of God in the transcendence, we have not yet reached the all-including term of love, for Q and S in their permanence are a state of oneness in the immanence and W is the common realisation

mode of completeness ; but it is further, nor less utterly,
an absorption and indrawing which takes over the other
self, the two operations proceeding concurrently, neither .
by one degree or tittle yielding ground to the other, so
that there is paradox of all paradox, seeking equation of
paradox, something beyond duality, even beyond union,
a state undeclared and unknown through all the world of
seeking ; but as to the attainment there is no record on
earth concerning it. The mind may conceive it faintly
as an eternal progress in eternal approximation, in which

of that state. Beyond these there is that which is indeed as a Supreme
Triad, being W—the communion of saints, as here distinguished—X,
the transcendent God—X indeed—and Y, the term absolute of love,
when W and X enter into a state of oneness. This is what eye hath
not seen and what it hath not entered into the heart of man to understand. But Z is the eternity of this state, when the cosmic Christ of the
immanence gives up the Kingdom to the Father, and God is all in all.

Now, we have no canon of criticism by which we can determine the
comparative values, based on mystical experience, of

L=God abiding within us.

N=The soul abiding consciously in God.

P=Consciousness in its realisation as the immanent God, postulated
by Christian Doctrine, or He Who is within—actually, here and now,
the Christ and Word of God.

But it will be seen that the reason is ready to our hands, because M
is God-consciousness, O is God-consciousness and Q is God-consciousness.
The result in each case is liberation for so long as the state lasts. But
we return afterwards into our normal, external mode, it being impossible
furthermore on the testimonies to affirm that the transient experience
has comprehended within its duration the state of permanent attainment—as this is preconceived intellectually—or whether it is an adumbration only, beyond which there is still that which God has prepared for
those who love Him and which the heart still has not conceived. Those
who affirm on one or another side of the whole mystery in either of
these aspects know not what they do. And this, once more, is why mystical
experience—howsoever the remembering mind may debate thereon—
can offer us no evidence in defence of pantheism, or in opposition thereto.
Our intellectual excursus leaves us in the same position. This being so,
the comparative intellectual value of these alternative hypotheses will
appear at best indifferent to the subject in hand. But we may see later
on that, after all, there is perhaps a middle way between them which is
not indifferent but vital.

thirst is never quenched, nor is hunger ever satisfied, though ministration has no suspension. But these things are on the threshold, words in which the true essence eludes, because—as I have said—we are speaking within the limits of the human order, measures of subject and object. But mystical experience in the zenith of attainment testifies to a love-state in the stillness, and it seems to me that what opens therein makes such terms as absorption and oneness but frigid substitutes and heavy clouds of veiling. Such vistas lie far beyond experience, at whatsoever zenith, and though one knows, or dreams of knowing, that such a mode sleeps at the term of all, there is nothing in the records to assure us, or even to hint.

But in this life, because of imperfections and disparities, the separation between subject and object, we have a plenary experience of love's inhibitions, of love's frustrations and see only as at an infinite distance its promised fulness. Those who would debate this do not know love ; they are in the outer courts, where the dealings are in lesser measures ; while those who would deny the witness which I have borne in these intimations have not even heard of love, though they may have lived among a thousand pallid shadows which are its substitutes. It is of set purpose that I have, so to speak, interwoven here man's love for man and God. The disabilities are the same in both and the way of escape is one. No man possesses either man or God save only within him.

The experiment of the inward way is therefore in an ineffable way an experiment in the union. The great experiment of Mysticism is to attain the mode of direct consciousness, and this is why it is so difficult, nor indeed apart from danger for those who are inadequately prepared. The path of preparation is that of union with the will of God, which draws all the lesser aids towards us, in so far as these are needful, while itself is the greater aid. It is also a path of becoming, while the final state of indissoluble union is a state of having become. In the doctrine of identity the path is to realise that which we are of necessity.

While the rest in God and the union, as they are understood in this work, are an inward state obviously and only, they are not incompatible with activity here and now. Sometimes counsel is darkened overmuch on both sides of this subject, (*a*) as if union with God depended on localisation—of that kind, e.g. depicted in the conventional heaven ; or (*b*) on the side in contrast, as if place and time precluded it. While the state may become so deep that external activity cannot be connected therewith, it is certain that the more we affirm God to be within, the less does this need to be done with prejudice to the world about us.

When the consciousness opens to God and when He is realised therein, then is the state of union—of which there are many degrees. There is no need to juggle with words and to speak of states as if they were periods or places, to say that one intellectual apprehension of the states finds expression as the doctrine of identity but another as that of duality. The state is God realised in consciousness. He is all in us Who is all in all. By such realisation of God abiding within us, we ourselves are all in Him, Who is all in all. Those who will be at the pains of weighing these words—which have been weighed well before they have passed into writing—will see that they account for the unity-sense experienced in the state of attainment called Divine Union apart from any hypothesis of identity. The assumption of the latter gains nothing further. God remains and is all in all, in virtue of His immanence in the universe and, because He is not contained by the universe, He transcends all. The objection to conventional identity hypotheses in this place is neither theological nor philosophical, but simply that they do not help us to understand mystical experience better than we can understand it otherwise. They postulate an inward being-condition of which we have no normal apprehension, while there is no certitude that we reach it supernormally, because the apprehension so attained can be interpreted differently. Finally they are a check rather than an incentive to the great work of our existence.

There is perhaps only one point more. The mystical term is not to be understood as connoting—except at some remote distance—a certain analogy with intellectual concurrence, as in agreement over a proposition, or with simple concurrence of purpose, as when two independent wills coincide about a given course of action.[1] Coincidence differs from union. It is not to be understood as the attainment of a common desire, if the terms of desire lie outside the subjects postulated. We must have recourse indeed to the meaning of the word consciousness: it is all that which is implied in knowing with, in knowing as we are known—that is to say, a state of self-knowledge in common. I have chosen here these intellectual forms of definitions, because it seems better to avoid those of emotion, which are usually so many certificates concerning a psychic state.

To sum up now as regards this section at large: If God, as it has been said, is the Indwelling Spirit, such Presence in the consciousness accounts for all that can be affirmed of the Union. The testimony of all the schools can be harmonised and ratified by reference to this one statement. The "local habitation" of this spirit is the consciousness, it being understood that the term local is according to a manner of speaking only. All that follows from the Presence can be discerned in

---

[1] I need not say that the sense of union must be more than intellectual, if it is not to be less than vital. It is in the vital recognition of the union that we must seek not only the root-matter of any practical eirenicon between the Churches, but the realisation of what is signified thereby will restore to the official sanctuaries that something lost or withdrawn which—amidst all the offices of zeal—is still found wanting.

advance of the experience, even if it is through a glass and darkly, by recourse to our daily familiarity with the facts of consciousness. Let an example be taken from the testimony of universal experience on the external side—e.g. that $2 \times 2 = 4$. We have a complete intellectual realisation of this arithmetical fact ; we know that it cannot be otherwise, that—*pace* the late John Stuart Mill—it is an eternal truth of the understanding. The foundation is of course experience. When God enters into the consciousness we shall realise the truth of His Presence with the same certitude, again founded on experience. We shall know the one as we know the other ; and yet—as it is realised at once in the heart—there is no comparison between them. Again, let us take an example from an experience on the inward side, being that of our consciousness to itself testifying, and let us remember above all that it is a testimony of unity. The facts of external experience people the mind with ideas, but they do not add to or take away from the testimony of the self in consciousness.

That testimony is, however, in our normal intellectual estate not without a distinct and inevitable passage from subject to object. The same gulf intervenes in any natural realisation of God and His presence, whether in the world or the heart. It is the same quality of separation, though the distance may be indefinitely greater and the realisation indefinitely more vague. The union of subject and object is the one mystical end, and in the transcension of such union God will be known of the heart and the whole nature. The mystical experiment postulates this state as possible of attainment and the witness of Mysticism through the ages is a testimony to the state realised. But the state itself is like the theory of evolution, unconcerned with a beginning or an end and not throwing light on these. These are the last words and this is the message of the present chapter.

CHAPTER VI

ANALOGIES AND DISTINCTIONS OF ATTAINMENT IN RECORDS OF EASTERN MYSTICISM

It is essential to understand that the few pages which follow are in no wise designed as a thesis on Eastern Mysticism. This would demand qualifications to which I can make no claim and for which an opportunity would be wanting, whatever the equipment available. Between the eastern and western literatures of God and the soul of man I believe that there may be a true sacramental marriage when the path and nature of the Union have been reconstrued in both directions and when the whole spirit has been put into a new body of language ; but I indicate an enterprise to come and not one of my own performance, though I can see how it should be undertaken. Not on the critical, historical, external side, but on that which is of all most inward and intimate, must be the loving and plenary comparison of oriental and western wisdom, so that those who " speak the same language, because they come from the same spiritual country," may be shewn to do so plainly on both sides of the world. The old Vedic saints undertook the same journey and attained—as shewn by their evidence—the same term and no other as Dionysius, Ruysbroeck and he whose undisclosed name is written in the Book of Life—the author of *The Cloud of Unknowing*. They are not only therefore men of a spiritual consanguinity shared in common but brethren of the free spirit. To indicate this is the simple purpose in hand, and to learn if perchance in the East there were any who went further. It calls only for the general knowledge of a student and not that of the expert.

Now, we have seen that in accepting the broad facts of western mystical experience one is not committed to the interpretation placed thereon by the memorials thereof. The aftermath in recollection of all such privities and transports, however clear in respect of its proper subject-matter, is often an imperfect and sometimes a confused testimony in respect of inferences drawn therefrom. It has been shewn in particular that the experience does not offer a reliable guide to doctrine in the typical case of identity between God and the soul or in the converse of this proposition. In the East as in the West we must separate such doctrine from experience and for the same reason, being the incapacity of human consciousness in a postulated state of Divine Union to distinguish between the alternatives. A solution of this and the other great mysteries may await us in the undeclared hereafter.

It will be known and understood that there are many schools in the East which have originated from the same religious or philosophical systems, many accredited teachers of widely divergent views, and that there is also a cloud of criticism upon the general body of sacred texts. I am designing to speak only of the Vedic system and the Mysticism imbedded therein. According to the doctrine of Çañkara there is identity between Brahman and the world, because—according to the *Chândogya-Upanishad*—cause and effect are identical.[1] But there have been reactions against the theories of Çañkara, and the identity in question has been disputed, or a middle ground has been sought—e.g. that in a sense Brahman is one with the universe and yet is different. Again, there is the doctrine " that the world extended

[1] Paul Deussen : *The System of the Vedanta,* translated by Charles Johnston. Part II, sect. 19 : *The Idea of Causality.*

in names and forms is non-existent,"[1] is glamour, illusion or *mâyâ*, " which Brahman, as master-magician, projects, as the dreamer projects dream-forms." But counter-views on the subject appear to have prevailed at and before the age of Çañkara, who is referred to 700 or 800 A.D., and in later times, on the authority of the *Śaiva-Siddhânta*, *Mâyâ* has been held to be " eternal and real,"[2] "a positive entity, coexistent with Śiva," not an illusion like the *mâyâ* of the Çañkara school.[3] So also other speculations postulate the reality and eternity of matter. As regards the soul of man, it is well known that not only is there no trace of transmigrations or rebirths in the ancient Hymns of the *Rigveda*, but that this hypothesis is excluded by their eschatological doctrine.[4] The identity of the soul and Brahman is, how-ever, rooted in Vedic teaching ; it is " the fundamental thought of the *Vedânta*."[5] A modern eastern teacher terms the soul eternal, perfect and infinite.[6] Others have affirmed that the condition of complete rest is to break through the prison of the individual soul.[7] It is said also : " Learn to realise thyself as the ever-permanent Intelligence, the one without a second, having relin-

[1] *Ibid.*, Part I, Sect. VI, 2 : *Exoteric and Esoteric Form of the Vedânta.*

[2] Dr. L. D. Barnett on *The Śaiva-Siddhânta* in *The Light of Truth.* Vol. XI, Nos. 2, 3.

[3] "It is a means subserving the will of the Supreme to produce illusion, the imagination of a differentiated universe, in order that the alienated souls may therein consume their Karma and finally reach salvation by realising their unity with the Supreme."—*Ibid.* So also the *Śvetaśvatara Upanishad* affirms that Mâyâ is a mode of thought imposed upon the real consciousness or self by the Absolute Thought, which is regarded as a Personal Deity—i.e. Śiva.

[4] *The System of the Vedânta*, Part IV, sect. 29 : *The Eschatology of the Vedânta.*

[5] *Ibid.*, Appendix I, *Short Survey of the Vedânta System.* Dr. Deussen says that the statement contradicts experience.

[6] I.e. Swami Vivekanand. See his lectures delivered in America.

[7] According to the *Sarabha Upanishad*, the Eternal One is " the self of beings."

quished all delusion." And of the Yogi: "He is part of the Infinite Spirit which has loved the universe into being."[1]

These are a few broad features of mystical doctrine in the East and they contribute a moderately clear distinction from the teaching of western theology, as there is no need to say. But we enter under another aspect of things in considering the nature of the term attained, as it appears in the hypotheses and records of experience in the eastern schools.[2] Liberation, according to the *Vedas*, is release from the bond of existence and is attained in the path of knowledge. By existence we must understand, however, the state of separation in the manifest, not that the soul or real part of manhood ceases or can cease to be: it realises in liberation that it is Brahman.[3] A simple change of the terms into those of Christian Mysticism, the substitution of union for identity would leave this final condition itself unchanged, just as a similar transposition would be possible in the alternative case. The end is one: it is the formulæ of definition that vary.[4] Experience remains that which it is, un-

---

[1] Tāyumānavar—a teacher who died A.D. 1742—taught that the soul is not a part of God, not a spark from Him in appearance or reality, but an entity dependent on Him for existence and bliss. There is one respect, however, in which God and the soul are one—in that both are conscious entities. A modern commentator on the *Mandukya Upanishad* affirms that "just as body cannot be mistaken for Ātma or soul, so soul cannot be mistaken for God, for as Ātma itself vivifies bodies, God vivifies the soul."

[2] The communion with God, according to the Brahman conception of God, has been described tersely as (1) With God revealed in Nature by the method of works and formulated by the *Veda;* this is *Karma-yoga:* (2) With God as revealed in consciousness and formulated by the *Vedanta;* this is *Jñāna-yoga:* (3) With God as revealed in history by means of love and proved by the *Purānas;* this is *Bhakti-yoga.*

[3] "The condition of the liberated is rather that of indivisibility, for thus teach the words of the Scripture: That art thou."—Quoted from Çānkara by Deussen, *op. cit.*, Part V, sect. 38, on *Unio Mystica.*

[4] "It is a fundamental doctrine of the *Saiva Siddhanta* that our life is

affected *qua* experience by explanations or doctrines concerning it. It follows that there is an eastern way to God, an end reached in Him, and the *Ashtavakara Gita* terms it " repose in absolute intelligence,"[1] or according to other symbolism in " the great expanse of spiritual beatitude." This is " the bliss of salvation," attained in the realisation of God, or by uniting with Him, the path being one of meditation " performed with all the powers of the soul." In yet other terminology, " when the soul is cleansed finally of sin it dwells in God and God abides therein."[2] Then follows a statement which sounds like one of the Christian mystics already cited : " It has no perception of any distinction between itself and God or other beings." Such a perception would be impossible in such a state, and within an intellectual measure it seems to me that this pregnant sentence has the saving virtue of declaring a Divine Mode of Being and wisely leaving all other questions open. I might fill many pages with extracts from all sources of text and commentary and criticism. It would adorn those pages and serve a purpose therein, but the real purpose is sufficiently served already, and I will add only that as Christ is the Way and the Life for that great branch of Mysticism which bears His glorious name, so in the East is He who is called the Eternal Krishna for many hundreds of

a probation, a period of preparation for ultimate communion and fellowship with the Supreme."

[1] That is to say, the repose of intelligence in intelligence, of consciousness within consciousness, the individual units being integrated in the great whole. It is obvious that in this state the part can lose nothing, for it becomes the All. I may mention in this connection that Kapila lays it down as beyond dispute that there are individual souls, each of which has and retains a distinct consciousness eternally different from *Mūlaprakiti*, the primordial cause of matter.—*The Light of Truth*, Vol. XIV, No. 5.

[2] " There is eternal peace and rest in the pure condition of the soul, and from this there is no return."—*Tirumantram of Tirumular*. First *Tantra*, § 24, being on Temperance.

adept-saints, who affirm on the basis of experience that He can be " apprehended in every heart."

I have met somewhere in my searchings with two stages of successive attainment according to eastern testimony.[1] One is the acquisition of first-hand self-knowledge by the spirit or soul of man prior to the knowledge of God. Such a distinction is illusory if there lies behind it the doctrine of identity, because experience of the one is in this case that of the other. There is a further thesis which says that in stillness of sense and in emptiness of mind—presumably of the logical mind—there supervenes a mode or state in which (*a*) the spirit knows itself, and (*b*) knows itself one with God. Some Christian Mystics would testify rather that in ceasing from the objective concern of self-knowledge Divine Union is attained by the soul, and this is a key by which I shall hope later on to open the Door of Union. This would mean that sacred concentration takes place upon the Divine Presence within, which concentration begins in a thought-act and becomes an act of life. We must remember, however, the catholic axiom that if God is within He is within the consciousness and that what is called the inward path is throughout an adventure in consciousness—being the mystery of the Divine Being realised in the self-knowing part. Subject to the hypothesis of identity, and ignoring this, the same notion is expressed in the eastern method, its self-knowledge being a realisation of union. When stripped of doubtful and unphilosophical extremes of language, the Vedic root looks sometimes as though it were reducible to terms which would harmonise the East and West. There is a very true sense in which the self contains that which it conceives, and the awareness of God grows in proportion as God is more and more the encompassing

[1] I do not think that it is accredited ; it may be merely a sequence of confused inferences ; but it has been current talk among some of us and requires a word of reference.

subject—the undiverted preoccupation—of life. The Absolute is in our consciousness by conception, the Eternal is there. We have conceived all, and it is ours to explore all—to reach into further realisation. So long as we picture God as without and apart from ourselves who are leading the unawakened life of the normal world, I do not understand how there can be a real growth in Him. Moreover, the true knowledge of self is knowledge of God, if He be within the self, and this is not identity but immanence,[1] realised so deeply and vitally that it seems to open a path into Divine Transcendence, for between these there is no dividing line and there is no barrier. The Divine Transcendence is God in so far as He is not realised within us and Divine Immanence is the one and same God in so far as we are awake in Him. So has it been said otherwhere in eastern teaching that the act of God transforms into His own likeness the mind which receives Him.[2] I conclude therefore that —whether in the East or West—the commentaries of great masters on great facts of experience are expressed in terms which leave much to individual gifts of understanding, but that their true interpretation and harmony in peace of the holy light will not be in fine wanting—if only the gifts are present.

It remains therefore that, whether in East or West, no mystics have borne testimony to other than one term of experience. They concur also by their insistence that there must be a preparation for the indrawn state in the outward and inward life. That which we have sought to understand as the higher mind—Tauler's *Synteresis,* Ruysbroeck's apex of the soul—opens like a divided veil

[1] On the simple ground that whatever is within the self-knowing intelligence is not apart therefrom.

[2] It seems also to be held in the East that " to assert oneself in the true nature is purely a self act," as indeed it could not be otherwise ; but in this case the work is a dilatation of self so that it may operate with the All.

and reveals the Divine within it ; but that which parts
the veil is holiness, by all the counsels and according to
all the high experience. We must not go unclean into
that which is called contemplation, or we must take
with us a firm desire and intention to be cleansed therein.
It is not till we are cleansed that we shall gain anything,
save shadows and deceptions of the threshold. They
are part of the cloud upon our sanctuary. But we must
bring also a righteous understanding of our high estate,
of that which Peter Sterry called the " race and royalty
of the Kingdom of God in the soul." He who says :
" In myself I am nothing, in Thee I am all "—is only
bearing witness to the fact that he is still in a state of
illusion. " O bring me to that self which is in Thee," is
really another mode of *mâyâ*. It should be rather :
" O bring me to that realisation in which I shall know
that Thou art in me, even as I am in Thee." This is
the threshold of that state in which we know even as we
are known.

I conclude upon all the warrants—having put aside
things that are negligible, like debatable points of doctrine—that the distinction between God and the soul
in western Mysticism is in respect of that which God
hath put asunder for the high end of individual being,
while the oneness of God and the spirit according to
eastern Mysticism is in respect of that which God shall
join together for the most blessed end of reunion. How
deep the union may become in this life and in the world
that we call eternal no one can tell in words, even when
the sacred language of the logical mind is married to
intuitions which we must believe are gifts of God, so
divine and great are they. There is a world unknown of
experience beyond the world of vision, and recognised
but not expounded by mystical theosophy. We get
glimpses of it there and here in the literature ; we find
its intimations perhaps in the deep heart of our hearts,
as we do those of the timeless mode when the sense of

an eternal now postulates itself strangely within us, in a hush of the mind-processes. In this direction we must seek the substance of our desired eirenicon between East and West. It may be thought tentatively to correspond with the implicits of that magnetic word " Absorption."[1]

There is yet another item for the loving work of memory, that it may dwell and have fruition therein. When the soul has taken God into itself, so is it also taken, that God may be all in all. The vision signifies in terms of symbolism and sacrament a beatification of the eyes in that light which is desired by the eyes. It is indeed, as I have said, the condition of eye to eye. It is the contemplation of Divinity in the glory which encompasses Divinity. But as to any state of absorption I can say only that " eye hath not seen, nor hath ear heard." Yet it is a term descried by the mind, even while those who have reached it do not come back to testify. The great secret is this : that human consciousness merged in Divine Consciousness remains in the primary root and the ideal principle that which it is ; it remains that which knows, but with the individual self no longer. It knows with the All-Self. It has put away the final and temporal and has become conscious in the eternal and infinite. No man ceases in God.

In considering the mystical experience, as the testimonies stand respecting it, we must bear in mind that after a comprehensive and at the same time an accurate manner, there are only two states of consciousness known to us normally : one of them is the state in which we think, after whatever manner, and the other is that in

[1] It should be mentioned that absorption in the mystical sense precludes the notion of identity, more especially as understood in the East. Things distinguished from each other only by an error of sensation or of thought—howsoever we may choose to express it—being one *ab initio*, do not tolerate the word. God is to be regarded as all in all in the purpose sense, not in that of substantial identity.

which we feel. These may be and are interpenetrating continually throughout our daily life. If thought gives birth to desire, " the wish is father to the thought " in many cases, as the common proverb affirms. But those are the two states. The question arises whether there is a third in any extra-normal mode. I heard once from a woman-mystic that, over and above the two, there is a state of being, and it so happens that it was defined—I believe, on a basis of experience—as a state in which universal identity was realised. The affirmation illustrates one way in which antecedent beliefs miswrite the evidence of experience. The *tertium quid*—if there be any—is the Dionysian state of emptiness in mental suspension, when that which supervenes may be consciousness of pure being divested of relations, and therein the inward nature may open on the world of God. This is the end of separateness, of the distinction between subject and object, the synonym of which is non-realisation. I am speaking of the end, however, and not of the way that leads.

That the path of mystical realisation is a path of (*a*) thought, (*b*) emotion, or (*c*) of the two in their conjunction is made evident by the fact that no experience presented for our analysis proves to be of another category. Even the witness whom I have cited said otherwise that love was the motive and desire the path; but we must realise here that thought is postulated in both. It has to be observed, furthermore, that the terms of mystical attainment in the expression thereof are terms belonging to states of emotion, however deeply thought may be involved in expression. This is an essay in distinction rather than in criticism. To affirm that the mystical experience is reached in a state of love, that it is the fruition of love, and that such fruition is emotion fulfilled at its highest, is not for that reason to question it. The love is stilled at the centre, if I read Dionysius rightly. It is then comparable to molten lead, at that temperature which does not burn the hand.

The theosophical doctrine of unity is that nothing can come out of the Godhead and nothing return thereto but that which is implied in the Godhead, that which belongs thereto. At the root therefore all things are one in Him—the universe of which He is the Cause and individual spirit placed therein (*a*) as a spectator in part, but (*b*) as an actor also. He has created that to which He can manifest, namely, conscious being, for the increase of eternal beatitude, according to our human manner of speaking—He being *beneplacitum termino carens*.[1] That which remains is the fact of our time-long quest, amidst suffering in search of joy, amidst separation to reach into union, and I believe in the attainable term which is these. I believe also that there is a substituted infinitude of individual being, multiplying world without end, that the rogations and raptures of quest, the ineffable glories of consummation may continue and be extended everywhere. So grow the hierarchies and the holy choirs, Amen, for ever and evermore.

Is it not true that in the face of these intimations identity and separation are both figments of the intellect, playing fast and loose with a notion of dimensions which may be false in both degrees ? We are the container and the contained. The more we grow in the Divine the more do we grow in the oneness, but it is we and no other. We grow in the self with God. The doctrine that the spirit of man is Divine Spirit is true on these considerations, and the meaning is that God is in communion with it, not as the hills which stand round Jerusalem are in communion with Blessed Zion, but in

[1] Expositors of the Advaita philosophy admit that no illusion is possible without a sentient being who suffers the illusion, and to say that illusion itself is the object of such illusion offers a contradiction in terms. The modern tendency is to regard the Māyārvāda theory of illusion as futile.

the sense of coming forth and becoming again into
return. What therefore is man's spirit ? What also is
God ? Both escape definition. As regards the Divine
Being the Easterns speak of THAT ; but the word implies
remoteness, and our own spirit, like God, is nearer than
hands and feet.

In conclusion as to the whole subject, and coming back
to the starting-point, the beginning is in God and the
end is like the beginning ; but that which is intermediate
is not *mâyâ*, masking identity. The latter, from a mystical
standpoint, is left where it is desirable to leave it—in the
hands of the logical understanding to carry on the debate
as it wills, for where experience testifies to either side of
the argument it exceeds its province.

Something must be added on alleged cessations of the
cognising Ego in alleged mystical states, though it is
done with reluctance, owing to extravagant notions.
The subject is, however, with us—at least in certain
circles.

There are many things which reflect from the East and
reflect badly enough. Among others, there are attempts
to substantiate pantheistic notions by experiences based
upon practices drawing from Oriental sources. It has
been said by several deponents that in certain deep states
that which is called the personal ego ceases and is replaced (*a*) by liberation, so called ; (*b*) by consciousness
of union with all things and beings—interpreted as a
kind of identity ; (*c*) by isolation from what is understood especially as self. The attainment of this state
has been brought about, it is said, as a result of particular
practices extended over a considerable period, for example, four years, including several hours—three to five—
daily of fixed concentration. Persons who have attained
it have been in a sense psychics, but not headstrong
hunters after psychical experience. It has indeed taught
some of them to forsake such paths of experiment, or
at least endeavour to do so, perhaps on the ground that

images and pictures remain in their places, not ascending higher. It is itself a state apart from pictures and images. By the hypothesis also, it is spiritual, and the fruits of it are over-lighted by a spiritual cast. Whether it actually exceeds a certain refined and uplifted phase of psychic feeling is a difficult question, but the increment arising therefrom is most certainly in the part of emotion and not in the part of mind. Among the alleged fruits may be mentioned a certain golden dawn of universal love, specified as apart from the personal—which is quite contrary to fact—reaching out towards all humanity and tending towards active service. After what manner the greater does not comprehend the lesser, by the hypothesis, in a business of this kind must be left to those who can resolve the question. We are not concerned therein, as the deponents deceive themselves. It seems to me part of the incapacities and contradictions in expression which supervene so frequently in the attempted diagnosis of inward states by persons unqualified to clothe them in clear and consistent language. There is said further to be a new sense of life, and it is believed even that bodily health is established, but I know of other cases in which the mind veered perilously towards wreckage. Withal there is an experience of detachment, of standing as one apart, doing everything as if it had been done previously, yet as if one were not doing it. I have no records of permanence in the condition attained; on the contrary, the living actuality of the experience faded, though there was always a certain presence in memory. I suppose that one is never the same after as before such states, though all darkness is possible and does not fail to be entered.

It would not have been worth while to cite these instances had it been intended to say that they were *per se* of no consequence, were mere delusions or were confused inextricably. Their recital contains no evidence of that which they set out to prove, but I believe them to represent serious efforts in ill-trained mystical practice. Their aftermath in memory has, however, tampered with the chief issues, because—as I have hinted—the minds of persons concerned had no logical efficiency and no ordered language for representing their inward states. The affirmation that such an experience takes place outside and beyond the ego is an irrational postulate and exposes the experience unarmoured to the derision of thinking minds. There could be no consciousness of a state which is in separation from one's own identity—supposing such a state were possible; there could be only complete blank. We shall do well on our part to remember that although individual intelligence may receive at first hand communications which convey an impression of some universal state—by way of adumbration or otherwise—if in a few moments it returns to what it was, and so remains normally, it has never ceased to be individual—as indeed I have implied already. General mystical experience is an evidential illustration of another mode of realisation which is possible to man. He is, according to the testimonies, united therein with that purpose which animates the universe. But that which is so united is the conscious individual self and it is in his consciousness, as in one place or state, that the whole drama is enacted.

In conclusion as to such mystical experiences, the fact that there is memory of these—however partial, or otherwise imperfect—shows that they took place in the ego, or part of self-knowledge. It is too arbitrary for discussion to suggest that the ego is capable of remembering experiences in which it never shared. To say this is to play fast and loose with the firm meaning of the word; it is to postulate another and distinct consciousness in one individual being; it is to say that the unknown consciousness X separates from the known consciousness A, has experience in the state of separation, joins on again to consciousness A and reflects so much of its experience therein as consciousness A can receive. Or if X = the unknown is in permanent separation from the known consciousness, the hypothesis is in the still more ridiculous position of affirming communication without bridge or channel. The experience postulated is explicable always as a realisation of the Divine in direct knowledge, consequent on which the soul enjoys for the time being some foretaste or reflection of an universal mode.

Apart from suspension of the Ego and similar stultifying dreams, one has good ground for questioning an alleged consciousness of being all things and all persons simultaneously. The examination of such a condition might lead to fantastic results; but of course there has been misdescription as usual. That which occurs most frequently is a simple exaltation of consciousness, and it does not follow in any certain manner that the recipient draws nearer to God.

The last words of this section can be these only. (1) If Divine Union was attained, as the testimonies affirm, by virtue of those methods which once prevailed in the West, it is not possible to go beyond such an attainment as the result of another process. It is possible, however, and has been recognised, that the state of union may deepen, and must obviously tend to do so by the fact of its implied perpetuity. Some of the eastern witnesses, who use a peculiar language, seem to indicate a fuller realisation in consciousness, but this is largely because of their identity formulæ, which are themselves only a fashion of metaphysical expression, guaranteeing nothing outside it. In any case union is absolute, is itself and no other, in the East and the West alike. The eastern literature is a great study, calling for a great dedication, and those who can follow it prudently should be rewarded by reaching a canon of distinction as to whether intimations of deeper states

do or do not lie behind the individual veils of language.[1]
They should be able to determine also whether temporal
states of union lie within the measures of the will on the
part of those who have once attained true spiritual
experience and whether they last longer than is shewn
by western records. Suggestions in these directions are
not wanting in the testimony of Indian mystics; but
they belong to a branch of the subject which calls for
great care and discrimination before any decision can
be reached. The worst possible guides are the ready-
mouthed western people who have tried their apprentice-
skill at a little oriental reading and a little, very much
qualified, oriental practice and are eager to lay down
the law when wiser heads are almost afraid to speak.
(2) Let us recognise that man is here and now in that
state which must be termed normal separation, and this
being so we are justified in believing that he has entered
therein not as part of a cosmic mummery but as a work
of Divine Providence in his regard. He was to this
extent put asunder, as I have indicated; but still it was
from God that he came forth, or from Him in Whom all
things are one. It is also to God that he must return—
that is, to Him in Whom all things will again be one.[2]

[1] A merely casual reader like myself meets with strange intimations,
as—for example—in a perfectly obscure and recent commentary on the
Tiruvuntiyar of Uyyavanthadeva of Nāyanār. In the work of establishing " a complete unity of consciousness," the soul arrives at its last stage.
" It has cut asunder the attachment of the body." It has entered into
Divine communion. " It has resigned all acts." But there remains a
last vestige of duality, being the affirmation that " I am in *Śiva-yoga*,"
or one of its analogues. This is removed " by dwelling with the out-
pourings of love on the true nature of the Lord " and by realising fully
" the non-dual experience of bliss." The soul is then merged " into its
Being " and the Lord Himself acts through the soul. " This is the way
to be and to become Him." An English poet once said paradoxically :
" I love but live no more." This is a realisation of the identity of being
and love.

[2] And according to William James, that which India calls Yoga—
at once a doctrine, a practice, a thought-mode and a state of life—

The Way of Divine Union

So therefore in respect of the East, the way is ours and theirs ; the end also is one. But I shall always think in my heart that a formulation of the way as Christ is that which of all is perfect and that this Master is He Who is truly ours. Eastern Mysticism shews us that there is more than one figurative veil of attainment. One thing, however, seems certain. The East or the West counts little towards the path of realisation until we have come to understand the veridic significance attaching to the word detachment, as contradistinguished from its conventional and ascetic meanings. It is a cessation from cleaving to that which is extraneous to ourselves, and above all to the substituted unions conditioned in the passage from subject to object. These unions may be innocent or not in themselves but they are not in the law of unity. Those which are pure among them can be brought under that law, and therein they are part of our way to God.

means categorically the experimental union of the individual with the Divine.

CHAPTER VII

THE PATH IN CHRISTIAN MYSTICISM

WHEN that which responds in the consciousness to the great and the last things, as they are called by the masters, speaks and is heard in the heart a new world reveals its vistas in the mind, and the path through which it is entered is known by many names. I have spoken of it on my own part as the path of realisation, but this presupposes foreknowledge as to the end attained in its travelling. The consideration which I propose concerning it is a consideration of the ways and modes of that quest which ends in God.

The path of Christian Mysticism, according to the records of the past, is a path of detachment, a path of ascetic life, a path of deep contemplation or prayer; but above all things and in all things it is a path of love. We have to see after what manner these conditions or principles were put in practice by the witnesses of experience and after what manner they can be understood and accepted by ourselves. As a clear line of demarcation between these two points or aspects of the subject is not in accordance with my scheme, I shall adopt another method.

It has become almost a familiar saying that many paths lead to the centre, and if I added on my own part that all those paths are straight, it would be merely a derivative from the symbolism—a working from the circumference inward. Images of this kind do not offer as a rule any considerable illustration of their subject, because analogies are approximates only, yet as they serve a purpose often by the way of stimulus it might have a touch of the ridiculous to examine their warrants too seriously. Perhaps if those who to-day are indifferent—but I will speak rather of the day's zeal, because I have known it better—would recognise that there is such a path at all and a term possible to attain, they might come to believe that many paths are open and many paths lead—in another form of symbolism than that of the circle. But mourning and sorrow abide in the evil ways, and there are courses which lead into great worlds of loss. Wise are they who avoid them, even if an issue can be found from each and any towards the bourne of life's desire. On the other hand, there is no joy comparable with that of the true paths—which go straight to the end.

A practical lesson that follows from life itself, and from the symbolisms, is to beware of saying that there is only one way, and this is the more needful because there is a sense in which it is true.[1] There is one kind of dedication, one sanctifying life, one work of the will, one zeal actuating, one transmuting love; whence, if these are the path—as they are indeed and surely—then it is true to affirm that the path is one only and that all have walked therein who have entered into real knowledge. But if it should be testified that the *via dolorosa* of ascetic life is the path which all must follow, I hold that the witness errs; while if another should affirm that it counts as a path only by some error of enthusiasm, he errs also in the condemnation of a method which has taken many thousands forward through several ages and nations.

---

[1] It is only *qua* wayfaring man that the man on his way through the world errs in any of the paths. There is nothing that leads more truly than ordinary life itself, when that life is sanctified. But the reason is obviously that it ceases then to be ordinary, in the common—which is the unclean—significance of the word.

The Path in Christian Mysticism

Passing to a different aspect of the realm of images, it is not well in any rigid sense to speak of the true path as one of crucifixion, though herein is living symbolism, because the progress of the mystic is capable of description under a variety of emblematical forms. All glorious warrants notwithstanding, we may dare at need to discern that this form is not in many cases the best descriptive mode, because it is open to misconstruction—as if suffering were of the essence of progress, whereas it may be an accident only. The truth is that life is individual and to each therefore shall a path at his need be given : in the catholic sense it shall be one, in the particular its variations shall seem infinite. He who is lame and walks goes differently from him who is sound and rides horseback ; but they may take the same road. It shall be admitted at least by every man who has travelled under true direction that suffering dissolves in glory, and that the will at a certain height does not know of the cross. If, however, we cleave to the symbolism and speak of a way of the cross, it follows that there is a point of crucifixion, and there it ends ; there is also another point, which is that of coming down from the cross, so crucifixion ends also. Finally, if that which dies within us at the term of the crucified life is that which does not belong to us, it is salutary to realise that dwelling unduly upon either passion or cross is attributing overmuch consequence to what is no part of us, which is with us but not of us, which dies in our liberation therefrom, so that charity is misdirected alike in respect of its pains and its penalties. Now, it is certain that no cross exists except for purgation and the death is final cleansing.

There is another point of view, from which the path in its proper understanding is one of roses. This, too, is a personal question ; some of us shoulder much baggage and some are clothed lightly ; some of us multiply cares, some cast them all aside ; God carries the cross of some of us, while the cross of some is a Satan. A few elect souls know that the cross is themselves, and these cease from bearing it. The understanding throughout is that no one can make a start in the absence of certain conditions which I began by defining, but these postulated a beginning can be made anywhere. It is much better to be a Christian in this our glorious day of freedom, but among the great cohorts of salvation in the ages which lie behind us the elect have reached the vision and the end under the ægis of other names. I conclude that the free choice is everywhere and the free quest : the end also is everywhere. The work in the first instance is one of awakening to a sense of the Divine within us and to the Divine in the universe.[1] According to Christian mystical doctrine such work is the part of God, for the sleeper needs to be awakened. In this case, it is certain that God stands at our door and knocks ; our part of the work is to answer. But it is truer symbolism to say that the Divine within us will not fail to open the door unless it is kept fast from without by the sense-life. Even so, it may open from within.

Respecting its essential nature, the definition-in-chief of the path has determined that it is an inward way.[2] As such, it is a way in consciousness, the word path

---

[1] It was said by Richard of St. Victor, " I would that a man learned him to know the unseeable things of his own spirit, ere he presume to know the unseeable things of the Spirit of God."—This is from the paraphrase of the *Benjamin Minor* printed by Pepwell and edited with other tracts, under the title of *The Cell of Self-Knowledge*, by Edward S. Gardner.— See c. x. The Latin text is in Migne's edition of Richard, *Patrologia Latina*, Tom. CXCVI.

[2] The term is a state and the path is a succession of states. The first, *ex hypothesi*, is permanent hereafter only and is now for most of the witnesses a matter of mere moments. The others are preparatory and so far as they are actually internal are classified in many ways. Sœur Jeanne-Bénique Gojos experienced thirteen interior states, ending in the perfect union of her soul with the Sovereign Good. This is, of course, an outward side of the path.

being accepted as a process leading to an experience. That experience is catholic to all periods and peoples: it is not contained therefore within the horizon of one faith or company of the elect. The developments differ, but it is the same in essential nature everywhere, though it has not led those who share it to the same exegetical conclusions. The field of consciousness is without limit in reception of experience, but it remains that which it is. No man goes out of consciousness in the experiment of mystical life and no man returns thereto. It is the self entering into a state of knowledge with God. When the manifestation of consciousness is suspended by physical disaster, it is because the brain-organ has been for this or that period damaged. The faculty of consciousness is distinct from the vehicle through which it works to sustain correspondence with the world which is called external. It should be needless to dwell on these points when a mystic offers his understanding of mystical doctrine and practice to those who are themselves mystics, or acknowledge a call or disposition to the inward life. But there is much loose speculation and even risky experiment on several sides of the subject.

There is a good deal of talk in these days about the art, secret, or practice of " going inward ": some of it is tolerably good, a little has the air of reflecting veridic experience and may be practical after a certain manner ; but I have not found that those who make the experiment attain any certain ground. If they are psychics, the seekers perceive psychically and return with pictures and pageants. If they are mystics they get intimations which are sometimes profound, sometimes even permanently helpful ; but as to the states entered I have never had one intimation that can be called intelligible from the amateurs of Divine Science. I have heard them described fantastically as liberation from a lesser personality. They are nothing of the sort ; there is no lesser personality, as we shall see in its proper place. It is a figment of debate, an economy of discipline, a fashion of speaking which is used by many because it serves easily and saves a good deal of trouble in explaining phases of consciousness.

If we ask them whether their inward experience occurred within or without the consciousness, some of them will answer that it was within, in which case the experiment, with any result attained, was in their own selves, in their very own nature ; but others—within my knowledge—venture to say that it was without, and that which is outside conscious intelligence is not experience but blank nothing. Those who come back to tell of it are raving. There is, as we have seen, an attempt to save such a situation by distinguishing the normal from another order of consciousness, and as every new experience is—as such—abnormal in respect of the individual ego, therein concerned and thereby affected freshly, this distinction is true enough ; but it does not help the case. Normal or supernormal, it is still an experience in consciousness. I may be hallucinated and have visions which are in no relation to reality ; yet it is I who see. So also the veil may be lifted and I may behold that of which St. Paul says that it is not lawful to speak : yet and again for ever, it is I who see.[1]

Now, we stand in the normal consciousness as on the threshold of that great world, mentioned at the beginning of this section. We look down its shadowed vistas and discern, however dimly, the vastness that spreads beyond. The beyond is also the within, and the path to eternal life is the path of man in himself. But before we enter therein it seems certain that the ground of

[1] According to Fichte, the Ego is the supreme principle of philosophy. It is this certainly as regards the philosophy of quest and if it were possible to have one of attainment I do not see that the ground would be shifted from consciousness, for in the state of union it is still the ego which knows with God and in Him.

faith must be determined, apart from personal hypotheses. There must be an assumption based on the records of experience, with a view to the repetition of experience, so that we may know at first hand that those who gained it previously have borne a faithful testimony concerning the greatest achievement which the heart of man can formulate. As regards the fact of the records, it is as if some travellers testified that they had found Mont Salvatch in the Pyrenees ; that, when questioned, they told an admirable story respecting what they had beheld ; but, as to the Holy House, that they had added : " Go and see." It is as if, when we were pledged so to do, they proffered many directions and left for our better guidance a map or an itinerary, very carefully drawn and specified. What is necessary in such case is a certain high confidence to follow the instructions.

Let us take therefore, in the first place, the counsel-in-chief of the path. The preparation of the soul for mystical attainment is made in love, and about the use of this word there is no qualification or symbolism, though much may be said hereafter on its true understanding in the high regions of thought. All things else in their failing may appear as economies, or modes and fashions of speaking, belonging to the images of mind ; but this is literal and is not cast out in any state. Here the appeal in proof is to all mystical experience. The Path of Eternal Wisdom is therefore to this extent a path of the emotions. Though I have said elsewhere that true love has no body of desire, there is desire in the soul of it. After the path there is a state, which is a state of peace, a state of living fire in stillness—as though it were fire centralised. One of the lesser rewards is termed a " new savour and sweetness " in all creatures and the manifestation of God in all. It is then a new love declared in Heaven and upon earth.[1] We may be

[1] The last degree of love is described by Castaniza as that in which the Beloved is enjoyed perfectly by the soul, the soul being transformed

led to see in this manner that the process is one of slow growth and that as love in its external developments does not proceed by leaps and bounds in the common course of things, so here it is, for the most part, very gradual. Yet if this rule obtains it shall stand with due respect to what happens in some cases suddenly—since there are many modes of working in these mysteries.[1]

The aim of the mystic may be described therefore as the term of union reached by the path of love. I have spoken of many paths, but all begin in this or must lead thereto. In the mystical darkness of Dionysius it is by love, as Corderius tells us, that we are joined with God.[2] The quality of the love is ecstatic and the word of the union is absorption—*totus absorptus in Deum.* Now, this has authority from the pseudo-Areopagite himself, who says that the lover of God is intoxicated and lost in God.[3] But the testimony of Ruysbroeck affirms that such love in its perfection seeks not its own profit, whether in beatitude or otherwise, being kindled for God Himself and for His eternal honour. Therein are we united, therein have intercourse with Him, in Him abiding and He also in us. This shall be sufficient on

in God. There are in all seven degrees which are expressed in the way of counsels as follows : (1) To languish after God ; (2) To seek God ; (3) To fear the loss of God ; (4) To suffer for God ; (5) To be weary of delay in the satisfaction of love for God ; (6) To run lightly, confidently and meekly unto God ; (7) To enjoy God and to live in and with God eternally.

[1] Dean Inge suggests that the knowledge of God passes into love of God, and *utrum amor possit esse absque prævia cognitione* is an old debate. See Antonii a Spiritu Sancto *Directorium Mysticum, Tract.* I, *Disp.* I, § 4, for the view which postulates knowledge and for authorities. The debate becomes a question of the will, *quia voluntas dicitur appetitus rationalis* and Aristotle has ruled that appetite postulates cognition. The debate is arid, but I mention it to add as a rider that there is love at the first report in respect of God as there is love at first sight among men.

[2] See the annotations of Corderius on *Mystical Theology.* Migne's Codex, Vol. I, fol. 1011, 1012.

[3] Treatise on *Divine Names, ib.* I, fols. 709, 710.

the subject, but it is understood that there is a cloud of witnesses.

Another condition of attainment, in respect of which there is no licence possible, is summed up in the word sanctity, of which it is the crown.[1] But it should be understood that this is not the condition of an hour, a day, a novena—as if in preparation for a feast. It is a word which stands for life—by which I mean the whole life of dedication. As, however, there are degrees in sanctity, so there is also a certain distinction in its qualities: we have therefore to establish a canon of criticism in this respect. And above all there is the question of environment, which corresponds—broadly speaking—to what is called the state of life. It is not to be affirmed —even from the standpoint of old ascetic literature in the world of the West—that mystical attainment is a reward reserved exclusively to the monastic state, though—prior to the dismemberment or partition of the West into places of sects—most practising mystics were monks or nuns.[2] It is not to be put forward as the exclusive crown of celibacy, understood as a virgin state, though again most mystics have followed this imputed counsel of perfection. Once more, the condition is not one of ascetic life otherwise—on the sum of the Christian records—though most records are those of ascetics. We have to set aside therefore these states, environments and atmospheres in any final consideration of our subject. No one denies that they have been aids,[3] but we have seen in the succession of Christian

[1] I have not thought it necessary to speak of the gate of morality, for it is obvious that we must pass therein if we are in search of the Absolute Goodness, and would know at first hand what it signifies to say: "Holy, Holy, Holy, Lord God Almighty."

[2] This is on the evidence of the records which are in the open face of day; but there are traces in traditional literature of an experimental process which has nothing to do with asceticism and was in view of an attainment of which the ascetic methods seem to offer glimpses only.

[3] Celibacy, for example, accomplished a most peculiar work—of

mystics who followed the ascetic period that there appears to have been a certain change in the admitted notions of attainment. That period would seem, however, to have passed, like that of its aftermath, and we stand now on the threshold of a new order. We have come to recognise the sanctity of life in all forms and the law of its salvation in all departments which bear the seal of purity. We have come, further, to discern the inherent sacredness of every physical gift and that all may be aids to redemption. It follows that the counsels of perfection have to be re-expressed and the closing taken in respect of some old vocations. But this is to be done with the reverence of due ceremony, in love, not in disdain, as becomes those who have found a more excellent way.

The Blessed Henry Suso, who has left us a precious record in his own memoirs, is perhaps the most typical example of the ascetic life, its titles and its errors ; but the annals of sanctity, from the days of the fathers of the desert and *The Palace of Palladius* to those of Madame Guyon, who wrote memoirs also, are the chronicles of the subject at large and the life of the cross as it was practised by multitudes who knew of it only as an instrument of suffering, abnegation and shame, a cross of death, not of true life and glory. I have no pages to fill with details of practice ; they are familiar enough and, moreover, the case against them does not need setting out. But it is essential to insist that the sense in which the path of mystical attainment is one of ascetic life belongs to the region of wont and habit rather than to that of a rule imposed. In any direct and categorical way it was not imposed at all. The counsels were those of detachment from the things of earth and restriction

which we as yet understand too little—by the transfer of repressed and starved sexuality to a spiritual plane. The Reformation vindicated Nature and put an end to a particular modality of mystical experience. At the present day there are vestiges of a new mode of realisation.

of the demands of sense ;[1] but that which was intended by detachment to divert the mind of the Christian from undue concern in transitory things was turned into hatred or contempt for all that belonged to the world, including personal love of creatures ; and that which was designed by restriction to place the mind of the Christian in authority over the sphere of his passions was turned into a rule of self-torture and the search after filthy humiliations became supernatural virtue and a part of heroic life. The main root is to be found in the erection of celibacy into a counsel of perfection, and this in certain directions threatened to poison the well-spring of one of the Church's own sacraments.[2] So far on the side of impeachment, but it has to be recognised on the other that every mystical saint of the Latin Church was a great ascetic and would have covered this criticism with contumely. So it comes about that we must look for another way.

We know, and it is of old agreement, that there is that within us which is neither satisfied with seeing nor filled with hearing, nor fed by ministries of the palate, nor does it enter into the ecstasy of plenary union by the

[1] On the principle of Cardinal Bona : *Sensuum occasus veritatis exortus est.—Principia Vitæ Christianæ*, I, 25.

[2] There was once an Alexis—whom God has forgiven long ago—and he is said to have been inspired by an extraordinary desire of perfection, in the gratification of which he " tore himself away from his bride on the first night of their union, and never returned to her." There are books going about in which things of this kind are treated like a dainty morsel to be turned in the mouth of the writers. What of the duties involved by the state of life into which it had pleased Alexis to call himself, or which he had consented at least to assume ? And what kind of counsels are those which justify, which laud even a monstrous act of self-seeking because in virtue of some hypothesis the search was called one of perfection ? Compare the records concerning Nicholas of Basle, who renounced his contract of marriage on the marriage morning itself. But the situation was saved in this case by the disgraced lady ultimately condoning the insult and entering conventual life. See Frances Bevan's *Three Friends of God*, a rag-fair of protestant sentiment.

physical organs of intercourse. But this is not to say that all these instruments of sense are to be kept in a state of inhibition, a deprived and macerated state ; they are to be used for the service of our real selves, as pages of honour, not as serfs or slaves, for to them also belongs the liberty of children of God. The governors must be of course upon them, so that they do not get out of hand, till they also have attained their measures in the stature of Christ. Let us remember in this connection that everything clean and true and just which is given us to do is in the nature of a sacrament, and in the worthy performance thereof a holy grace may be received by the soul. The senses are natural sacraments and the instituted sacraments work with them and through them. The false law of suppression is rooted in the notion, conceived by theology, pampered by ascetic writers and drawn through lowest deeps by irresponsible guide-books of devotion, that human nature *per se* being hateful in the sight of God until it is redeemed by Christ, must be hateful through all its stages to him who is seeking redemption.[1] It is the impeachment of our proper personality, and here is what it forgets. God is personal in respect of our personality and He dwells in our consciousness consciously, while in respect of our

[1] So also in devotional works—*Le Directoire Spirituel*, for example, and a multitude of text-books—the mystical counsel to know oneself is imposed for the purpose of exploring the depths of our misery, degradation and inquity.—*Op. cit.*, c. XXVIII. This is the fundamental standpoint in any case and out of it the other considerations arise in their due order. The mode of reaching self-knowledge is by examination of conscience, so that we may the better discover our infamy.—*Ibid.*, c. XXX. Compare this kind of conscience, its sifting and the mystical exploration of self on the quest of God. The protestant l'Abadie goes to work with the same intention ; his *L'Art de se Connaître Soi-Même* is to sound the unplumbed wells of our abasement, and the charge against pagan morality—including that of the Portico—was its ability to elevate man, not to humble him. It is just to add that in the opinion of this witness the humiliation contemplated by Christianity was to remove the pride of the soul without reducing its dignity.

The Path in Christian Mysticism

highest states there is a true symbolism which affirms that He is the Spouse of the soul in us. He is all things to all of us in all that can have part with Him. In so far as we are life, He is in us, with us and by us, the life of life, and that life is everlasting. Hereof are our titles and dignity, which it serves no purpose to deny, but makes indeed for hindrance, seeing that every high estate has cares, as it has duties also, thereto belonging. It is good here to remember the extent of the soul's prerogatives. This manifest world is a witness to intelligence: there is its first reason, its chief object, being part of the truth that manifestation is only to consciousness. Above all there is the nobility of that which can dream of union with God and, by the testimony of many lords and princes of the life within, can also attain it. There is nothing which calls to be renounced on the inward way but that which does not belong to our high and true estate.[1]

There is a path or method of attainment which is called nothingness by Molinos, but here the term has to be distinguished from its use in the sense of Dionysius, Erigena, or the author of *The Cloud of Unknowing*. It is not, I mean, a counsel of attainment in Divine Darkness, where the uttermost of Divine Transcendence is withdrawn, according to these mystics, and yet a corner of the veil is lifted for some most favoured souls, so that they gaze in rare moments into that ebon deep, as into something which is within them, and is in the true understanding a *plenum*, not a void. On the contrary, it is for Molinos a nothingness of the soul itself, and that is assuredly a false counsel which seeks to magnify and approach God by disparagement of the one vessel that, within our direct knowledge of the cosmos, is capable of realising His presence by a reception in consciousness.

[1] We have recited too often our *Domine, non sum dignus* in the spirit of those who abandon every claim, instead of expecting the day of the *Nunc dimittis*, as of those who have done their work.

The Way of Divine Union

It must be merest commonplace to say that the belittlement of that which is called " creature " must be a poor compliment to that Other which is called " Creator "; and the pity of it is that few things savour more strongly of hollow pretence, with all its poor devices.[1] This art or science of grovelling has been regarded too long as the first science or first art and craft to be acquired in the spiritual life. " Sink thyself down to the dust in His mercy," says Böhme, and a long literature of quotation is possible at need on the subject. The basis of all is a coarsely conceived analogy between God's relation with man and the position of suitor or mendicant at the gates of an eastern tyrant. One implicit is of course the fall of man and our own personal guilt, which contributes to its perpetuation. But the king's son cast down at the feet of his father will remember that he is the king's son.[2] It is time to make an end of these laidly reflections from monks of Africa and hermits of Palestine, which are like an open sore upon the fair body of the Christian centuries of sanctity.

Out of it has come the long-drawn way of the ascetic life, with its beginnings in the counsels of discipline and side-issues leading through all refinements and exotics of self-punishment and torture. They failed, it would

[1] These things notwithstanding, the truth is not in Rudolph Eucken when he says that the older Mysticism was the offspring of a worn-out age.—*Life's Basis and Life's Ideal*, English translation, p. 247. So far as Christianity is concerned, the ecstasies like the aberrations, the conquests like the renunciations, were products in their prime instances of a young and imperious age, which was put to school hardly and was intolerant of curb and rule.

[2] That counsel is sufficient which has been left by Richard of St. Victor. " He who desires to see God must cleanse the mirror of his soul. When the soul is cleansed by the fire of love, that which is seen is our own unworthiness and God's goodness." But the love of God is not " the desire of the moth for the star "; the soul which conceives it knows that her Beloved awaits her; and His love swallows up all unworthiness. By all the mystical hypotheses He raises her to the throne of union—that is to say, into His own estate.

156

seem, to understand in those past days that the spirit of the world, in which Christ has not anything, dies to each of us when we shut our doors and leave it in outer darkness. Thebaid solitudes and purlieus of the Palace of Palladius are really more difficult than the cities by the great waters, the crowded streets and houses of exchange, because they circumscribe the field of possible spiritual activity. It is not exactly that temptation is necessary—and in any case it comes always, wheresoever we may be abiding or hiding in the external part—but rather that growth outward towards Godhood and not inward only is in the city rather than in the wilderness.

For the rest, self-conquest is one thing, but that which exceeds these measures in the ascetic ways leans to and attains self-outrage, or a dishonouring of the image of God within us. It is not on account of our imputed vileness, our miserable plight and the compassion which this state may be presumed to kindle, but because of our genealogy and because of our implied possibilities, that God has given to His elect all that which we know to have been given. If there be a part of man for which humiliation is salutary, there is a part also which must be so raised that it shall attain its own. There is a false pale of ceremony in respect of self-abasement which needs to be broken, that the vindication of God's honour may enter therein. In place of its exploded doctrine I dare to offer the glory of human personality in its marriage with Divine Will.

This is, therefore, so much consideration offered towards a rejection of the ascetic life because of its implicits, and because I look for a more excellent manner of the life purified. As it was followed in the past, the ascetic life is a great example of the heart that had found no weariness in its exploitation of the outward ways.

The path of mystical attainment is called by universal consent a path of contemplation, but it requires to be understood in a particular manner. I do not propose

to cite the witnesses at length on this very important
subject, as was done in the case of the holy term itself.
There would be endless repetition involved, with
variation in detail or form of presentation only. At the
beginning, and on the question of fact, one distinction
is needed. We tend in ordinary speech and writing to
use meditation and contemplation as if they were
synonymous of a single working of the mind, and the
custom may pass tolerably where nothing of moment
is involved. It is otherwise in the spiritual life. Meditation is there always regarded as an initial state. It is
discursive ; it reflects and compares : as such it is purely
intellectual.[1] *Ex hypothesi*, an intellectual knowledge of
God may be reached rationally in the work of meditation ; the latter is therefore comparable to natural
theology. Contemplation is an ascent of the inward
path where it has passed above reason : it is comparable
to revealed theology.[2] The one is a figure and shadow
of the other. Meditation is water, contemplation is
wine. The sanctifying motive of love is necessary to the
first, but the life of contemplation is the life of love
itself.[3] It will be seen that the general sense attaching

[1] Compare St. Teresa's state of mental prayer, as distinguished from
contemplation. It consists in thinking over and realising what, and with
Whom, we speak, etc.

[2] The practice of the Presence of God, the practice of Divine Love and
the practice of the Union were not an automatic work of conventional
or formal concentration. This is mechanism, but they were life itself.

[3] "Contemplative life consists in perfect love . . ., in a true and certain
sight and knowledge of God and spiritual matters."—Walter Hilton,
The Scale of Perfection. It has three parts, which are (1) knowledge of
God and spiritual things ; (2) affection ; (3) these two combined, or
knowledge and perfect love of God. Richard of St. Victor had already
distinguished six kinds of contemplation : (1) In imagination and according to imagination only ; (2) In imagination according to reason ; (3)
In reason according to imagination ; (4) In reason and according to
reason ; (5) In something which is above but not against reason ; and
(6) In something which is both above reason and apparently in contrariety
thereto.—*Benjamin Major*, Lib. I, cap. 6.

The Path in Christian Mysticism

to the word can have little if any correspondence with the particular and exotic meaning.[1] There is, unfortunately, no light in Dionysius as to his intention in using it. That which he prescribes is contemplation pure and simple—as a condition into which the postulant casts himself inwardly; but there are no particulars, save only that it is an increasing exercise, while it follows from the context that the experimental research of mystical theology is followed in a world outside thought. This has its limits and hence cannot be a way of communion with that which is unconditioned. Moreover, as normally understood, the contemplation which has God for its object of necessity produces an image. This is a form of thought and as such is in our likeness, whereas it is postulated that in the deep states there must be no forms. It is possible that a practice within measures of the accepted sense may lead in this direction up to a given point and is therefore a door; but beyond the experience lies too deep for the operation to continue further.[2] There is a suspension of faculties in the process, a closing of avenues through which the mind works, so that intelligence is thrown back into itself, seeking to operate directly and not in a reflex sense. There is no search after objects; but, according to the old thesis, God is within and God discloses Himself.[3]

We must take this key of obscure intimation and carry

[1] The most comprehensive and the noblest definition is perhaps that of the Jesuit Corderius, who says that "contemplation is Divine Intercourse."

[2] The definition of Richard Rolle is memorable: it is "ravishment out of fleshly feeling and ravishment of the mind into God." *The Fire of Love.*

[3] The delineation of Pascal, already quoted: "God known of the heart," is the gate opening on the whole mystery of experience. Where does the abyss of the Godhead open for those who seek it? In the heart of love. Where does the height of the Godhead reveal itself? In the mind of love. Where are all the unsearchable treasures concealed by God? In those who love Him. All is within the self.

it with us through the centuries. St. Thomas Aquinas defines contemplation as *simplex intuitus*, not of the thought category but of direct inward seeing, and the Venerable Augustin Baker annotating hereupon, suggests that the clear sight is a consequence of diligent research.[1] There are great developments in Ruysbroeck. Contemplation is knowing apart from mode, abiding above reason, though not apart therefrom. It is a capacity for gazing inward with an eye uplifted and open to eternal Truth. It is also simplicity, stillness and utter peace. Above all it is a loving longing of the soul to be with God in His eternity, a turning from self into the freedom of the will of God. Richard of St. Victor says that the eye of the soul is opened to behold God and all manner of ghostly things.[2] The mind is ravished therein. St. John of the Cross draws many threads together when he affirms that purgation, detachment, poverty of spirit and contemplation are one and the same thing. He gives us also many definitions: (*a*) Contemplation is a lofty union with God attained in this life, though He is not revealed distinctly; (*b*) It is a loving infusion of God which sets the soul on fire with love; (*c*) It is the dark night of the soul and the wisdom of God utters discourse therein; (*d*) It is a reception of the highest wisdom in a silent spirit, detached from all sweetness and particular knowledge.[3] But according to St. Teresa perfect contemplation signifies conformity between the human and Divine Will.[4] It is not, there-

[1] He says also that this is the occupation of beatified souls.

[2] After all the workings, he affirms it to be the gift of God without desert of man. But I have said already—and we know in the words of the Master—that God stands at the door and knocks.

[3] It is also (1) a purifying fire; (2) that which absorbs the soul and brings it near to God.

[4] She says also that highest perfection lies in the conformity of our will to that of God.—*Foundations*, c. V. It is passive at first, being contained in the notion of surrender, but afterwards it is active, and here begins the great work of Mysticism.

fore, a work of concentration but an attitude, a habit, and herein is the true way to mystical life, without postulates, without processes—a simple, uniform, undeviating modality of the whole nature.[1] It can be laid down on this basis that the first steps in union with God are steps taken by the will of man, and are a continual affirmation of possibility by the mind to the mind itself, apart from all images. It is the planned application of a recognised principle.

The various classifications or tabulations under which mystical progress is set out are all stages of contemplation and contemplation is literally the life. One of them is well known, being (a) Purgative, (b) Illuminative, and (c) Unitive. It is the chief favourite of all, and I should be retracing a beaten track to describe it.[2] St. Teresa

---

[1] All that has been said of contemplation in the modern schools and of its processes calls therefore to be re-expressed from another standpoint. The emptying of the mind must be performed with a new intent. The whole is a work of the will and the object is realisation : it is that always and that only. But if realisation is of God Who is within, the will working towards it is not the business of a moment but of all life, all thought, all action and all sleep. The supreme exercise of the will is that apparent suppression which Dean Inge mentions in *Personal Idealism and Mysticism*, p. 144, in virtue of which " God can think and will and act freely through us, unimpeded by any wilfulness on our part." But in this connection there is a statement which may cause misapprehension on the part of unwary readers, being the affirmation that " there is no room in the universe for more than one will, existing in its own right." Dean Inge is, of course, pointing out that our free will in opposition to God is intolerable, not that it is impossible in fact.

[2] Antonius a Spiritu Sancto says that in the first stage, which is that of neophyte, the chief concerns are abstinence from sin and repression of concupiscence, because these are opposed to charity. In the second, which is that of craftsman, the dedications are to progress in goodness, that the life of grace may be strengthened. In the third, which is that of master, the mind is transformed completely by love, fruition of God, and the desire to be dissolved and to be with Christ.—*Directorium Mysticum, Tract.* I, *Disp.* I, Sect. VII, Nos. 124–128. The reader may compare the tabulation of *Mysticism in Christianity*, p. 18 *et seq.*, under the heading of *Scala Perfectionis*. It contains several good points.

enumerates degrees of prayer: (*a*) Mental Prayer, which is meditation properly understood, including recollection of the senses. (*b*) Prayer of Quiet and recollection of soul. (*c*) Prayer of Union, being sleep of the powers of the soul, mystical death to the world and union with God. (*d*) Prayer of Fruition, a state impossible to understand and much more to describe.[1] There is suspension of bodily powers and entrancement of soul faculties. It lasts less than half an hour, but the effects and their sweetness abide, at least for a time.

Eckehart's idea of the Union and the mode of its attainment recalls Dionysius, but in the sense that one who has reached some knowledge at first hand concerning the hidden mysteries may recall another who has searched the mysteries before him and with whose testimony he is acquainted. The likeness is with due regard to independence and leaves untouched the individuality of the later mystic. In one state of the soul it enters into comprehension of the Holy Trinity by its capacity of intelligence, and with that which it has comprehended it becomes one by grace. By the capacity of the will—but this is in another state—it plunges into the unknown which is God. These are obviously degrees of what is called otherwise the unitive life. The path is that of sanctification, which is placed by Eckehart even higher than love; but this is a confusion of terms, as it is certain that sanctification is love in its activity approaching God by the road that we can alone approach Him. Sanctification itself he describes,

---

[1] It will be seen even by the beginner that these brief descriptions are sufficient to separate the degrees from all which attaches commonly to the practice of formal prayer. We shall do well to remember in respect of every aspect—from the least even to the greatest—that prayer does not change the order without, but it does change that which is within, and this is more important, for the institution of a new order within means a new relation to the order without, and this is how prayer is answered. In this symbolism, the last stage of prayer, or that of fruition, signifies that the great work has been performed.

in terms similar to Dionysius, as that race or running which is "none other than a turning away from all creatures and being united to the Creator." Eckehart adds that when this state is attained by the soul "it loses its own distinctiveness, and vanishes in God, as the crimson of sunrise disappears in the sun."[1] Here is an irresistible text for a discourse on German pantheism in the fourteenth century by those who fail to understand the deep things of preoccupation in God, and are unqualified by capacity or experience to gauge the unmeasured possibilities which open their vistas in the world of human love.

According to Ruysbroeck, God created man that He might confer beatitude upon him. He created that He might have love distinct from His eternal self; that He might lose Himself in us; that we might find ourselves in Him—having first lost ourselves in order to find Him, in Whom is all. The path is that of contemplation in unity of spirit, on the understanding that the holiest is he who loves the most.[2] When the spirit is transformed in love, it enters into the possession of itself, in the sanctuary of its created being. The eternal sun rises therein; beyond reason and beyond even love itself, the man is rapt at length into the naked vision

[1] It is difficult to decide whether Eckehart is speaking of the hereafter or here and now. I am certain that the implied absorption is a bourne which is very far away—perhaps with many worlds intervening. There is, however, all that which follows the incorporation of Human with Divine Will.

[2] This being understood, the thoughts are to be kept bare and stripped of every sensible image, the understanding to be opened and uplifted lovingly to Eternal Truth, the spirit to be outspread in the sight of God as a living mirror. There are four modes of the practice : (1) Entering within the self, free of earthly things, with the heart raised to God. (2) In simple purity of spirit, by love and reverence, to stand unveiled before the Presence. (3) To see God as in a lucent glass of vision. (4) Uplifted and illuminated exercise of love, according to the beloved will of God. Mysticism is the Art of Love and its literature is the Art expounded.

and reaches the mystery of unity, as this is accomplished in the spirit. The spirit is united by a triple tie to its eternal type—principle and source of life—or that Christ Who is, I conceive, understood as the form of all souls, the latter being regarded as the redeemed body of the Church, even as each soul is for theology the form of that whole personal human nature which it sustains and animates. Those who can receive this may be partakers of another and more deeply theosophical view of the Inward Christ and the Marriage. " We are beatified in His Divine Essence," says Ruysbroeck, and this is the attainment of the Kingdom of those who love God—*Regnum Deum Amantium.* The fruition therein is likened in Dionysian terminology to a perpetual nescience. And this, says *The Book of the Adornment,* is that dark silence, wherein all loving spirits do love themselves after a certain manner.

With the author of *The Cloud of Unknowing,* the great work of seeking and attaining God is a work of Divine Love for God's own sake and of man for the sake of God.[1] It is a long following of the course of common grace in a cleansed and purified conscience. It is a work also of prayer, which differs, however, both in kinds and degrees. It is a casting out of knowledge, even as of sensible passion, and a service both of body and soul, in the subjection of things earthly to things ghostly, so that the bodily personality may be as if nowhere, while the spirit is in all and everywhere. To this end, however, there is more than one class of hindrance which must be overcome, for the operation of the rational understanding does not lead to God's

---

[1] We may compare with this the stages specified by Richard Rolle in *The Form of Perfect Living* : (1) The world is forsaken—with its vanity, covetousness and lust. (2) God leads in the lonely way and speaks to the heart. (3) God causes the heart to be gathered up and fixed on Him only. (4) He opens the gate of Heaven to the eye of the soul. (5) The heart is purified by fire. (6) The man is ravished in love.

knowledge, and here the author of *The Cloud*—quoting Dionysius—testifies that " the goodliest manner of knowing God is to know Him by unknowing." This is the kind of life and the practice is a passive contemplation, an abstraction of spirit, in which—says the Venerable Augustin Baker—a man " loses the feeling of his own being " and has " being and living in God." It is a state of perfect union, removed from soul itself, as well as body, and dwelling in the height of the spirit.[1]

After Ruysbroeck there is the admirable Tauler and there are his *Institutions*, very noble in conception and yet, like the rest of his work, rather a practical guide to men in the way of the world who would keep God in their hearts and live in the sense of religion, contented if they can walk in the more conventional narrow path, but feeling that the great heights are beyond them. He could not discourse of the high things without reflecting Dionysius, unawares or otherwise, but no doubt he knew of the texts. In the 35th chapter of the work mentioned I find some prudent counsels on the banishment of all mental images and on cleaving to God by an inward act which is apart from the forms of thought. Such a course should have been preceded by long contemplation on the purest and most sublime images of Divine things. Yet these are ways only by which we may be led to the simple and naked truth, which is attained in disengagement from everything, by veiling the eyes of the spirit and proceeding on the way of love, holy desire and pure, Divine intention. It is a path of crucifixion in the uttermost sense, for the price of essential truth in its perfect attainment is such an

---

[1] The steps and degrees of perfection, according to Castaniza are : (1) Faith, fear, dread of mortal sin. (2) Dread of venial sin. (3) Asceticism. (4) Inward exercises. (5) Resignation and perfect obedience. (6) Satisfaction with God only, but as yet unwillingness to surrender Divine favours. (7) Perfect contemplation—inflamed, absorbed, ecstatical, and therefore unselfed even in respect of favours.

emptying of self on the altar of love that the seeker is deprived even of that which he must attain, being the inward consciousness of God. It is this dark void which God at length fills in the state of inseparable union.[1]

I should have spoken at an earlier stage of Johannes Scotus, but this is not a chronological discourse, and if I mention him now at the close it is because he does not seem of the whole mind of our subject, his intellectual greatness notwithstanding, and notwithstanding that he translated Dionysius. He was an illuminated theologian rather than mystic, glorious in the life of debate rather than in annals of attainment, though we must remember always that he gave the root-matter of all its Mysticism to the Latin-writing West, in which sense the whole literature derives through him. In his work on the Eucharist he identifies true religion with philosophy—almost as if it were an intellectual study and not a practice for the attainment of life. His five books on Nature are a monument for their period, but I know scarcely where some of the speculations might have landed unwary minds. As regards the return of man's spirit to God, he distinguished seven stages of progression, the last being the absorption of all in Deity, whence—I suppose—that everlasting figment of debate, the charge of pantheism once made against him. Theology which does not recognise this state as the term of individual being, so that the end is like the beginning, is a doctrinal system in eternal separation, and is as much out of court as the vedic pantheism which travesties the

[1] We may not unserviceably compare the practices leading to regeneration according to the testimony of John Engelbrecht. (1) To fix the eyes upon God. (2) To follow God in holy doctrine and life. (3) To yield up self to direction by the Holy Spirit. (4) Ever to live in the Spirit. (5) To cease from living according to human reason. (6) Thus to become regenerate through the Holy Spirit. (7) To abide therein, becoming a new creature and partaker of the Divine Nature, which is an eternal, fiery, almighty, Divine Essence. (8) To live in God and God in us.

sacred and glorious universe by the substitution of illusion for sacrament.

The conclusion is that life is unbeginning, for life is in God. The spirit came forth from God, and the spirit in fine returns. It comes forth into separation by Divine Will: it returns into union, taking individuality with it. So ends the age-long pilgrimage of the soul. As regards the path itself, the findings of this section constitute to some extent a parting of the ways. The path to the Highest, however conceived and followed, can be only one of holiness; but the denomination belongs to all modes of life and is not to be circumscribed within the rule of anchorite and anchoress. It depends from the root-meaning of the word itself, which implies the doctrine of union, or conscious integration in the conscious whole which is God. There is no question of external observance but of an inward mode of being, the fruition of which is the term of mystical life and the quest of which is the path. So long as the Divine Object is apart from the soul, or is so conceived, there is no conscious integration, for herein the passage from subject to object is in fine transcended.

CHAPTER VIII

SYMBOLISM OF THE CHRIST-LIFE IN THE SOUL

THE path and term of attainment in Christian Mysticism are presented under two palmary and recurring formulæ of symbolism. One of them sets forth the inward mystery of the birth, life, death and resurrection of Christ in the heart and soul of the mystic ; the other conceives an ineffable union between Christ and the soul in mystical espousals and marriage. It is realised by both in a definite and plenary manner that Christian Mysticism is concerned with the realisation of Christ within, whether as the *absconditus sponsus* or as the Lord of Glory, hidden and declared in Bethlehem, Nazareth and Galilee, on Calvary and in the rock-hewn sepulchre, even unto the mountain of Ascension. In each case a root of the symbolism is to be found in the New Testament, but in each its presence is by way of a vestige only. The two formulæ are so distinct from one another that they appear as mutually exclusive, and it is of vital moment to recognise this fact—whether ultimately they can be harmonised or not—if we have to judge between them in respect of their comparative values. If there are cogent reasons for exercising a preference between them, and if both have found their development within the same school, how shall we explain their co-existence ? But if in the main the formulæ characterised divergent or successive schools, does the discovered superiority of one symbolism signify that the school which adopted it is the higher and truer school ? Or are both imperfect as

168

formulæ, and does any ulterior question remain open after setting both aside ? It so happens that there are difficult aspects of these questions, and no answer is therefore ready to our hands. For example, the Christ-Life symbolism attained its chief development and final elaboration in post-Reformation schools, but it did not originate there. On the other hand, the symbolism of mystical marriage was perfected in the Latin school but was taken over by protestant mystics, though it was not their favourite formula. Again, it must be said that each embodies a vital symbolism, so that one is disposed to recognise that they are full of grace and truth ; the suggested preference between them is not therefore easy, if indeed possible to exercise. Moreover, the Christ-Life formula is concerned chiefly with the path, while that of the Spiritual Marriage is both of path and term. In fine, if neither be perfect, the explanation may well be that there are points at which all symbolism fails, that it intimates rather than expounds, and that its sacramental value is along broad and general lines.

The root of the Christ-Life formula is to be sought in Pauline epistles and arises therefrom. There is the personal testimony of St. Paul when he said, " I am crucified with Christ "[1] and " Christ liveth in me."[2] There is the testimony of his mission when he said to the Galatians, "I travail in birth till Christ be formed in you,"[3] and to the Ephesians—" that Christ may dwell in your hearts by faith."[4] He said also to the Romans : " If any man have not the Spirit of Christ, he is none of His."[5] Once more : " If Christ be in you, the body is dead . . . but the Spirit is life."[6] With these scattered references must be compared the recurring counsel on the part of Christ Himself to take up the cross and follow in His own way, as also St. Paul's affirmation that " our old man is crucified "[7] with Christ. I have called

[1] Gal. ii. 20.   [2] *Ibid.*   [3] *Ibid.*, iv. 19.   [4] Ephes. iii. 17.
[5] Rom. viii. 9.   [6] *Ibid.*, viii. 10.   [7] *Ibid.*, vi. 6.

169

these things vestiges, and their symbolism, if it can be so denominated, is of the simplest kind, while that which was developed therefrom not only became complex but so began. The governing idea was, however, exceedingly natural, namely, that the life of Christ as the Incarnate Word on earth is the prototype and pattern of the spiritual life in each one of His followers. That which was enacted by Him and in Him when for our sake He assumed the flesh of humanity has in us to be re-enacted, that the Divine Mission may be fulfilled efficaciously for and within each one of us. So in the mystical as in scriptural formulæ Christ was to be formed or born and to abide within us, we being crucified with him to the world and spirit thereof. It came about therefore very early in the Christian centuries that Justin Martyr speaks of the indwelling Logos, and the Epistle to Diognetus says that " Christ is ever begotten anew in the hearts of the saints," being the reverse side of that symbolism which speaks in the *Epistle to the Hebrews* of crucifying the Son of God afresh.[1]

The mystical theology of Dionysius and the letters arising directly from that text are devoid by their very nature of all conscious and express symbolism, and it cannot be said that the idea of Christ has any office in the mystical work indicated. There is, however, his putative master Hierotheos, of whose *Book of the Mysteries of the House of God* I must speak at some length, but without discussing whether the tract in question anteceded the texts which pass under the name of Dionysius. It exists in a Syriac MS. and the nature of its content is known solely by a pamphlet[2] of Mr. A. C. Frothingham, published

---

[1] Heb. vi. 6.

[2] This was the subject of a study by Mr. G. R. S. Mead in *The Quest*, October, 1911. He describes the work of Hierotheos as an " epic of the soul setting forth the mystical stages of the ascent of the mind or spirit to the Supreme." His study is more sympathetic than that of Mr. Frothingham.

in 1886. It describes in the first place how the soul is prepared by purification not only in its own part but that of the body. Thereafter the aspirant passes through opposing and chastening hosts in " the purgatorial realms of Hades." At the end of this he attains spiritual re-birth and ascends " beyond the firmament " into " the heavenly realms." There are mysteries, however, which are beyond those that are understood by the word heaven and its experiences, and their path is the Way of the Cross. The travelling of this path is followed by crucifixion of the entire human nature, the mind or spirit being on the cross in the centre, with soul and body on the right and left hands. A mystical death follows, and the mind is laid in a sepulchre to rest for three days, after which—or on the third day—it rises from the dead and " unites to itself its own perfectly purified soul and body." Here, however, is in no sense the end of the process, for after all the mystical experiences a root of evil still remains in the aspirant and this has to be eradicated. There is a second descent into the depths of Sheol, another crucifixion therein, followed by a baptism of the spirit ; and it is thereafter only that " the Mind passes into that state " when the " mystery of union with the Universal Essence " begins. Yet is it still a place of strife and trial rather than of rest. The mind has once again to descend, even to Sheol and Hell, armed with a mystical sword. The reward of its final victory is attainment of universal purification, when its undivided will is " to be united with the Arch-Good alone." In virtue of this will the re-ascent begins by way of resurrection and ascension. It is thereafter that the mind is really and perfectly united with the Universal Essence and " embraces all in itself."

At any risk of imperfection and the suppression of important points for critical appreciation, I have endeavoured to reduce this involved system to the simplest part of its elements. It suffers on the surface from the expression of personal and inward experience in cosmic terms, and as there is subsequently a cosmic part, which I have left over, it is at first somewhat difficult to decide where the one ends and the other begins. The line of cleavage is, I believe, indicated by the words of my last quotation : to embrace all in itself means that the mind has become part of the Divine Activity operating through the universe. Prior to this, the three successive passions seem in correspondence with a redemption of the part physical, the psychic or desire part, and that which is called mind, being the part of purpose and will.

The procession of this imputed mystical experience is exceedingly interesting, its confusions notwithstanding, because at so early a period—whatever date may be finally assigned to the text—it is a presentation at large of what I have called the Life of Christ formula, of the great symbolical principle which belongs to one side of mystical literature in Christendom. It tells us, like the later witnesses, that the mystery which began at Calvary and ended—so far as the visible plane is concerned—on the Mount of Ascension has to be enacted within each of us before it is of effect in us. So much as we know of Hierotheos gives the symbolical pageant and not the doctrine ; Dionysius furnishes the doctrine, not the pageant. Over the principles at work in the process both pass lightly ; contemplation is the keynote of one, purification that of the other ; and these are words which stand doubtless for years of preparatory toil.

Outside the Syriac MS., the text of Hierotheos is non-existent ; it has practically no history ; and I do not find that it has exercised the slightest influence, in any direction whatever, on Christian Mysticism. There seems good reason to question whether it was the work of him whom pseudo-Dionysius saluted as master under the name of Hierotheos and from whom he quotes thrice, but from *The Book of the Hidden Mysteries* never. However, the question on either side is little of our own concern.

It is sufficient for us that the strange voice of those mysteries found no echo in Christendom. The Christ-Life formula, as represented by the literature of Mysticism, remains almost as simple as we find it in the New Testament. For St. Augustine, in each pious soul a Christ is born again, and for him we have been made in Christ.[1] For Abelard, the material ascension of Christ was a type or pageant of that spiritual ascent which occurs in the souls of those who have received Him as their life of life. Eckehart is first to bring the symbolical hypothesis into that fuller realm of application which was exploited, I might say, at all costs by one at least of the later non-Catholic mystics. For Eckehart, " the Father speaks the Word into the soul, and when the Son is born "—I should say rather, conceived— " every soul becomes a Mary."[2] It does not require an advanced grade of intuition to see all that may follow from this. Tauler goes further in saying the same thing. " The Father begetteth His only begotten Son in the

[1] Compare Eckehart, who says : " The Heavenly Father begetteth His only-begotten Son in Himself and in me. I am one with Him, and He has no power to shut me out. In the self-same work, the Holy Ghost receives its being and proceeds from me, as from God." There is little wonder that the voice of condemnation was raised against such modes of symbolism.

[2] Eckehart says elsewhere, with his customary daring : " It is more worthy of God that He be born spiritually of every pure and virgin soul, than that he be born of Mary."—See the Sermon on the Angel's Greeting, translated by Claud Field, M.A., in *Meister Eckart's Sermons*. The Word is spoken " in the purest, loftiest, subtlest element of the soul." The condition of the conception and birth is that a soul must be " absolutely pure and must live in gentle fashion, quite peaceful and wholly introverted."—*Concerning the Eternal Birth*, translated by C. de B. Evans in *The Porch*, Vol. II, No. 2. Concerning the soul and Mary, compare Plotinus, who says that " in the intelligible world the celestial Venus reigns," that " every soul also is a Venus," and that this is obscurely shewn forth by the nativity of Venus and Love at the same time.—*Of the Good, or the One.*

173

soul, as truly as He begetteth Him in eternity, neither more nor less. What is born when one says: God begetteth in the soul ? Is it a likeness of God, or a picture of God, or is it somewhat of God ? Nay: it is neither picture nor likeness of God, but the same God and the same Son Whom the Father begetteth in eternity and naught else than the Blissful Divine Word, that is the Second Person in the Trinity." [1]

Here is the utmost extent to which the subject of this symbolism seems carried by the Latin mystics. I find nothing to add from Ruysbroeck, *divinissimus contemplator* as he is ; St. Teresa is taken up almost entirely with the sacred marriage formula ; and for St. John of the Cross, who is in like case, even the cross figures as a sign of betrothal. [2] But a certain change comes— though a little insensibly—when we pass over to that other school which resounds with the voices of non-Catholic Mysticism. The formula of the Christ-Life recurs continually in Böhme. " Man is impotence and nothingness until Christ is formed in him " ; and if the sacrifice of the cross is to avail in the soul of the Christian, it must be wrought in him. " The Father must beget His Son in my desire of faith." [3] So also many other

---

[1] Tauler gives elsewhere an account of the rule to be followed by those who would experience the birth of Jesus Christ in their hearts. It embodies the usual ascetic counsels of self-abasement and denial, so that the outer man may die to all things for the elevation of the interior man and his direct progress towards God, looking neither to the right nor the left.—*Institutiones*, c. XXXIII.

[2] It is of course to be understood that *The Ascent of Mount Carmel* and *The Dark Night of the Soul* are documents of the life of crucifixion, but they do not contain developments of the symbolism with which I am concerned in this chapter.

[3] Christ in the first place having " generated us again to the paradisical image."—*The Treatise of the Incarnation*, Pt. I, c. 4, pars. 6–8. It is said elsewhere : " Christ is that virgin-like image which Adam should have generated out of himself with both the tinctures."—*First Apology*. " All souls have communion or sympathy with that one soul of Jesus Christ."—*The Way of Christ*.

174

intimations of Böhme convey symbols of the Word being born in us, the understanding of which is the true way to Christ. The whole procession of Divine Life in Nazareth passed before the spiritual eyes of Valentine Weigel, who defined true faith as the life of Christ within us: "it is being baptised with Him, suffering, dying and rising again with Him."[1] Gichtel speaks of " Christ united with us in the deep places of the soul " ;[2] and Marsay, a French mystic, who draws from Böhme, supposes that the Divine Man was separated from Adam by the Fall ; but the work of Christ in each of us is " to put us again into that state in which God created us." He speaks also of receiving the life of Christ Jesus,[3] which is mentioned in similar words by John Saltmarsh[4] and others of the Rebellion period in England who were rather in the outer court than in the mystical Church of God. His counsel is to have the life of Christ within us, to " incarnate Him over again." Bromley in his *Way to the Sabbath of Rest* draws out a symbolism recalling that of Hierotheos, as follows : (*a*) Death upon the mystical cross, (*b*) descent into hell, (*c*) transition thence into the Eternal Paradise, (*d*) the Eternal World, entered by ascension.[5]

I suppose that at this day there are few who remember George Keith and his *Way to the City of God*, but he also preached the inward coming of Christ, " a Divine Seed sown by the Father in the heart of every man," out of which there is raised, as it were, a body of holiness, and

---

[1] " Of the Life of Christ, that is of True Faith," 1648. Translated from the German.

[2] Gichtel says further : " Christ Jesus is nothing but love, and the more we thirst after love by imagination, by a strong appetite of mind and soul, the more we draw the love of Jesus into our inward hunger and desire." [3] *Discourses*.

[4] " The Foundations of Free Grace Opened," 1645.

[5] I believe that *The Way to the Sabbath of Rest* was reprinted some few years ago in America, but I have seen only the original edition of 1710, to which another tract was appended.

this is God's image. The work requires a " supernatural concurrence of the soul," after the manner of an earthly mother, to conceive it in the inward nature.[1] This is like a reflection from Eckehart, not that the one borrowed from the other, but that they drew rather from the same source of spiritual insight and came to see in this manner that there is a working within the soul which leads up to the Christhood. I might speak, in this and similar connections, of testimony which arose in the English Philadelphian school, at the end of the seventeenth century, concerning the new birth and restoration of the Divine Image in man, the crucifixion with Christ, the mystical death and resurrection, and the ascension which crowns the work of the Christ-Life.[2] These things are in Jane Lead and in Robert Roach, but in each case the root of derivation is Böhme, who is presented more clearly and with a better grade of realisation by William Law.

He speaks on the authority of Böhme of that likeness or image of God in which man was created originally, in virtue of which he also was a trinity in unity, having the Son of God in his soul. This likeness was broken up by the Fall, and the scheme of redemption by Christ is to restore the Son within us and the presence of the Divine Ternary.[3] It is the new birth or regeneration. In other

---

[1] *The Way to the City of God* appeared in 1678.

[2] See in particular Jane Lead, *The Heavenly Cloud now Breaking*, 1681, *passim*.

[3] See *The Grounds and Reasons of Christian Regeneration*. According to Latin theology, the unitive presence of God in the soul is an union with the Three Persons of the Holy Trinity, because these are undivided. It follows that in so far as God is conceived as a Trinity, that Trinity also is within. The work of our redemption is to know by experience that he who goes to the Father goes inward to find that Father; that he who would be saved by Christ finds that salvation in Himself; that the descent of the Paraclete is into the inmost man. When God is born within the individual soul, He is called Christ. So is the Word made flesh and dwells among us. Therefore, by the hypothesis of Christian doctrine, the Trinity in Unity is from eternity that which we may become in realisation, when we have been remade by Christ in Its image.

words, Christ must be formed within us and so we are re-formed in Him.[1] Not in an external sense but as an inward Saviour does He come to raise us, entering as deeply into our soul as sin itself has entered and restoring all things. He comes as a seed at first, but out of it is formed " the inward and new man," destined to grow into that spiritual creature " which was first created in Paradise." There was ordained " the whole process of our Saviour's incarnation, passion, death, resurrection and ascension into heaven," because fallen man is " to go through all these stages as necessary parts of his return to God."[2] The pageant of the Christ-Life in Palestine was therefore a devised ceremonial, a procession of events which goes on, as one might say, for ever, and the incarnation of God in man is everywhere repeated in that part of humanity which is brought into the Divine Scheme. " Nature is overcome by a birth of the life of God[3] in the properties of the soul." But that which is called a birth of Divine Life is also a birth of love.

We come in this manner to the last witness of all, to the final development of the symbolism by L. C. de Saint-Martin. We have been presented so far with the heads of a spiritual experience in correspondence by affirmation with the manifest life of Christ, but as to what we should understand by these there has been no

[1] *Ibid.* But see also *Some Animadversions upon Dr. Trapp's late Reply*, in which the parallel between the soul and Mary is drawn out with considerable clearness.

[2] *An Appeal to all that Doubt or Disbelieve the Truths of the Gospel*, c. 1, where it is affirmed that " regeneration is the real birth of a Divine Life in the Soul," and that a Christ Who is not born within us cannot be for us, meaning that He cannot profit for our salvation.

[3] *The Spirit of Love*, Pt. I. This is Law's distinction between intellectual and vital religion. The latter is not notional apprehension or historical knowledge; it is an experimental discovery, a reality, " living, speaking and working " in the soul.—*The Way to Divine Knowledge*, 3rd Dialogue.

instruction. It is true that Hierotheos presents the pageant of a greater initiation, as it might have been enacted in a Hidden Temple of the Word, corresponding —*mutatis mutandis*—to Egyptian or Greek Mysteries ; but I have said that it is pageant only. Eckehart, Tauler and the succeeding witnesses leave us with the whole position undetermined, except that the ascetic life prevails therein. But Saint-Martin comes forward with an entire volume on the subject and we must expect that which was previously as a mere summary of chapters in a projected work to appear as full text of the thesis. It must be stated, however, at the outset that Saint-Martin was neither in the Latin line of succession nor in that of the post-Reformation groups. When he wrote *Le Nouvel Homme* he was an independent, unattached mystic drawing from his own spiritual consciousness. At a later period he came under the influence of Böhme without appreciably moving from his proper ground. There is not the least reason to presume his acquaintance with the great mystics of the past and the fact that he enters into the chain rests purely on his own warrants, which were those of inward experience, as in the case of the other witnesses. Within definite limits he could not help using similar formulæ to represent a similar knowledge attained spiritually.

In a more considerable study of *Le Nouvel Homme* than can be attempted in this place, I have said that the Christ-Life is represented by Saint-Martin as a new life conceived and born within us.[1] It was also—as in other witnesses—a restoration of that which had been lost by man when he passed into his fallen estate. This appears reminiscent of Böhme and his disciples, but obviously it was common property of the symbolism at large. The stages of personal experience of the inward Christ are presented as stages of suffering, from con-

[1] *The Life of Louis Claude de Saint-Martin*, Book V, § 2, p. 259.

ception to crucifixion.[1] " Before Divinity can penetrate and occupy us in its splendour and glory, it must possess us in its pain and passion."[2] The succession of inward events embraces all chief details of the Christ-Life in Palestine and may be tabulated somewhat as follows, presuming only that there is firstly a triple purification of body, soul and spirit, perhaps like that of Hierotheos, and that these parts of our personality are restored to a virgin state.

(a) The soul is then like Mary, and Divinity announces by its angel that she shall be overshadowed by the Holy Spirit and that He who will be born of her shall be called Son of God.[3] (b) The soul becomes aware of conception.[4] (c) The soul recites her *Magnificat*.[5] (d) The neighbours, being presumably witnesses already in regeneration, salute her, like Elisabeth.[6] (e) The birth takes place within us, as in a stable at Bethlehem, being that of our natural humanity.[7] (f) The Son Who is born is Divine Love, but also a Son of Suffering.[8] (g) He is worshipped by shepherds and angels.[9] (h) Offerings are brought to Him by Magi.[10] (i) He is pursued by Herod.[11] (i) At the age of twelve years He confounds the doctors of doubt, darkness and false teaching in the human heart.[12] So did the child Jesus grow in grace and beauty. (j) He enters upon definite ministry and receives baptism at the hands of one who is termed His Guide, faithful companion, or a spiritual creature, our guardian angel in fact.[13] (k) It is said in some un-

---

[1] It had been pointed out by William Dell in the seventeenth century that the crucifixion of Christ began with His assumption of human nature, though I think that he misses the true aspect when he says that this crucifixion was in the fact that the flesh of Christ was crucified and dead to the desires, delights and ends of the flesh.

[2] *Le Nouvel Homme*, 1796, p. 31.   [3] *Ibid.*, p. 32.
[4] *Ibid.*   [5] *Ibid.*   [6] *Ibid.*
[7] *Ibid.*, p. 51.   [8] *Ibid.*, pp. 53, 54.   [9] *Ibid.*, p. 52.
[10] *Ibid.*   [11] *Ibid.*, pp. 52, 53.   [12] *Ibid.*, p. 90.
[13] *Ibid.*, p. 171. Saint-Martin does not actually say that the Guide is the Guardian Angel.

demonstrable manner to be a corporal baptism, though performed with water of the spirit ; but the whole question is involved, perhaps inextricably, with a doctrine concerning the angels, this doctrine belonging to the strange school of Martines de Pasqually. Saint-Martin writes in his most cryptic way concerning it, and though I know from what quarters some of the intimations are derived, the question is far too large and much too distinct from our subject for its treatment in this place. Moreover, there would be nothing to explain the baptismal office of the Guide. I add only that when the Rite is finished and the New Man has issued from the water,[1] a voice from heaven proclaims, as in the old story, that " this is My Beloved Son, in Whom I am well pleased." That Son does not appear to have recognised His own estate prior to such declaration, or to have been conscious fully of divinity. (*l*) To meditate thereupon He passes into the desert of God and the Spirit, where He cleanses all His universe of being and casts out all those who work evil therein.[2] (*m*) He is tempted like Christ and defends Himself, like His Prototype, by the power of the Word.[3] (*n*) He changes water into wine at another marriage of Cana.[4] (*o*) He goes forth into the world within Him and preaches on a mystical mount to personified powers within Him which are capable of redemption.[5] (*p*) He testifies of the kingdom that is at hand, collects apostles, is encompassed by disciples, performs miracles, accomplishing the conquest of that realm over which He should rule of right.[6] (*q*) He is transfigured upon Tabor and in this experience attains the knowledge of His Source.[7] (*r*) He makes triumphant entry into His own Jerusalem, riding on the ass of His old nature.[8] (*s*) The Last Supper follows in due order,[9] and then (*t*) the Passion with all its details, from the

[1] *Ibid.*, p. 173. [2] *Ibid.*, p. 178. [3] *Ibid.*, pp. 179–181.
[4] *Ibid.*, p. 196. [5] *Ibid.*, p. 202 *et seq.* [6] *Ibid.*, p. 228 *et seq.*
[7] *Ibid.*, p. 296 *et seq.* [8] *Ibid.*, p. 334 *et seq.* [9] *Ibid.*, p. 356 *et seq.*

Garden of Gethsemane to the yielding of the spirit on the cross.[1] (*u*) He goes down into Hades, as into His own abysses, for judgment and redemption therein.[2] (*v*) He comes forth into risen life and manifests to His own within Him.[3] (*w*) He ascends to the Father,[4] (*x*) that He may pour down the Spirit upon the personality in which He has dwelt and worked, the Church and the world thereof. He departs,[5] (*y*) but returns again for the ministry of final judgment and to raise up the Zion of individual nature into the Blessed City, after which manner[6] (*z*) the redemption of personal humanity by the Christ-Spirit is in fine accomplished perfectly.[7]

I have mentioned in my previous criticism that there are many and transparent defects and a few inextricable confusions in the long pageant of symbolism which I have thus summarised.[8] The account in brief may give an impression that the book is really a prose-poem, but on the contrary it is an exhortatory work and is so described by the writer, who says that he would have written it differently had he then known the deep revelations of Jacob Böhme. One illustration will suffice as to its mixture of elements. We have seen that Mary is the soul who conceives the Inward Christ; yet at the close of the mystical drama the soul is not *mater dolorosa* at the foot of the cross but Maria Magdalena speaking with the angels at the sepulchre on the morning of Easter.[9] It would seem also that St. Peter when it is said to him: " Lovest thou Me ? " and: " Feed My sheep "—is the

---

[1] *Ibid.*, p. 388 *et seq.*   [2] *Ibid.*, p. 408 *et seq.*
[3] *Ibid.*, p. 419 *et seq.*   [4] *Ibid.*, p. 420.
[5] *Ibid.*, p. 420 *et seq.*   [6] *Ibid.*, p. 425 *et seq.*
[7] *Ibid.*, pp. 430–432.

[8] It is obvious that the summary does nothing to justify the various allocations of the symbolism—e.g. the personal inward sense of the transfiguration on Tabor. These things are not too clear in the work itself and do not admit of explanation in a brief space.

[9] *Ibid.*, pp. 416, 417.

soul again, or there is a curious confusion about scriptural references.[1] However it may be, a thing of this kind can scarcely escape imperfection, for the greater the detail in symbolism the more it exposes weakness. The most interesting point about *Le Nouvel Homme* is that it closes the allegories of Christ-Life in the soul with a great ceremonial mystery comparable to that of Hiero-theos, in which they began. Between these two elaborate memorials there are only intimations and outlines. One could write commentaries still more elaborate in defence of either or both, but after all the special pleading they would stand for that which they are—strange devices of invention—and the question arises concerning them which Saint-Martin once asked in another connection : Master, is all this needful to attain God ?

I write as one who regards the story of Christ as a synthesis of the mastery, but it is in respect of the broad outline and as regards minute particulars I look for better light than I have met with so far in the literatures of the soul. It may be that this light will come. Meanwhile individual inward progress of path and term are repre-sented in the Divine Memorial of Palestine by (*a*) the conception and birth, (*b*) the hidden life of nurture and preparation, (*c*) the ministry and (*d*) the mystical death, burial, resurrection and ascension. The ways of all the Mysteries have met herein, so that it derives from every-where. The treasures of the four quarters of mystical experience have been drawn together for the building of this temple of types, and it is what Zion was fabled to have been, a centre of all things. But the Christ of such symbolism, as it seems to me, is the Cosmic Christ and is He Who was of Palestine in the sense that this Christ was declared in Jesus of Nazareth. Jesus of Nazareth came, by the hypothesis, to shew forth the mystery of salvation in the way of the Christhood. As such, He goes before us eternally, rising from grade to

[1] *Ibid.*, pp. 417, 418.

grade in our consciousness, drawing all things after Him. Yet the path of mystical attainment remains in the Cosmic Christ—Divine and Eternal.

The symbolism of the Word born in each who is called to the Christhood places the soul in the position of Mary the Virgin, and in this connection never did speech of parable shadow forth a greater mystery than the miraculous conception of Nazareth. When the genealogy of Joseph is recited as of Him Who was not born according to the flesh, a keynote is given to those who can use it. It is void as to the descent of Jesus from the line of David, being the genealogy of a foster-father. But it is of all truth mystically as a story of election through the ages. It was on becoming the Christ that Jesus of Nazareth entered into the line of royalty, and it was the soul of Jesus of Nazareth who was Mary the Mother of Christ. But this was a soul which was truly and literally *vas insigne electionis.* To her belong all the titles of the Litany of Loretto.

It is needless to say that this understanding of the mystery has never entered into the heart of doctrine, nor into the heart of any mystic, howsoever removed from the courts and temples of theology.[1] From the standpoint of the Christ-Life formula, as it has passed into expression in literature, the great initial question is how to prepare the soul, that it may become wise and a virgin. It is obvious that we must take Mary as she is presented in the Gospels and not as the doctrine has been developed concerning her in high Catholic theology. The soul of Mary in Scripture is not set apart from other souls in her history, save in respect of the child that she bore and the way wherein she bore Him. So

---

[1] The difficulty regarding the genealogy of Joseph is of course obvious, and for all I know it may be a stock argument with several classes of writers. Since the words of the text were written I have met with it in a curious mystical periodical which appears in America and is entitled *Ek-Klesia,* edited by the Rev. Holden E. Sampson.

also the soul of the aspirant on the threshold of the mystical path is not *virgo intacta*, and though it may return into purity, it is never free from blemish, according to theology. Set therefore side by side with her who " conceived in her heart before she conceived in her body," her who is *fœderis arca, stella matutina* and *advocata nostra*, we can see why Catholic Mysticism does not lean overmuch to any developed Christ-Life formula. That which *ex hypothesi* is conceived in iniquity has no analogy with that which is conceived immaculate, nor is that which sin has prostituted capable of virginal conception. It is the soul of man which itself has to be born again, and we know the wide appeal of this symbolical formula through the mystical centuries. We know also that it corresponds to a real event in spiritual life. The protestant types of Mysticism were not in the peculiar difficulty which I have indicated here. They could and sometimes did postulate a peculiar position in the sense of personal sanctity for Mary, the Virgin Mother, but as they did not hold her to be conceived immaculate there was an analogy possible between her who bore the Christ and those souls of election in whom Christ could be born spiritually.

The alternative position of the two schools over a point of high symbolism does not bind us to a decisive choice between them ; but it is easy to see that when Saint-Martin made a sincere attempt to take the whole field of Divine Life in Palestine as his province, he produced a large result in fantasy. Only a small part belongs to the life of the soul. And this leads me to one more point of contemplation as appendant to the whole question.

The high message, the moving eloquence, the life, the glory of the Passion of Christ are the more deeply convincing to us in proportion as we are capable of raising that Passion into a great enacted Ritual, quickening with messages to ourselves, rather than a tale of human wrong and suffering—great and holy as it is within these measures. The "man of sorrows died," and here is one moving message, but as such it is of the natural order only; it moves but maketh not alive. However, the Divine Tragedy is also " a symbol and a sign," and we may become acquainted in this manner with consequences unlooked-for in the external ways. The official sentiment concerning the Passion, which makes the Sufferings of Christ a subject of rather hectic devotion, might be dangerous rather than unhelpful, except that anything which promotes a personal love for the Christ of Nazareth is, in its own degree, on the side of salvation. The true purpose of the Passion and Death was to declare the Lord of Glory, Who is our one and sole concern, as He was for St. Paul evidently, when the Apostle to the Gentiles laid all his stress on the resurrection.

Jesus of Nazareth is our Exemplar in one of two ways —apart from ecclesiastical teaching, though not in the second case opposed thereto: (*a*) in the sense of the naturalists, who regard Him as a great spiritual teacher giving His life for the truth, but as to the values of this sense they do not exist for mystics; (*b*) in the sense of those who regard His birth, life, death and resurrection as a synthetic presentation in ritual form of the spiritual history of each individual who attains in God. This is not to say that the great story of Palestine is like a ceremonial pageant in Masonry, though raised to a higher plane, and is without an historical basis. It is at once actual and symbolical; the side of symbolism places it on the Divine Plane, while the side of literal realism brings it—with saving warrants—into very love of the human heart. He knew whence He came and why; He knew that it was for the working of a mystery; He knew that this mystery was an epitome of the experience of each individual soul on the way of return

Godward. He went through the high dramatic enactment with a conscious and plenary realisation of every element therein, from the most even to the least ; and hence for us there is vitalism and grace in all.

I am indicating here very roughly, and as if in words of one syllable, the findings of a secret school, which tends to hold that there was a plan prepared through the ages, in virtue of which He Who was to come arrived at the due time, and in Him was the plan fulfilled. He took flesh with knowledge. It is held further that Mary the Mother was prepared, the mystery of whose conception was the mystery of a withdrawn Sanctuary, while the whole event was one of Divine foreknowledge. Whether this is to be understood literally or in a deeper sense ; whether in the one case the Sanctuary is of this world or is withdrawn from the simple senses ; whether in the other my own understanding is in correspondence afar or near with that which is intended ; I do not claim to know.[1] We shall see as we proceed further. Meanwhile, as one who is assured that there have been many saviours, I feel on my own part that He Whom we call Christ, being last, is also the first. He carried with Him throughout the whole crucifixion, which was also the concealed glory of His earthly life, a consciousness of His Divine Nature and Destiny. As real man He suffered, but as Divine Man He knew. We are only on the threshold of understanding the scheme of Christianity, its great work of redemption, its universal import. I hold therefore that one school of the mystics has given us a true key when it teaches

---

[1] I am not putting forward the notion otherwise than as a mystical hypothesis. So far as I am aware, that on which it rests is a sequence of intimations rather than anything that can be called evidence. Its serious consideration would raise one very difficult point. Supposing that the Christ history had been put forth from a sanctuary of adeptship and were pageant, parable or myth, if it delineates the way of the soul in realisation, is it of the same vital consequence as if the Christian orthodox scheme were of very fact as well as very truth ?

that the mystery which began at Bethlehem in the land of Juda and ended—so far as external history is concerned —on the Mount of Ascension has to be enacted within each of us before it can be of effect in us. This is a path of our redemption, and here is one great tabulated scale of our ascent. But after all symbolism remains within its own measures, and if several schemes are without prejudice to one another while making for the same end, we can take our choice between them. Each after its own manner is true in symbolism. I believe in fine that there is an undeclared part in us which, when we awaken to consciousness therein, can say unto each : I am the Resurrection and the Life.[1] But it is only far down—and how far ?—the path of mystical quest that we can hear it speak within us.

Notwithstanding recurring allusions to the symbolism of birth, life, death and resurrection, and notwithstanding the possibility that I may have yet more to say of them as our quest draws to its close, it seems needful here and now, at the risk of future repetition, to define that which they embody, though I have assumed some understanding of the subject in those to whom I appeal. The birth is that which in the symbolism of Christ is a process of being born again. The life is that new being which the second birth produces, when those who have been kindled by the spirit maintain the fire within. Of the death it is less easy to speak, but it is really (*a*) a Dionysian death—in fixity of heart—to the images of sense and mind ; and it is (*b*) a death into life, for in the stillness of this state the life of God is realised in the intelligent and self-knowing part.[2] This is termed, in the

---

[1] So also, but in an earlier stage, there is a part of us which is not in redemption but is capable of redemption, or " I know that my Redeemer liveth " would be a testimony against truth and reason. The Christ-Life formula is a symbol of the working out of our salvation.

[2] Compare R. P. Avrillon's dying to all, to live only with God, " blessed if this mystical death," for which the soul suspires, shall unite the soul to God for time and for eternity.—*L'Année Affective*, p. 551.

language of spiritual alchemy, the shining of the sun at midnight. The resurrection is into glorified being thereafter.

We shall see in the next chapter that one of the questions formulated at the beginning of the present section is answered by shewing two points at which the Christ-Life formula and that of the Spiritual Marriage meet and join hands, notwithstanding their apparent divergence. They do not therefore exclude or reduce one another. I can give bare indications only, for reasons which will there appear.

CHAPTER IX

SYMBOLISM OF THE MYSTICAL MARRIAGE

THE revelation of the mystery of redemption and its completion of human nature is illustrated in the mystical literature of Christendom by another form of symbolism, being the intercourse subsisting between the Inward Christ and the soul who becomes His Spouse. The banns of marriage are published in faith, the marriage itself is made by a mutual concordat, and the union that follows passes eternally into consummation. As with the Christ-Life formula, the root of this symbolism is found in Holy Writ, where the relations between God and the Church of Election in Israel are represented by certain prophets as those of marriage. " Thy Maker is thine Husband,"[1] says Isaiah in his adjuration of Zion, " the Holy City." So also Jeremiah, speaking in the person of the Lord, says: " I am married unto you ";[2] and he reminds the faithless city and people concerning the kindness of its youth, " the love of thine espousals, when thou wentest after me in the wilderness, in a land that was not sown."[3] There is finally the promise of Hosea concerning the union of Israel and Judah in the days that shall come to pass, when the Lord shall betroth His elect people unto Himself for ever, in righteousness, loving-kindness and faithfulness.[4] I must set aside *The Song of Solomon*, because it is given over to every interpreter, so that he may do what he wills there-

[1] Is. liv. 5. [2] Jer. iii. 14.
[3] Jer. ii. 2. [4] Hos. ii. 19, 20.

with. Moreover, it would involve a long excursus on fundamentals of Zoharic theosophy. We know how the great canticle is regarded by Christian commentaries, and some of us may hold a defined opinion of their exegetical value, which is comparable to the gratuitous in-readings of chapter-headings prefixed to the sections of Isaiah's prophecy, in " authorised " and other versions. The canticle is really a poem of espousals between Messiah the Spirit and the Human Soul to which He was united in the flesh. The motive of the other references that I have quoted was taken over into the canon of the New Testament by the writer of the Apocalypse, where the Bride, " the Lamb's wife," is shewn to the seer of Patmos in the spirit as Jerusalem the Spiritual City, " descending out of heaven from God."[1] The combination of irreconcilable images is not less stupefying than the wildest dreams of Kabalism, but apocalyptic pageants of the period must be judged by canons of their own and not by those of the logical sense in literature. It remains that in the New as in the Old Testament Jerusalem is presented " as a bride adorned for her husband " ;[2] and the city is also an elect people, a holy assembly, or a church in more strictly Christian terminology.

Of visions on Patmos St. Paul knew nothing naturally, but he remembered the prophets of old, and in his doctrine of grace and the Christian life in earthly marriage he drew something from Isaiah and transmuted it in the alembic of his mind. There is scarcely an excuse for quotation, as the counsels are household words within the fellowship of faith, and with the side of material espousals we are not concerned here. But the pattern of relations between man and wife in the Lord are those of Christ and the Church,[3] which Christ presented to Himself as a part of Him—" holy and without blemish." The symbolism is that of a head ruling the

[1] Apoc. xxi. 9 *et seq.*   [2] Apoc. xxi. 2.
[3] Rom. viii. 1–4 ; Ephes. v. 23–32.

190

body and its members, and is not therefore a marriage symbolism, but it is made comparable to marriage in the world on the ground that Christ and His Church are one, as in the joining of personalities in wedlock the two become one flesh, by the testimony of Adam in Genesis. Now, the Church is *ex hypothesi* archetypal and is not constituted of its members, who are rather integrated therein : this is illustrated by the apocalyptic vision. In virtue of that integration—and not otherwise —the individual soul is joined with Christ according to the symbolism.[1] But out of the scriptural elements there grew up in Christian Mysticism the idea of a purely personal relationship between Christ and the soul, in which the more catholic union dissolved or passed out of sight, while remaining as a root of doctrine. A state which is characteristic of the whole is characteristic of its parts also, and though one cannot help feeling that the symbolism was never intended to have a personal side in the Scriptures of the New Law, they cannot be held to exclude what is involved by their own images. I think therefore not only that the mystics were right but that they gave a life to the symbolism which is wanting to the abstract conception of a church in wedlock.

From such small beginnings the idea was extended gradually and very slowly through the centuries. While most of the earlier fathers saw only the Church as the bride,[2] there are beginnings of the individual view—for

---

[1] A study of the word *pneuma* would shew us that the Greek fathers might have been in some difficulty over marriage-symbolism in respect of the individual soul, for this word is neuter ; and as regards the feminine substantive *psyche*, although this is used for the human soul in the New Testament, it was applied to the soul of animals by the best Greek writers, who are followed by the Septuagint.

[2] St. Just, Bishop of Urgellensis in the sixth century, wrote a commentary on the *Song of Solomon*, in which the Church is the Spouse. "Let Him kiss me with the kisses of His mouth" is her voice speaking. In "Thy breasts are better than wine," the reference is to the breasts of Christ; but these are apostles and evangelists. The "odour of

example, in St. Gregory of Nyssa, as we have seen, and when Tertullian speaks of the soul as the Bride of Christ. Things of this kind are vestiges, and it would serve no purpose to multiply the witnesses. We must pass to the twelfth century, when the symbolism was elaborated contemporaneously by two great writers—St. Bernard and Richard of St. Victor, the one in *Sermones in Cantica Canticorum*[1]—eighty-six in number—and the other in *De Quatuor Gradibus Violentæ Charitatis*.[2] St. Bernard is busy about many things in his mighty collection of discourses, from the desire of the Israel of old for the coming of Christ to the quest of the Church after union with the Divine Word, and it is only from time to time that we hear of the personal soul in communion with the spouse of the soul. On the other hand, the work of the Victorine gives at full length the story of the Lover and Beloved with comprehensive solicitude, alike in plan and detail. There is no understanding of Solomon's glorious song like that of the Zohar, but the sermons of Bernard are a museum of many types curiously interpreted. It is the Church who cries: "Let Him kiss me with the kisses of His mouth." The mouth is that of God, the kiss is the Holy Spirit, and the fruit of the kissing is knowledge of the Holy Trinity.[3] Longanimity and benignity are signified by the breasts of the Spouse, Who is Christ.[4] The mountains and hills of the canticle are heavenly spirits, or from another point of view they are (*a*) angels and men, (*b*) demons.[5]

vestments," signifies words and works. It will be seen that the commentary is a little book of high fantasy.

[1] The editions are innumerable; I have used that of the *Opera Genuina, juxta editionem Monachorum Sancti Benedicti*, 1845. The *Sermones in Cantica* are in the third volume.

[2] See Migne's *Patrologia Latina*, Tom. 196, containing the remains of Richard of St. Victor and other writers belonging to the same foundation.

[3] *Sermo* VIII.   [4] *Sermo* IX.

[5] *Sermones* LIII, LIV.

Symbolism of the Mystical Marriage

The lilies are good works.[1] These things and others may make for edification and did no doubt in their day, but for conviction they do not make, at least in this day of ours. For the rest, in the primary sense it is the Church which is the Bride of Christ, but the universal dissolves into the particular. The soul is the Bride thirsting for God in Christ;[2] she is likened to heaven in her holiness,[3] and receives Christ as the Bridegroom when she is in that estate. He is her physician in fragility and sickness.[4] But if she is chosen out of thousands, the Church of the elect itself, of which she is part and a member, was chosen before the ages began. And so from one to another aspect of the subject the monk of Clairvaux passes and repasses, as he is moved by the spirit within him; but often and too often he is far away from his text, among things connected with and arising therefrom in his mind.

We are on other ground with the monk of St. Victor, and I think in the first place that he had the courage of his symbolism in the sense that St. Bernard had not, or alternatively he had fuller realisation of its deeps and its high places. The kingdom of celestial espousals[5] is prepared and eager to suffer all the violence of love in the liquescent fire of his text. We do not hear much of the Church, for the more fully that personal union was realised as the need of man, the more difficult it was to dwell upon the alternative side of the symbolism. A Mystical Lamb with a Mystical City for His Spouse was after all an unthinkable proposition in imagery, but that which was possible to grasp was the Church as an *urbs cœlestis, urbs beata,* and seemingly it was a place of many bridals but one *Sponsus.* This of course is very difficult

---

[1] *Sermo* LXXI.   [2] *Sermo* VII.
[3] *Sermo* XXVII.   [4] *Sermo* XXXII.
[5] Betrothal, according to Scaramelli, is an earnest of the Spiritual Marriage. It is said to take place in a suspension of the outward and inward senses, in the intellectual instead of the imaginative part.

symbolism, but I do not find that the *crux*-in-chief ever occurred to its orators, nor the way of escape therefrom. The Christ of their espousals and union was unquestionably the Risen Christ of Palestine seated at the right hand of God the Father Almighty in the glorified body of His earth-life. There was little realisation of that which is now called the cosmic Christ,[1] the Second Person of the Trinity and the *Verbum Dei* by which the world was made. This was in the transcendental region of doctrine, not in that of experience in a world of desire spiritualised and ineffable bliss of soul. The Eucharist communicated an undivided personal Christ to each believer, who lost no particle of the Divine Body and Blood because there were myriads of communicants. So also each soul in espousals and marriage was in a state of jealous and exclusive union—for this and another moment of experience during earthly life, and afterwards for the eternity to come. A more vital understanding concerning the communion of saints would have removed the technical difficulty, which offers the Spiritual City of Wedlock to the irreverence of sensuous minds in the guise of an houris' paradise. It lay behind the symbolism but was not excogitated. By the hypothesis, it is only in virtue of integration in the Church that the soul can enter the nuptial state of the spirit, and all souls who attain it are one bride therein. It is in this sense that the Church is the Bride of Christ, as well as in that of the archetype already mentioned, and if therefore the Spiritual City is, as I have said, a place of many bridals, there is not only one *Sponsus* but one *Sponsa* in union. Perhaps from this point of view the apocalyptic text really saves the higher sense of the symbolism by sacrificing the outer body in a grotesque combination of images: it leaves nothing that can be

---

[1] The Christ-Spirit entered into potential matrimonial union with all souls when It assumed the soul of Jesus of Nazareth, and this is why the doctrine of the Incarnation is the great doctrine of all.

wrested sensuously by the mind of sense. If in this attempt to rectify an understanding of the Spiritual Marriage the risen body of the personal Christ passes out of view it is so much the better for the formula at large.

Richard of St. Victor's four grades or stages of *caritas violenta* are those of Betrothal, Marriage, Wedlock and Fruit of the soul in Marriage. The first offers some correspondence with St. Bernard's thirst of the soul. The second is a state of vision,[1] and the soul is said symbolically to behold the Sun of Righteousness, by another mixture of images. The third is union, glory in God and Christ, a state of vital transfer : it is called also deification and transfiguration. The fourth can be best described as the condition of the tingeing stone in alchemy ; it is one of life communicating life to others. The *Sponsa Dei* is said to be now *Mater divinæ gratiæ.* These stages are in perfect correspondence with those of mystical birth, life, death and resurrection, according to the Christ-Life formula, and as these are developed ceremonially by certain Instituted Mysteries of the Rose-Cross type with which I am acquainted. The birth is that of the soul itself, now in time and in the world, taking place in the stable of our human personality as in another manger of Bethlehem. In truth there are many Christs, or manifestations of Him Who is always in the world, Whose mission is to manifest everywhere. The life is hidden for the most part, but this also tends

---

[1] The classification and its distinctions are of great interest, but in the spirit of its symbolism I think that the real correspondence is between Espousals and Vision. The separation of Marriage and Wedlock is somewhat arbitrary, for in all the correspondences the Bridal Day is assuredly the beginning of Union. It is worth while to indicate this because of what has been said previously of the Blessed Vision passing into Perfect Union. The Blessed Vision as a state of unchanging beatitude is, mystically speaking, a substitute. Indeed it is a picture-state and as such a sequence of symbolism. Taken as a rigid doctrine, it is the eternal division between subject and object.

towards outward expression, because it is not possible that it should do otherwise. The death puts aside the old order entirely, as if the veil of the external temple were rent in twain ; and the risen life is that of Divine Mission—again corresponding to the symbolism of the tingeing stone.

St. Francis of Assisi was assuredly a mystic in experience of a certain quality and grade, but he was not a writer on Mysticism, and though I think that St. Bonaventura, the seraphic doctor, is passed over much too lightly by some of us in these days, it is scarcely through more than an aphorism that he belongs to this part of the subject. In *Itinerarium Mentis ad Deum* he bids us remember that " the highest wisdom must be sought of the Bridgroom, not of the Master,"[1] so that his soul had rested after its own manner in the arms of the Beloved. The Blessed Jan Van Ruysbroeck has left us a heritage for ever in literature of the spiritual life, a testimony of his own attainments in expression of the higher mind and an opening of vistas of things that are beyond expression clouded in light of glory. In particular he has left us an *Adornment of the Spiritual Marriage*, which is the psychology of Divine Bridals.[1] But as St. Teresa conceived of a state which is beyond union and which she happens to have called rapture, because a better word failed her, so in Ruysbroeck we seem to hear continually—not indeed that he so says, but by way of intimation only—of things that are beyond marriage for consubstantiality and oneness. And thus it comes about, I suppose, that the specific imagery of the symbolism is not overmuch with us as we tread the wonderful mazes of his labyrinth. Indeed it is lost altogether in the most advanced stages. He has simple things to tell us of the languors and im-

[1] There is the Latin translation of Surius in the *Opera Omnia* of 1609 and the French rendering of Maeterlinck, of which there are several editions.

patience of love,[1] deep things concerning Divine contacts,[2] things which pass into language with difficulty on the possession of God in a repose of unity, taking place in essential comprehension, apart from all intermediaries.[3] It is a state of incomprehensible light, an unplumbed deep of modeless rest, the abyss of God calling upon the abyss within. The self-sense of the soul—which can mean only our mode of self-realisation, and which, it may be presumed, is the last intermediary—is lost (that is to say, is exchanged) in the wild darkness of God ; and there God encounters God. These intimations and outlines are above the measures of marriage symbolism, as we meet with it in other writers. They are drawn from the text which I have named ; but the path and term of union are the subject of all writings of Ruysbroeck. *The Book of the Twelve Béguines* has many precious indications.[4] The union with God is said to be in our prototype, or the image of each individual soul which pre-existed eternally in God and is in close correspondence with the Zoharic *Tsure*, that divine part of our nature which never leaves *Atziluth*, the world of Deity.[5] The body, the heart and the senses are affirmed

---

[1] *L'Ornement des Noces Spirituelles*, Livre II, c. 23.

[2] *Ibid.*, c. 52.   [3] *Ibid.*, c. 56.

[4] This has been translated into English by John Francis, 1913. In the Latin rendering of Surius it is embodied in *De Vera Contemplatione Opus*, forming the first sixteen chapters.

[5] I shall recur to this subject in the next chapter. In the *Speculum Æternæ Salutis*, c. VIII, Ruysbroeck says that this prototype or *imago* is the Son of God, or the Divine Wisdom in which all things have subsisted eternally. In virtue of this highest portion of our soul, we are the living and eternal glass of God, which glass is ever exposed to the Face of God, reflecting It and shining therein. Compare Francis Rouse on *The Mystical Marriage* : " There is a pure counterpart of thy nature, and that pure humanity is immediately knit to the purest Deity. And by that immediate union thou mayest come to a mediate union. For the Deity and that humanity being united make one Saviour, Head and Husband of souls, and thou being married to Him Who is God in Him art also one with God—He one by a personal union, thou one by a mystical."—Chapter I.

to participate in the life of union, flowing out from the soul therein, for God so clothes our human nature that he is with us both God and man ;[1] but this is rather an attainment of the fulness of Christ's stature than a part of nuptial symbolism. So also when the treatise on *True Contemplation* enumerates four modes of the soul's love for God, the end is to become a living Christ.[2] The message of Ruysbroeck is summed up thus, almost in his own words: The fruition of the soul in God is a quiet, glorious, essential unity, above the differentiation of persons. It is that state which I have termed so like absorption, though not termed absorption ; and it testifies to the union of all souls in the realisation of God, so that the beatitude of the blessed in Him is one only joy, without differentiation. It is the joy of the universal Bride-Soul in unification with the Spouse to which I have referred. This is the Communion of Saints and the Church Triumphant in Heaven.

Meister Eckehart is connected with Christ-Life symbolism rather than that of the Marriage. Tauler, on one occasion, defines the mystical end as becoming the bride of Him Who is King and Lord of the universe.[3] Suso, another disciple of Eckehart, had experience in his own case of an espousal with Eternal Wisdom ; but he was a man of many visions and when it came about therefore that he prayed to look upon her she appeared to him as a beautiful maiden, but again as a noble youth.[4] In this kind of experience our subject has no part. Nor do I think that we need pause over *The Celestial Revelations of St. Bridget*, called " the beloved bride," containing the communications of the Lover as also of the Blessed Virgin and other visitants. She and her espousals are *nihil ad rem mysticam*, and as much

[1] That is to say, in the realisation of love towards God. See c. VII.
[2] See chapters XXIII–XXVII. [3] *Institutiones.*
[4] See *The Life of Blessed Henry Suso by Himself*, translated by T. F. Knox, edition of 1913, c. IV.

must be said concerning the espousals of St. Catherine of Siena in the presence of a glorious company, which included the Queen of Heaven. She belongs to a different category and is greater than St. Bridget as a woman and a saint; but even when the world of images is filled with " speaking likenesses " it is still the world of images and not that of mystical realisation in the still centre of the soul.[1]

We come therefore to St. John of the Cross, who in *The Living Flame of Love* and in *The Spiritual Canticle* of the Soul and its Bridegroom sets forth the whole subject. These texts do not lend themselves at all readily to analysis, nor is it necessary to my purpose, more especially as they are readily available in English.[2] For attainment of the Spiritual Marriage the soul must not only be purified but must have great courage and exalted love, so strong and so close is the embrace of God therein. She attains in this state a transcendent grade of beauty and also a terrible strength. The Author of the Spiritual Union is the Holy Ghost, and the soul is in communion with all Persons of the Trinity.[3] The

[1] With the records of both these saints we may compare the *Revelations of St. Mechtilde* and that experience in particular when she was made one with her Beloved, after having drunk " deep draughts of all deliciousness and sweetness " from a wound in the heart of Christ, and having eaten " an exceeding sweet fruit " drawn forth from that heart. It came to pass also, " while she was at prayer, and crying with a fervent heart after the Beloved of her soul, that of a sudden the power of God drew her soul so deeply to Himself, that she seemed to herself to sit down by the side of our Lord. Then our Lord pressed the soul against His heart in a sweet embrace." It is vision of all vision and psychism of ultra-psychism. See *Select Revelations*, 1875, c. V.

[2] See *The Works of St. John of the Cross*, translated by David Lewis, M.A. 2 vols., 1891.

[3] Another deponent concerning the Spiritual Marriage affirms that God descends therein " under the form of the Trinity," to dwell in the inmost place of the soul. There is an intellectual vision of the indwelling Trinity, presumably as a Presence realised. God is not seen face to face. St. Teresa is cited in this connection.

experience is above all things ineffable and a marvellous bliss of transformation even in this life, though it is not so essential and complete as it will be in the life to come.

St. Teresa was a bondswoman of Divine Love, but we have seen that she favours the Prayer formula and that of the Spiritual Marriage she uses sparingly, except in certain *Thoughts on the Love of God*,[1] based on versicles of *The Song of Solomon*. Here it must be said that she is not to the manner born of the symbolism. In *The Castle of the Soul* she refers the experience itself to a state of ecstasy and says that the soul therein dwells with God.[2]

Last among the Catholic witnesses there is Jean Avrillon, a Minorite friar in the first years of the eighteenth century. He was regarded by superiors of his Order as " speaking from the fulness of a heart penetrated with Divine Fire." I do not think that his long commentary on *The Song of Solomon*,[3] to which I have alluded previously, is marked by any great insight, but it is a deeply devotional work, and his summary concerning the Mystical Marriage is representative enough in its way. " It is in the most secret place of the soul that this admirable union comes to pass. God draws her to Himself, or descends within her, amidst ineffable ardours, splendours and sweetnesses. She sees Him, feels Him, touches Him ; she unites with Him . . ., and embraces Him so closely that nothing can separate them.[4] All natural powers are raised to a supernatural degree. The soul is stripped, and again the soul is clothed, according to the words of St. Paul—stripped of its own qualities, clothed with those of God. Whatsoever is carnal and earthly is consumed by a devouring fire, which fire again

---

[1] Œuvres de Sainte Thérèse, traduites en Français par Arnaud D'Andilly, 2 vols., 1855 ; Vol. II, p. 553 *et seq.*

[2] See Part VII, *passim*, especially Chapters II and IV.

[3] See *L'Année Affective*, edition of 1727, pp. 548, 549.

[4] All this symbolism veers perilously towards the side of psychic vision.

is love and God, at once and together. The soul lives henceforth in God only, because He is her life and the Divine Life is within her." Chancellor Gerson is quoted to shew that the soul is changed into God, she in Him and He in her—dwelling, working, possessing. In his own words, " she is lost in God and comes forth never from Him."

The non-Catholic frequenters of this path of symbolism are few and far between. I will mention J. G. Gichtel in passing, who bound himself to live with Jesus in a conjugal bond of love, and Jesus was his " Heavenly Helpmeet." The imagery is confused, for the Helpmeet is called also Mother.[1] He says that Christ Jesus is " nothing but love," thus defining the only possible relation between the Lover and Beloved in the work which is love or nothing. But the most curious testimony of all—as coming from a protestant source—is contained in a rare treatise of Francis Rouse, entitled *The Mysticall Marriage*. It was published originally in 1635 and the author in after years was one of Cromwell's councillors of state. The sub-title describes it as " experimental discoveries of the Heavenly Marriage between a soul and her Saviour." An engraved additional title to the edition of that year alters the main title to *The Mysticall Marriage between Christ and His Church*, but in the text the term Church is applied to the individual soul. I have called it curious, but there are precious intimations also, and though here and there the senseside of the symbolism intrudes somewhat, it is sane and restrained on the whole. I do not quite understand how it has been so long in a cloud of forgetting, but it may yet emerge on a day. It is said that the soul is divine

---

[1] Compare the Virgin Sophia of Böhme, which suggests a Divine Womanhood as an object of spiritual espousals, in the case of a mystic who is male in manifestation, as counterpart of the Divine Manhood to Whom the soul is espoused in Latin Mysticism. Fortunately the symbolism was not developed, but Gichtel has it in embryo.

and heavenly in her origin, essence and character.[1]   As
a spirit she must find happiness in the Highest Spirit.[2]
She fixes her love thereon, but the union is attained only
in Christ, with Whom the soul becoming one spirit is
joined to God.   The Spirit of the Lover passes into His
beloved and makes her of one heart and will with Him,
and this conformity of the will with Christ is true holiness.[3]   The soul beholds Christ Jesus with open face
and is visited with abundance of blessings, for the marriage state is a time of plenty.[4]   The progress is from
earnests to full performance, from beauty to beauty,
from grace to glory, from glory to greater glory, from
faith to vision, from God in His shadows or reflections
to God Himself.[5]   The end is beatific vision in an eternal
life hereafter.   All this, says Rouse in his preface, is
doctrine which brings strong consolation, being that of
a sanctuary within us into which the avenger may not
enter.[6]

Having regard to all the testimonies, we should have
no ground for supposing that any physical vehicle comes
to the bridal between the Spouse and self-knowing
intelligence of soul, though so far as the experience in
this life is concerned it cannot but share in the results
within its own modes and their limits.   But there is the
body of resurrection to be reckoned with by Francis
Rouse, as by all mystics under the ægis of Christendom,
and it is to this he refers presumably when he says that
the body is to be put on again glorious and holy.   " Then
it shall be a fit garment for the soul in the day of her

[1] *The Mysticall Marriage*, p. 1.
[2] *Ibid.*, p. 248.   [3] *Ibid.*, p. 257.
[4] *Ibid.*, pp. 169, 170 *et seq.*   [5] *Ibid.*, p. 220.
[6] There is another excellent book which I can mention only in passing.
It is *Christus in Corde :* or " The Mystical Union between Christ and
Believers," by Edward Polhill, 1680.   It is a much more reasoned treatise
than that of Rouse, though it does not breathe the same fervent spirit of
devotion.   It may be read and compared with Dr. John Collings' *Intercourse of Divine Love betwixt Christ and the Church*, 1676.

gladness and capable of the consummate marriage with the King of glory."[1]

In conclusion as to the whole subject, Christ is the lover of the soul, according to this symbolism, whether she is located in a male or female body. The external differentiation, however important in itself, is of no consequence respecting the Divine relationship, because male and female are one in simple intelligence. The operation of desire between them in earthly life is a striving after this union. Regarded as understanding and consciousness, the soul has, however, a female aspect. It is true therefore to say that the spirit of man is the Spouse, for the Spirit of the soul is Christ, though this Spirit has been called by other names. It is the catholic centre of Divine Experience through the ages and nations, the Divine in the universe and in us. Speaking still within measures of the symbolism, there are—from one point of view—two mystical marriages ; the first is celebrated in this life, while the other may be begun here but is only completed hereafter. It is the real and unending marriage, for it is certain that Christ goes back with the soul to the Eternal Father when God becomes all in all. This is a high prize at the end of a long journey. Perhaps it would be more correct to say that we are betrothed here and wedded hereafter.[2]

Having discussed by no means exhaustively but to the extent that my limits will allow, and perhaps indeed sufficiently, the two paths of symbolism which are characteristic of Christian Mysticism, there is one question which remains, and it is one of the first importance.

[1] *Ibid.*, pp. 5, 6, 223, 224, 294.

[2] I see that Francis Rouse gives expression to the same view. "The highest knot of blessedness on earth "—meaning of the spiritual order, for he writes obscurely—if compared to " the consummate marriage in heaven " may seem " but like to a betrothing, yet even this betrothing, compared to earthly marriages, casts a shadow of darkness on them."— *Op cit.*, chapter III, pp. 43, 44. It is one of the veils on our sanctuary.

When the adumbrations of symbolism have been set aside, do the witnesses of attained union in their memorials concerning the term put on record anything belonging to the region of experience which shews indubitably that the notion of union with Christ is not interchangeable with that of Divine Union in the simplicity attaching thereto ? In so far as the records lie within the measures of psychic vision, or in the world of forms and images, the two denominations are certainly not interchangeable ; but we have removed these from consideration as belonging to another order of experience. In so far as they lie beyond those measures, or not in the world of forms, the two denominations are actually used interchangeably by practically all the witnesses. Pseudo-Dionysius may open his discourse on mystical theology by invoking the glorious Trinity, but his thesis on the way of Divine Union belongs to pure theism only. It is the same with the Dionysian successors extending the mysteries of realisation concerning the Divine Object of love, with Ruysbroeck on the *pelagus Divinitatis*, and so of the rest. Let any one recur at this point to the collections embodied in my third and fourth chapters ; they can make their own conclusions. The doctrinal beliefs of the mystics are one thing, and about these there is little question, but in their heights and deeps of attainment there is no distinction of Persons in the God of their research. It is different of course among the exponents of the Christ - Life and Mystical Nuptials formulæ ; but it is vital to remember my intimation that the first of these, as excogitated, belongs to the path rather than the term, of which it falls short invariably.[1] It has missed entirely the true interpreta-

---

[1] The mediatorial office of Christ is included in the idea of the Way, and the Way is not the Term. Path is not goal, exemplar is not archetype. And this leads to another consideration : if Christ differs generically and *ab origine* from every man, then He is not in the category of examples. Mystically, however, He is our great exemplar, and it is in

tion of death and the way in which this corresponds to betrothal in the alternative symbolism ; it has missed also the analogies between resurrection and spiritual marriage. These things are in reservation—I know scarcely why—among the keepers of certain Instituted Mysteries, until some one who is not in such bonds shall be found having open eyes to see without special instruction—at least from such sources. Meanwhile, taken as that which it is, a symbolical presentation of the soul's progress towards the union pictured under a formula of risen life, the pictorial scheme does not contribute anything to the question here at issue, as it is simply a delineation of experience within terms of allegory. It is not less important to remember, as regards the alternative symbolism, that the idea of a mystical marriage between God and His elect was brought over—as we have seen—from Jewry, the Spouse of which was Jehovah, and it is therefore obvious that all the terms are interchangeable at need. It is a symbolism which has been used by several schools of Mysticism, and its most extended aspects are not in Christendom at all but in Zoharic and Sufic Theosophy.[1] Again, however, it is the delineation of experience in allegorical terms ; and once outside the paradise of seership common to St. Catherine of Siena and the other great psychics, to whom a literal personification of God was essential, it must be obvious to any student of the texts that an interchange of Divine Names can be made without detriment or reduction in respect of experience and its evidential value. It is patent, moreover, that the interchange is made con-

virtue of an essential equality in the potential sense, or because the state of oneness is attainable by us which was shewn forth by Him. Here is the end which He puts before us.

[1] In the Zohar, the Earthly Paradise is that union which is possible below ; the Higher Eden is that union which is attained above : in both cases it is a mystery of male and female. See, however, my *Secret Doctrine in Israel* on the mystery of sex and of the Holy Shekinah.

tinually in the texts themselves, and this was inevitable, because Christ was God for every mystic in the chain of Christian Mysticism.

This is how the question is determined regarding the two denominations; but my readers must beware of making unwarranted conclusions. I have done nothing more than exemplify by a new instance the point already determined that mystical experience contributes nothing to the for or against of theological or philosophical doctrine. We have tested it early in these pages on the alternatives of theism and pantheism; its findings were ruled out of court. We have now tested it, so to speak, unexpectedly and for quite another reason, on the alternatives of theism and tri-theism; again it is out of court. But the debate in the first case will continue henceforward; and in the second, which is of far other and greater importance, all Christian doctrine remains unaffected by the conclusion reached. There is no power vested in me to rule upon it, for this is not a theological treatise; but those who have accompanied me so far on the quest will know that I understand the cosmic Christ or Johannine Logos as God manifest and hidden in creation. " No man cometh unto the Father," but through Him, for the Father of Christian symbolism is the transcendent God, while That which is called the Holy Spirit is a bond of union between them by virtue of which they are one God. The cosmic Christ is known only by incarnation in each of us, and this high truth of experience was revealed to us in the West under many glorious veils by the incarnation in Palestine. The life of Jesus in Palestine is the archetypal history of the Incarnation and Christ-Life in every man who comes to the realisation of God abiding within him. It would be not less true if the story of Palestine were a mystery of Divine Symbolism, but for me it is a mystery of the sanctuary, and there may come a day in God's holy grace when I shall have entered so far into the heart of this mystery that I can bear faithful witness. But the time is not yet. Meanwhile the Christ Mystical is Christ the Path, so long as we abide within the limits of manifestation, looking for that time when Christ shall yield up the Kingdom of the universe to that Father Who is God in the transcendence and He shall be all in all. It is yielded up for and in each individual who attains the term absolute of union; but there may be also a close of the æons when the whole purpose of manifestation will have been fulfilled in all. This possibility is, however, not of our concern.

CHAPTER X

OF SOUL AND SPIRIT IN MAN

THOSE who would attain to the summit will do well to be quit of much baggage which used to be carried as intellectual aids, whether in East or West. Everything, or nearly everything that has been postulated and contended about the nature and aspects of the Union—on the doctrinal and intellectual side—has to be restated. A key to the whole mystery of path and term must be sought—as we shall see—in a revision of our notions concerning consciousness and in a change *ex hypothesi* possible, in certain cases and moments, taking place in our mode of self-knowledge. Everything that has been affirmed regarding personality and its denudation has to be unsaid. Everything that has been tabulated about the inward constitution of man in semi-mystical and occult schools, through all these recent days, has to be torn up and the fragments scattered to the four winds of heaven, more especially the multiple up-splitting of personality and its distinction from a putative true self. This is one of the intellectual scandals which distract several existing schools of Mysticism. On the one hand, the chaffer and traffic of new voices repeating old shibboleths count for little or nothing on the subject and are not in the real region of debate, while as to the old authorities, on the other, they are dead, and their records remain among us in this respect like lavender laid among linen.

It must be affirmed that individuality is the most sacred thing within our knowledge and the most peculiar, seeing that it stands alone.[1] The appeal of religion is thereto and so is the call of attainment. If Christ came to redeem that which is lost it is personality which He came to save. There is in the proper use of words no ultimate distinction between the terms personal and individual, but there is a fluidic distinction, as there is between the terms occult and mystical.[2] This distinction intimates, among other things, that we are subject to change in our outer, manifested or phenomenal part, yet the self is still one within. The people who speak loosely and glibly of a lower personality mean self in its phenomenal aspect.[3] The higher personality is within us, even as it is by us that the lower is manifested : they are one and not two. Consciousness also is one thing. When it is directed to concerns that are highest it may be called highest consciousness, but it is more correctly the subject of realisation to which the term belongs.

Our personality is not that which shuts out union ;

[1] Compare Carl Du Prel : " Only one thing we shall see really attained by our earthly existence : the exaltation of individuality."—*The Philosophy of Mysticism*, translated by C. C. Massey, Vol. II, p. 309.

[2] While both terms are of Latin origin, as all know, it is to be remarked that the Latin *individuus* is not used substantively. There was the state *individuitas* and there was the *individuum* of Cicero, but this signified a minute body or atom. *Persona* is one man or woman, taken apart from the *genus*. The substantive term " individual " is late in English and is of course used colloquially as an equivalent of " person " ; it is not a form of the adjective adopted to create a distinction between the noumenal and phenomenal man ; this is a very late device, but it serves legitimately enough when the etymological position is defined.

[3] Massey, who was a remarkable thinker, with an inborn faculty for metaphysics, speaks, in his introduction to Du Prel, of " transcendental individuality in distinction from the personal consciousness and functions " ; but his words do not signify essential difference, for he adds later on that there is " nothing unintelligible in the distinction between personality, understood of a certain fixed state, or preoccupation of consciousness, the reactions of character on the special circumstances of a life-time, and the individuality of which these conditions are but a particular and transient determination."—*Op. cit.*, Vol. I, pp. xvii, xx. Therefore they are modes of a single being.

it is that which has capacity for union, on which account it is among all things holy and sacred.[1] We have not to eradicate but complete it. The great personal desire is for God: it is only in our aberration that we suffer the external distractions. It is therefore a fatal mistake to condemn *per se*, like too many of the mystical schools, that which is native to the heights because it is often in the depths.

The distinction between a personal and true self is either a commonplace confusion or it implies a gratuitous postulate.[2] If it means that the body perishes and that what is liberated therefrom is and will remain the real man, it is a truism and can be ignored as such. If it means more than this but does not understand by the true and higher part that universal Christ-Spirit—called by so many names—which unites with the soul when the soul attains its term, then it postulates something which is unknown both as to nature and office, which explains nothing and should therefore be set aside also. If it means the Christ-Spirit, all that we know concerning It is that It is found in realisation to be within. This also is a state of knowledge in self and the key of another mode therein.

Man's life, through all its ways and length, is like a quest of individuality, so that we may realise the vast region which can open within us. If it is possible to know God, it is in virtue of our individual consciousness. We have to reach behind our own phenomenal modes, preliminary to which is a realisation that those instruments through which we function in the external are not ourselves at all. The instruments are most sacred

---

[1] " Self-knowledge is a condition of union."—Castaniza.

[2] Novalis says that our so-called *Ego* is not our true *Ego*, but only its reflection. When this is translated into terms of accuracy, it means that our consciousness under the ministry of things that are false or seeming is in a false state, but consciousness illuminated by the good, the beautiful and the true is in a state of truth-abiding.

and have to be maintained as such, but they are not to be confused with our proper being. The senses are great hallows and they have capacities for our service in sanctity of which there is no conception amidst the conflicts, cross-purposes and chaos of daily life, and to which church-teachings have blinded us after their own manner. Till they have become ordered and plenary channels for the grace which they are meant to communicate we must be in the place of the mastery. Thereafter they will communicate in peace according to cosmic laws; we shall receive in peace; and their ministry within Nature will be the sensible ministry of God.[1]

The mystical life is solely and only an exploration of that which is called self, in search of that which is termed the All.[2] If we affirm that God or Christ is within we must suffer the logical consequences involved thereby. It is more self and fuller that we want, which means more realisation in consciousness, its deeper, wider, estate. It may be true in a manner to say that there is a higher self which is in God, but it is true also that God is in the higher self. It is again a question of realisation, and again because God is within; it is attained only with Him and in Him, yet it is not apart from any man. It is presumably the *synteresis* of which Tauler speaks, or alternatively that writer who assumes his name in *The Following of Christ*.[3] It can be understood

---

[1] Eckehart says that the lover of God " is the guide and conductor of the five senses, and shepherds them, so that they follow not after their craving to bestiality." He should so shepherd them that within their own measures they might fill his world with beauty.

[2] The Christian mystic, whose process is not the extinction but rather the extension of our self-knowing part, is aware that it is on this side of his being that he derives from God, as also that he returns to Him. The joy and sorrow of the universe both help him on the road.

[3] The word connects philologically with ςωτηρια, which is *salus, incolumitas, conservatio*. It is called (*a*) the highest power of the spirit, (*b*) the understanding faculty, (*c*) that which is brought back to its first nobility by the Passion of Christ. It belongs therefore to the integral

only as a potential state of consciousness, not as a part arbitrarily separable from the rest, if only to serve a purpose in mental classification.[1]

The axiom is therefore: Know thyself. It is the one thing necessary in order to know God, and growth in the knowledge of God is an extension through the self for ever. In the right understanding of things, the way is not long to Heaven, which way is within, as the Kingdom is also. In the fluidic and inaccurate sense of things, it is perhaps tolerable to say that, by a process of purification and casting out, we relinquish the lower in search of a super-excellent self. It might be argued further and equally that we have many selves, but it is still the self that we seek, and the distinctions are a fashion of words. When God shall fill our consciousness in the depths and heights thereof we shall attain that realised self which will be ours for ever.[2] We are in the

unity of our inward being. It is said also to be the protector or salvation principle, suggesting that it is Divine grace, but theologically it would be false doctrine to regard grace as a part of personality.

[1] Marsay terms the spirit the centre of the soul. It is from this centre that the new man manifests. An anonymous book of 1743, which is a store of deep simplicity, speaks of God as the centre of the heart, in virtue of which we are His entirely, and He is all for us. Life should be therefore a continual tending towards Him, continual adherence to Him, unbroken union with Him. I conceive that this and this only is the real sense in which a man is true to himself. The same work gives intimations of an invisible and spiritual resurrection which takes place within us when the soul issues from the grave of its imperfection in conversion, awakening and renewal.—*Conversion de l'Ame à Dieu.*

[2] We speak inevitably in terms of space and time and can approach things unseen only in a language of symbolism, borrowed from the world of sense. I have spoken of height and depth, but it has been affirmed that the soul has neither, and this is true, with all that follows therefrom, if the soul or consciousness is not a space entity. " It has no parts, neither is there any difference between its interior and exterior, for it is uniform, nor can one part of it be more enlightened than another. The centre of the soul is God." On the hypothesis obviously, the last statement contradicts the rest, for the centre implies a circumference and both are space terms. The words within and without also postulate space.

midst of new terminologies, and it is desirable at this point to lay down that the subconscious is not an equivalent of the transcendental self. The self that is superconscious would be nearer, if we elect to make up words like this.

The redemption of personality is in the realisation of the Divine. The opening of consciousness towards God is like a descent of God into our nature, but the *latens Deitas* is already there, in what mystics call the secret place of the soul, which—in virtue of Divine Immanence —is a place of the Presence, and the work of reaching towards it is one of realisation. We have to remember that what are called in one of the symbolisms the new and the old man are both within us ; that the mystical or transmuting death of the one means fulness of life in consciousness for the other ; and that mystical rebirth is resurrection in this form of symbolism. It is as if, in the words of Christopher Walton, there arises in the man a new holy nature or spirit, having free communion with God—free at least in comparison with normal experience. But that and that only which is new is the experience itself. The great sacrament is to keep ourselves sacredly and all our avenues of communication open to the Divine Messages and Quickenings. This is the beginning and this also the path. They can enter through all the ways. We question, we doubt, we deny, and it occurs to few of us that if we open the door of the heart God may Himself come in—or be discovered—and possess the whole man.[1] We shall not have need to distinguish in that day between a higher and lower nature ; or to split up our consciousness into sections and set apart those which entertain the Divine Guest and those which

[1] And it is assuredly the whole man which must prepare for his reception. I do not therefore agree with Franz von Baader when he says that " we have to open the higher regions within us " to " know the Divine Manifestations therein."—*Fermenta Cognitionis*, § 1. Yet it is a *façon de parler*, and behind the words one can discern what he means assuredly.

must be content with His shadow. Sort as we may in these manners, all such devices dissolve in experience itself. For this reason, I do not believe that metaphysically or in fact of being there is anything to justify the separation of the soul into several elements. It is an unity of self-knowing substance, and in its relation to the universe it receives the testimonies of manifestation from all the worlds.[1] I have sometimes described this reception as an opening of various doors in consciousness, but it is understood that the expression is analogical only. There is, however, a door which does open into another mode of self-knowledge, and the inscription of the lintel is love. The multiplication of parts in personality confuses the real issues. The so-called outward self is what is called otherwise the animal man, but this is self of manhood—not of another animal. The inward man is the spiritual principle, reflecting its self in the external, consciousness being turned outward in the so-called lower self, but inward for the realisation of that which is greater—also so-called.[2]

---

[1] An example of the aberrations into which the alternative speculations may lead us is given by Marsay, who dreamed that the divine man imparted to Adam by God when He breathed into the nostrils of Adam was withdrawn at the Fall. It was this spiritual man which was of the same nature with God and in His image. Adam's disobedience was rebellion against this spirit. Christ restores to man the Divine Life and the Spirit.

[2] Du Prel says : " If consciousness in even our highest ecstasies does not exhaust our whole being, leaving beyond an immeasurable fund of the Unconscious . . ., then certainly man appears as a being of groundless depth."—*Op. cit.*, Vol. I, p. 142. The speculation seems to put individuality outside consciousness. The groundless depth of our being lies in the potentialities of consciousness—as, for example, that we can grow in knowledge with God, even as in knowledge of the outside world. For this reason, I do not understand Tauler when he affirms that " there remains no residue of myself left outside of my perception." If God is within, the great residue remains, at least until the day of perfect union. Hence—in the order of the spirit—there are always worlds to conquer. Alexander could have done better had he known better.

Of Soul and Spirit in Man

The Ego is therefore the vessel of reception, and this reminds me that the common counsels about " overcoming the I-ness " are also leaders into confusion, though they stand about a real mystery of experience. One truth which lies behind them is that consciousness operating in and with the external, through the brain-processes, shuts the greater doors behind it ; but in the realisation of God within those doors open and another state supervenes, which is the threshold of integration in universal consciousness. There is only one kind of consciousness in man, but it turns there and here, being extensible without known limit in either direction. There is a state possible and actual when that which is without at its highest becomes like that which is realisable within ; then all things are made new, with a new heaven, a new earth and a new man in all his modes of being.

The views here expressed may stand for certain implicits which actuated western theology when it abandoned the triad in humanity on the official side of doctrine ; but having dealt with many confusions on the modern side of transcendental thought, it is necessary to indicate certain extraordinary difficulties which arise on the other. According to Latin theology, the soul is spirit, and as such it is like God. Soul and body, part that is noumenal and permanent, part that is perishable and phenomenal—these are recognised only. The words soul and spirit are therefore used interchangeably, so far as man is concerned. It is this which constitutes the distinction between human and animal natures, for the animal soul—*ex hypothesi*—has not the nature of spirit. There is nothing in mystical theology which contradicts this, though there is a recurring tendency to recognise the subsistence of a higher part,[1] and the word spirit is assigned

[1] See, for example, Ruysbroeck and what has been said previously of the work attributed to Tauler. Tauler distinguishes elsewhere (1) the outer, animal man ; (2) the rational man ; (3) the highest, god-like man,

to it on rare occasions, by way of distinction. It would be an error for this reason to think that more than two parts of the natural personality are recognised in the annals of Christian Doctrine—understood either as Latin Christianity at large or as Latin Mysticism. It is not a distinction as between two natures but of a higher and lower grade in a single nature ; it is a higher part of the soul and not an unknown quality by which the latter is overshadowed. It corresponds to the modern formula of higher consciousness, but it happens to have been in the hands of logicians and not of irresponsible speculators in fields of metaphysics who tend to multiply confusion at every turn of expression. I suppose that, in all simplicity, it is a stage of the growth of consciousness in the knowledge of God and the deeper experience of union with Him. It is the ascent of a ladder of sanctity.

So far I think that Latin theology holds up a clear mirror to human personality ; the greater the divisions of this, the more—and to no purpose—is our mirror clouded. But it is said further that the spirit of man, *qua* spirit, has " total freedom from the laws of space

or spirit—*gemüth*= emotional, feeling nature—" the very highest part of the soul," evidently the *synteresis* of *The Following of the Poor Life of Christ*. This is reflected from St. Jerome, who identifies the highest faculty of the soul with the Divine *Logos*. Ruysbroeck speaks of an " uplifted part of our being, where the intellect must be kept open, inclined towards Eternal Truth, and the spirit like a pure and living mirror, spread before the face of God and ready to receive the Divine Image."—It is the high summit of the spirit, pure and naked and turned within. It is the Christ-Spirit that speaks to the human spirit in this region. We shall begin to see, by the help of these intimations, that the marriage of the soul with Christ may be reduced to much simpler terms than prevail usually among mystics. Once more, the Christ is within : there is no descent or ascent on one or the other side. The marriage is a work in consciousness—a work of realisation. The soul is self in manifestation, acting on things outside and reacted on thereby : the espoused soul is the self turned inward and united consciously to the Christ immanent within. That Christ-Spirit with which the soul seeks union in Christian Mysticism corresponds with what is termed Spirit simply in some other systems.

and time," which do not exist for such a purely immaterial nature.[1] Now, outside space and time it is not possible to postulate multiplicity, because this involves a space notion. So long as souls are incorporated their distinction from God and one another can be affirmed metaphysically and the experience of all life can be cited in support of the thesis. But what, according to theology, is the state entered by disembodied spirits during the postulated time-period which intervenes between death and the general resurrection at the close of the present order? Though a vehicle of some kind is implied by the whole *corpus symbolicum* of the intermediate state, a psychic or spiritual body is not recognised by Latin Mysticism, nor—so far as I am aware—by Latin theology at large. The reason is not for our seeking. If the soul after death were clothed in a body—psychic or quasi-spiritual—the purpose of physical resurrection would seem to be made void, while the resurrection body itself, being that returned into the earth, is described as spiritual by St. Paul.[2] The notion of a subtle body within the physical here and now, suggested within limits by the findings of psychical research, was of course outside the mental horizon, and the alternative notion that there might be two such bodies in succession would

[1] See *The Human Soul and its Relations with Other Spirits*, a very clear elucidation of the Thomist view, by Dom Anscar Vonier, o.s.b., 1913. See in particular chapter I on the "Nature of Spiritual Substances."

[2] The non-Catholic School of English Mysticism, represented by Lead and Pordage, remained undisturbed by this, for it regarded the complete man as essentially triadic—whatever was to be understood by the inward realisation of Christ and God—whence it looked for a resurrection in the flesh. A certain section of English thought at this day—though it is hardly represented by books—interpreting these writers and others of their kindred—regards the transmutation of the physical body as the crown of the regenerate state, so far as manifestation is concerned. Seeing that admittedly this crown is won very seldom in the life of earth, I should think that they also must look for a resurrection of the material body, to complete the triad for ever in all who attain redemption.

have been intolerable,[1] supposing again that it had ever entered into the mind of theology, as to which there is no evidence but that of antecedent unlikelihood. It follows that in the intermediate state between physical death and the Last Judgment the soul is without an envelope, which is a state of imperfection, or the resurrection doctrine would be again disqualified. The doctrine itself is of course outside my subject,[2] for whether it is mentioned or not by Christian Mystics there is no use for it in their system,[3] and it is indeed as great a burden as it is in Zoharic theosophy.

The alleged state of imperfection *per se* is also beyond my province. I am concerned only with the metaphysical fact that outside space and time we can postulate unity only, and that if therefore the spirits of men on the departure of each from the body are not held within those limitations by an envelope of some kind, they must fall back into unity, or—in other words—the spirit indeed returns to God Who gave it—that of the evil man and that of the saint, with all intermediate degrees, indifferently. This is an intolerable proposition from any theological standpoint; but it is not more intolerable, and—if it must be said—is indeed far less ridiculous, than the doctrine that souls, which are spirits, beatified in the presence of God, are in a state of imperfection till

[1] According to St. Gregory the Great, " the spirits which have no bodies are angels; those that have bodies and live after them are souls of men; those that have bodies and die together with these are the souls of cattle and brutes."—*Dialogues*, Book IV, c. 3.

[2] As the Beatific Vision and the deeper modes of union are possible and actual for all the choir of sanctity between the Particular and General Judgments, one does not understand what purpose is served by reintegration in a body of any kind. On the other hand, one can grasp as little the distinction between subject and object implied in the word " vision " as regards beings in a spaceless mode.

[3] I except of course the symbolism of mystical resurrection in Christian Instituted Mysteries, founded on a particular understanding of the mystery of the Risen Christ.

that is restored to them which, all transfiguration notwithstanding, is the body of this life.

Two other points may be added to these difficulties :
(1) If the soul is a spirit like God, we have no title to
postulate more than one quality of spirit, and to this
extent Monism stands justified ; (2) self-knowledge is
also one quality or faculty of being, and it is impossible
to draw any line of demarcation as to the root-nature of
consciousness.

It follows that Latin theology cannot help us except
in so far as it concurs with the definition of soul as an
unity of self-knowing substance.[1] The next point is
what is the position of pure Mysticism regarding the
relation of spirit to space and time ?[2] A mode of being
in independence of both or either is to us unthinkable,
and the question arises whether we are compelled to
postulate it. As regards the Divine Spirit, the com-
pulsion is because infinite spirit occupying infinite space
is an affirmation of two infinites, and this is impossible.
It is an old crux of metaphysics. But the spaceless,
timeless condition is rather that of the Godhead in the
unity of Its essential state. There may be Trinity within
this unity. That is a mystery of faith and is received
or not as such. But the point is that, Trinity or not, it
is unity. If in virtue of the doctrine and experience that

[1] It may be thought that if the soul is an unity of self-knowing substance there can be no change therein, and that therefore if self-knowledge
is reached now only by a reflex act she can never attain that knowledge by
the direct act which theology postulates in respect of God and, again
therefore, the state of Divine Union is unattainable. But in the first
place, as regards the postulate concerning change, there is a very necessary
distinction between nature and operation. Even for the mind of the
schoolmen God changed operatively when He proceeded to the work of
creation : yet His nature did not change. So also the soul does not change
in nature by cooperation with God in love, and Divine Love changes
the mode of self-knowledge without affecting the soul's essential nature.

[2] Reversing the more usual meanings attached to personality and
individuality, Autenrieth regarded the latter as the organ in space of the
former, which is not itself in space.

God is within we are to concur with theology in postulating, under the common denomination of spirit, some
kind of consubstantiality between the soul and God,
there is no question that our Mysticism is Monistic to
this extent in respect of our nature and origin. If in
virtue of doctrine and experience we concur with all
true Mysticism that the term in God and the Union are
attained by a reintegration of each self-knowing spirit in
the Divine Self-knowing Spirit, or a state of transmuted
self-knowledge in God and of God in self-knowledge,
then the end is like the beginning, and it only remains
to account for the intermediate æons and worlds. They
are behind us and they are likewise before ; they are
grades and degrees of manifestation ; but to postulate
manifestation together with succession therein is to
postulate space and time ; and within these modes the
spirit of man can operate only—as now—through vehicles
of one or another kind. Qualities as such and faculties
do not occupy space, but they have their root in entities
and are shewn forth in space. Spirit is activity, pure
force, potentially and *per essentias*, but these also require
space for manifestation. Activity supposes extension.
As in addition to our present obvious condition in the
body of flesh, the cloud of psychic manifestations at this
day offers at least presumptive evidence as to the fact of
psychic bodies on other planes of being, we have no
reason to suppose that a transit from space and time will
follow departure from earthly life.[1] We may rise in

---

[1] Gustav Theodor Fechner describes the state after physical death as
one in which " the life of the individual is interwoven with the life of
other spirits." It is " a higher life in the Highest of Spirits, with the
power of looking to the bottom of finite things." He suggests also that
" all our volitions and actions in this world are intended to produce an
organism, which in the world to come we shall . . . use as our new self."
An obvious contradiction in terms is involved here, but it is easy to get
at the meaning. Fechner says also : " He who lived here entirely in
Christ will be entirely in Christ hereafter ; nor is his individuality to be
extinguished in a higher individuality ; nay, he will be established and

the scale and pass from glory to glory ; we may reach a state in which our vestures and veils are no longer a seeming hindrance as now ; but so far as analogy can shew us the desired end of being, which is conscious absorption in God, lies far and far through the vistas.[1]

Now, this—as I conceive—may be the root-matter of a real eirenicon between the East and the West of Mysticism. It leaves to Thomist theology and the *corpus virile* of orthodox Christian doctrine the substance of their own findings respecting the nature of the soul, which does not differ essentially from eastern views. It offers a way of escape from intellectual confusion by postulating a vehicle for the personal conscious soul until the end of all our travelling, with which eastern theology seems to concur utterly. In agreement with western Mysticism, it recognises such an intimate relation of nature between God and the soul as the term " union " involves, but it forbears from a rigid definition of the term " consubstantial," and it does not therefore affirm psycho-pantheism, much less the identity of the universe with God. It leaves these questions in permanent suspension, because we are here at " the end

receive new strength." Again : " The consciousness which wakens in a child at its birth is only a part of the eternal and universal consciousness concentrated in this new soul." But it will not be re-absorbed therein, any more than the branches of the tree can be swallowed up into the trunk again. " The tree of universal life must grow and develop itself."— *On Life After Death.* It seems to follow that the state of the psychic body hereafter is determined by our motives, thought and conduct here. The counsel would be therefore so to live that it may become our robe of glory.—Compare Du Prel's *Philosophy of Mysticism,* Vol. II, p. 303. " Man is product of his own development . . . Our earthly phenomenal form is the product of our intelligible character. . . . After stripping off this phenomenal form we shall be that which we have made ourselves through the earthly existence."

[1] The middle way between theism and pantheism is in this final re-absorption of that which has come forth from God into separate existence but in attainment puts an end to separation. Many worlds may be travelled intermediately.

of knowing." Mystical experience—as we have seen—
offers us no criterion to guide our choice between the
yea and the nay thereon, and the intellectual debate of
centuries has brought none of the schools into peace upon
the deep issues. But in respect of the term mystical the
experience in its records speaks a language and recognises
a state which are at one in the West and East. The
eirenicon is offered, however, not as between theology and
theology but as a concordat between all forms of Mysticism. It does not tolerate (*a*) the necessity of a vehicle
for the perfection of the soul, more especially when the
soul sees God, nor (*b*) does it bear the grievous yoke of
physical resurrection in common with Christendom and
Jewry. It does not insist on emanation, though it
recognises that Jesus of Nazareth taught the Fatherhood
of God, which means that men are His children and
have therefore been begotten and not made by Him.
It does not postulate, with pantheistic Vedantism, the
identity of the unconditioned and conditioned and is
not therefore compelled to account for apparent distinction by an hypothesis concerning illusion ; rather
it recognises the unreason attaching to such a thesis. Illusion postulates distinction, since there must be something which deceives and something that is in a state of
deception, but it is certain that God cannot deceive
Himself. Finally, it will be found that it leaves untouched the two recurring formulæ of Christian mystical
symbolism, being those of Christ-Life and the Spiritual
Marriage, for both are concerned otherwise with stages
in the realisation of that which is already within, on the
hypothesis of Divine Immanence.

This is on the one side, but it has to be admitted on
the other that the whole question of time and space
calls for more extended consideration, as the attempt to
escape from these imputed limitations may not be
bringing us to the essential truth of things. There are
speculative regions in which we are apt to be hoodwinked

by our own ingenuities, and some modern views on action
outside time are not without perilous suggestions. After
all time and space may not be illusions but openings of
true testimony to our consciousness; and if this be so,
what is left of our eirenicon ? Well, I think that there
is an alternative view which may be allowed to stand at
its value after a brief delineation. Behind all the
ponderable and imponderable forces of the universe,
and behind all that is manifest there is that in which
they live and move and have their being. This is realised
by us as space, considered as bare distance between
points, and where all objects cease hypothetically it goes
on as a metaphysical postulate ; but it may be Infinite
Eternal Spirit, immanent within the objective world and
transcendent beyond it. God is in this sense all, which
all includes space and duration. So long as the spirit of
man remains in operative communication with any
worlds or planes of objective being, whether that among
these which we see now with the physical eyes or those
others beyond numeration which may be now to us
unseen, he abides within a vehicle, but thereafter may
still be a withdrawal from all such modes into the state
of ineffable union with that which I must term the
Divine Transcendence, as a formula for the adumbration
of a realm of Being which is not only ineffable but beyond
all experience. Within the measures of this utterly
tentative hypothesis, it seems to me that the eirenicon
remains.

A word must be added on trichotomy, or the division of
man into body, soul and spirit. I believe that it has
been condemned by the Latin Church, but it is virtually
restored in these pages, the soul being the vehicle of the
Christ-Spirit and thus comparable to the psychic body
recognised by the orthodox schools of the Gita which
adopt this triadic division and hold that the subtle body
permeates that which is physical here and now, much
as the soul in Latin theology is regarded as the " form "

of the human body.[1] The experience of all psychics endorses this view.

I conclude as follows : our personalities in the normal state of life are sacramental ; let us make them sacraments of grace and not of scandal.[2] We must beware of the crude distinctions between lower and higher personality, remembering rather the doctrine of purpose, understood as the direction of consciousness towards a vital apprehension of eternal things. There is a paradox of expression which leads some people—as we have seen—to speak of leaving their personality, passing into another mode and returning subsequently into that which is the accustomed mode. But it is obvious that A has not ceased from being A if after some period of recollection or of rapture he becomes A again. The fault is not merely through some alleged inefficiency of language—that last refuge of those who fail in expression ; it is the misdescription of an internal experience which is perfectly capable of diagnosis in rational terms. On the assumption that there is such an experience it can

[1] According to one eastern thesis, the subtle body is immortal, but this we have no title to postulate. The idea of successive vestures is more in consonance with the terms applied thereto, and it is also more deeply mystical, looking towards that state in which the spirit of man shall have passed from all life in the manifest. But the absorption which will then ensue is not more that of the human spirit by God than of God by the human spirit. It is the repose of consciousness in Infinite Love and of Infinite Love in consciousness. It is the sinking of the self into absolute realisation of God within it, or the carrying of the doctrine that God is within to its final term in life and practice.

[2] There is truth in the idea—drawn, as it is said, from Fichte—that " the spirit enlightens the sense-world by making it part and parcel of the spiritual world." The senses are *media* through which the spirit works. This is why they are sacred, why pleasure and pain are so utterly important in their ministry and counter-ministry, and it is why the nuptial intercourse of man and woman in purity is the most important physical act that can be performed in this world. I say, in purity, for all our acts can be consecrated by intention, and for this to consecrate it must be united with Divine Intention. Thereby and therein, its consecration is not for this world only.

signify only that the consciousness of A passes into another state. On such misdescriptions the question of personality and its criticism has rested throughout in the recent transcendental schools. Personality as we know it is a certain state of self-knowledge, and mystically that which has to be effected is a change in this state or mode. This is the secret of finding that God is within and that our intelligent being can partake of a Divine Mode.

CHAPTER XI

THE MYSTICAL EXPERIMENT CONSIDERED IN THE LIGHT OF CONSCIOUSNESS

For us, and for our salvation, the first great fact of the universe is that inward faculty of knowledge and self-knowledge before which the picture-book of the universe turns over the successive leaves of its endless volume. We also are as a book of pictures, written within and without, receiving as we do the communications from that which is external to ourselves and from another world which is within. The next primary fact—to us and all those who are made in our likeness—is that consciousness communicates with consciousness—all individuals with one another and the Divine with that which is human, for God is (*a*) consciousness or (*b*) that which is above and includes it, as the greater includes the lesser. The history of human life on this plane is one of evolution in consciousness, by which the glory of the world is more and more received into the sacred repository of the self and its meaning is more and more realised. The history of human life is one also of evolution on the inward side, by which the self and its divine deeps are to the self unveiled, but on that side of our nature we are at the threshold of knowledge only—in the *pronaos*, not in the *adytum*. All mystical experience is sought and attained in the self. The path is within us and there is the term also, the reason being that God is within.

A definition of consciousness is required in the first place, but there is no reason to dwell upon the bare fact

of etymology, which tells us that it is to " know with."
Now, to know presupposes the self, understood as the
known, and the term consciousness signifies in an imperative sense the state of self-knowledge—of the
knower and the known within. This state is reached
by a reflex act, or by the self becoming its own object.
There is further, but in a secondary sense, the consciousness of other objects presented by the outside world
through sense-channels to the knowing and self-knowing
mind. We have a more intimate realisation of the
self than of things external thereto, though these are
absorbed or brought within us in proportion as they are
known. We know them, however, in part only, or as
they are presented to the mind, not as they are—
essentially and noumenally. They remain objects, and
our hindrance lies in the gulf fixed between subject and
object. This is also—though in a lesser sense—the
hindrance in respect of self-knowledge, for the reflex act
opens another gulf and—all the intimacy notwithstanding
—we are students and even tyros in regard to our own
subject.[1]

[1] It seems desirable that something should be said briefly as to the
warrants of this theory. That self-knowledge is realised through mental
processes by a reflex act calls for no demonstration, as it is possible for
every one to make the experiment and see for himself in a moment.
That the self-knowledge of God is in virtue of a direct act, as simple,
immediate perception, is implied when it is not expressed by every doctrine of the Divine Absolute. According to the ideology of St. Thomas
Aquinas, in proportion as pure spirits ascend in the hierarchic scale
their enlarged intelligence operates through fewer ideas and this progression reaches its term in God, Who embraces all things by virtue of
a single infinite idea, which is His own essence. In the state of eternal
beatitude souls possess God less or more perfectly, and the objects
present to their consciousness are proportionately more or less. Here is
one distinction between St. Thomas and the mystics, but it will be
realised that the design of the mystical life is to permeate consciousness
with the sole idea of Divinity, while the union is that state when all
distinction has ceased, when the object has merged in the conscious
subject. Unity is therefore the goal of human intelligence, as Balmes

Chief among the objects presented to us by the manifest world is the multiplicity of other conscious beings in function about us, possessing self-knowledge like us, so that it is the common property of all, but in a separate or individual state for each. There is not one reservoir of universal self-knowingness which contemplates itself in all of us and finds its undifferentiated self everywhere; but there is a seeming infinitude of detached selves looking each into its own glass of vision and in that process never contacting normally another unit. And yet the word consciousness in its root-meaning seems to register an implied opposition to these patent facts of our universe. It suggests integration in a common source, the nature of which is not indicated. If this be the case, we are not really standing apart but are sharing one with another, wheresoever dispersed over the face of manifested things. It is, moreover, a state of knowledge with something that knows also, not with unknowing objects: indeed the term consciousness seems misapplied to our cognition of these. Such a state is more than one of self-knowing with all who know themselves in our separation from them and in theirs from us. From the mystical point of view, an integration of this kind is affirmed on the basis of experience. It is the recognition of a common kinship, or bond of union, between every individual self, in virtue of which it is possible for each and all to know with God, to attain the state of God-consciousness, which is His state of self-knowledge and the state of self-knowledge in Him.

In virtue of the Divine Immanence within us and the universe, it is the recognition of a spiritual consanguinity between our own noumenal part and the noumena of all

points out in his *Fundamental Philosophy*. See Book I, c. 4. This acute Jesuit held that the Blessed Vision was in effect Divine Union, on a thesis of identity united to representation, and he claims St. Thomas as his authority. *Ibid.*, c. 7. The debate is purely speculative and seems at issue with other parts of his work.

beings and objects by which we are environed and which are summarised in the word external, though the recognition cancels that word and substitutes a bond of union deep down in the nature of things. But this bond of union and this integration are realised by a few only, for the grade of experience involved has not been attained as yet by the great majority of men.

The validity of this understanding is otherwise evident—because " all-knowledge " is that which we predicate of God. Let it be observed that the word consciousness does not signify knowledge in God, because this is not the sense of the prefix to the verb *scire*, and yet all knowledge is in Him, as it cannot be outside or beyond. That we live and move and have our being in God is not less true by the doctrines of true philosophy than it is by those of religion. It should be observed further, and still in the same connection, that if, as the result of will and desire, exemplified in life, on the part of individual consciousness,[1] God enters into a fuller mode of communication therewith than obtains for the natural man, complete in his own degree, He

---

[1] I am told that Mr. R. C. Nettleship speculates about a state in which there would be (*a*) no individuals at all, (*b*) " an universal being in and for another. When being took the form of consciousness, it would be the consciousness of another which was also oneself." I suggest, however, that to be or to exist for another postulates individuality on both sides of the notion. So, too, does consciousness of another, more especially when that other is also oneself. Bishop Westcott spoke once of " a higher type of life, in which each constituent being is a conscious element in the being of a vast whole "— a very different conception to that which I have just cited. It is, in fact, that to which I refer in the text, the integration of human consciousness in God. As it is usually held by mystics that there are grades and degrees in the term and that vision, as we have seen, tends to pass into union, so also that which is called union may become what we term absorption ; but it is consciousness dissolved in consciousness, self in self, and those who say that anything ceases or is lost are raving. What should the soul lose when it finds the all ? Neither in God nor man does any man part from the supreme self of consciousness.

comes not to destroy but to fulfil. Such communication implies the recipient throughout. Did that remain no longer, there would be an end of consciousness—of course, in the specific instance—an end to that which has the faculty of " knowing with."

Why are we so unaware of our part of soul within us, seeing that the soul is consciousness, and that the question therefore involves a pure paradox ? The answer is that, placed as we are, the state signified by the word *conscire* is one of identification solely or chiefly with an external order, whether in our daily life or our inward realisations and reflections—the most objective part of ourselves and the surface-side of others. We do not know with our deeper selves, with the world that can open within us, if only we would begin its exploration by a gradual and continued method, apart from haste and violence. We do not know furthermore with the Indwelling Presence,[1] so that the Spouse has not come to us consciously. Thanks be to God—for this He is not the less overshadowing those who desire Him.

When Fichte and others tell us that consciousness, as realised normally, covers but a part of the field, the meaning is that we have not explored ourselves—e.g. on the quest of God. In the vast majority of cases we cannot be said even to have attempted such an exploration. We are limited to the testimonies of sense and the offices of material thought. The man who " goes inward " is the man who dwells in consciousness of determined purpose and who explores it.[2] If God

---

[1] The presence of God in the consciousness is not that of an individual and separable fact but of the all. It is a Presence which fills the whole nature, and nature is one with grace. This was the experience of St. Paul, when he said : " Not I, but Christ liveth in me." But if God shall possess us utterly, we shall possess all things in God, and this is true " cosmic consciousness," the sense of oneness with all, interpenetration of all spirits and the kingdom of heaven realised.

[2] The work is therefore one of the will applied in the sense of purpose. In other words, it depends upon a faculty which we know can

speaks, it is to our consciousness, by an operation within the bond which inbinds the soul with God. If God manifests to soul or spirit, this means that He manifests to consciousness. Do we seek first the Kingdom of God and His justice, believing—if you please—that all other things shall be added unto us; or—following a yet more perfect quest—do we seek out of very need, thinking nothing of what shall be added; we are undertaking a quest in consciousness.

The art of self-knowledge is then the art of exploration in our own consciousness ;[1] but we rest content to live on the fringes of the light, knowing nothing of the sun at the centre. We are at home on the outskirts of the great city which is within, though many testimonies assure us that there are towers of ivory, temples of gold, and houses of jasper and chalcedony. We hear therefore but have no awareness, while the faith which is apart from understanding, and does not enter into experience, leaves us cold and with scarcely a ray of life. To those who would know and understand, let me give this counsel: Do not await demonstration of the things that are greatest; expect this when it is possible to ascend into those heights of love which are called contemplation, realising that the significance of this word

be exercised by us, that exercise reshaping our whole life. But the successful exercise postulates a governing motive, and this is Divine Love.

[1] What is said by L'Abadie in *L'Art de se Connoitre Soy-même* concerning scriptural morality is especially true of the awakening in mystical consciousness, and it is worth repeating for the sake of those—still perhaps among us—who may regard a quest pursued within self as a quest of pride. " It raises man without inflating him and abases him without causing him to lose realisation of his inherent dignity. It casts out pride by the communication of true glory "—that kind which does not pass away with the world, because it does not belong to the world—" and it manifests his excellence, fashioning his humility by that Divine Commerce of our souls with God which religion makes known to us. Therein God comes down to us, losing nothing of His grandeur, and we ascend to God, losing nothing of our lowliness in His presence."

is apart from all conventional use ; cultivate in the meanwhile a desire and conviction respecting them which shall be great as they. Hereof are the untried ways of life, in the high places of life. Such things are not proved by reasoning, but they are realised by following a certain path of ascent—in most cases by degrees, with prudence and slowly.

What is their test of value and what are their titles, as these come to us at the beginning ? That we have conceived them within the measures of the sovereign reason of things. They are people of the solitude of the far-off places of our consciousness: let us seek familiarity with them, and it may be that they will testify to themselves in unlooked-for manners.

Behind the knowledge which comes through channels of sensation, and behind the offices of material thought, there lie the undiscovered realms, the life of grace, the city and the sun thereof, the high-uplifted temple on the holy hill. The vistas open, the great splendours shine, and it seems to me that in a deep sense of the words there is no end whatever. As the external world testifies to us and awakens our ever-present faculty of perception in consciousness, and as the purpose-faculty in consciousness can respond, increase and multiply the testimony on every side, so it may well be that what we recognise as the spiritual world, the world of grace, the Divine World, substanding and transcending this one, will begin also to witness. In other language, God testifies to the consciousness through senses and mind from within the manifest order immanently. It is the Divine Immanence without testifying to the soul and awaking the immanence within. We become conscious in this manner of that other order of being to which we ourselves belong. If we respond, as we do in the alternative case, this witnessing will increase also and multiply on every side.

The distinction which I am making is in a certain

manner analogical, and the mystic must always beware
of his own symbols, lest he enter into bonds thereby.
Their dangers are like hidden quicksands. Some of these
pitfalls lie within such definitions as " the consciousness
of God is within us " and " the consciousness is filled
with God." Expression has perhaps no alternatives
because language is symbolical, but both are juggles of
words. In reality, consciousness, not being dimensional,
is neither cup nor reservoir. It is a question of realisation. There are other pitfalls in the equally symbolical
terms of a journey to God undertaken by the soul. They
are part as such of an exile and return formula. The
expression of modes of consciousness in such language of
travelling is a taking form of imagery and is difficult to
set aside utterly. But in the last resource all these
analogies must go, with everything else that postulates
time and space,[1] though this it not to affirm that the
symbolism as such is false or that distance and duration
are mental modes merely. There is actually indeed that
which corresponds to a journey in the mind until
Brother Lawrence's *Practice of the Presence of God* has
reached its end, and the Presence is without the practice.
This is not the work of a day, but the hostages of
perfect peace are with us from the beginning. In
other language, the practice is what may be and is
so often called, by yet another convention of common
language, a preparation of the ground. It is to be
observed of this preparation that it is not a process of
thinking out, as when there is a problem for solution
presented to the rational faculty. It is not the analysis
of thought but a dwelling thereon and therein by means
of recollection in love. To approach it as a point to be
sifted by way of research is fatal to all real progress.
That progress is comparable to the " slow coction " of
alchemy, and it is attained chiefly in a stillness of mind.

[1] There is no need to say that qualities and faculties do not occupy
space, though they are manifested from a ground therein.

In such stillness, the light—which is light of Heaven
—falls into the heart. There is, in fine, that recurring
danger which lies in the familiar alternative between the
terms " within " and " without." Here it is necessary
to establish with great clearness, once and for all, the
true meaning which attaches to the word " within."
It connotes usually little but a misty vagueness. We
think of the soul or the spirit as of things and worlds not
realised, the fact that they are not realised being the
continual evidence concerning a cloud on our sanctuary.
It comes about in this manner that we believe ourselves
to be living permanently in a dark night of the soul,
but this in reality is an advanced stage of the spiritual
life. That in which we are abiding actually is, however, only another form of simple mental confusion.
Wherever and whensoever it is used in relations of this
kind, the word " within " refers to the world of intelligence. When it is said that the Kingdom of Heaven is
within, we are to understand that it is in consciousness,
and this is true also of the indwelling cosmic Christ.
I would say here that the door which opens inward is
not so much a closed door as one that is always ajar ;
it is not so much ajar as open ; it is not so much a door
as a curtain ; and indeed it is scarcely a curtain, for it
is an arch rather, with a free space beyond. When we
have done with confusions and their symbolism, we can
affirm truly of such inward world that it is there we live
and move and have our being. So is it nearer surely than
hands and feet. Regarded from this standpoint, it is the
external things which may be called remote by contrast,
though they are knocking at the gates of sense continually.
Having established these points, I shall continue—
like all my co-heirs in mystical literature—to use the
symbols freely, as if they were indeed the things signified,
not the signs and the sacraments.
The ultimate mystical process has for its object to
place the self-knowing part alone with God—that intent

being held attainable in a supreme state of loving stillness. Part of the method resides in self-emptying of all
images, suspension of the working of the mind and
realisation of the Presence in love. There are, hypothetically or otherwise, two ways in which the Presence
may be experienced. One is when consciousness is
filled with the knowledge of God and realises Him in the
innermost of its being, all things else excluded.[1] The
other would be manifestation of God as a Presence outside consciousness but testifying thereunto. The analogy
in the latter case must be sought in the manifestation of
the external Universe to our consciousness, through the
senses. The one is the way of the mystics and the other
is that of the official churches ministering to those that
believe.

The intellectual position is that Divine Union in the
self-knowing part has been preceded, temporally speaking, by a state when, so far as consciousness is concerned,
there was separateness from God.[2] It may or may not
have been the kind of separateness which consists with
a mental conviction that in Him we live and move and
have our being. It is compatible, in other words, with
a very full and keenly willing awareness of sacramental
union—such indeed as is often conferred in a high
degree by church channels of grace. There are many
instances in which this kind of Union—especially
through the Eucharist—seems to have approached an
ineffable degree. I think that we may venture to call it
at very least a valid substitute, the warrant being that

[1] This is a general mode of expression; there are two particular
formulae : (*a*) the consciousness is immersed in God and lies naked
therein, divested of all intermediaries ; (*b*) God fills the consciousness
to an exclusion of everything. There is no canon of criticism to determine the comparative value of these alternatives. On the contrary,
they are one at the root, the self possessing and being possessed, permeating and being permeated in either case. Consciousness is there and
there is the presence of God.

[2] It is only separation which desires union.

235

mystical experience postulates a more exalted state, while evidence seems wanting that the one herein specified exceeds in most cases the higher emotional and psychic modes. It is clearly not union of consciousness with consciousness, for the production of one transcendent mode of being in consciousness; it is not a state of being immersed or of self-immersion.

Now, we know—on the Dionysian and many succeeding testimonies—that in high mystical states the senses and the image-making mind are shut off, by the hypothesis, or that the mind at least is emptied, and that the communication which constitutes the experience comes straight into simple consciousness. This is the expulsion of symbols, to make room for that which they signify. It is an attempted transcension of the sacramental order, and that which supervenes—also by the hypothesis—is a state of pure being, apart from objective vision—whether of sense or mind. It follows from the last statement, and will be understood forthwith, that the self is also isolated, not on the ground of objectivity and the cloud of shibboleths it connotes, but because in the reflex act, by which it is realised, the self becomes an object.[1] The conditions being thus defined, we can see, I think, readily why the experience which follows—however characterised—is one of exceeding brevity and great difficulty in attainment. The period for which

---

[1] I observe that according to Dr. Rudolf Steiner we stand in self-knowledge within the object. There was never more crude imagery, if it be intended to illustrate the fact that man realising himself becomes his own object.—See *Mystics of the Renaissance*. This kind of thing belongs to the characteristic looseness of occult metaphysics. Our inevitable limitation is that, antecedent to active self-realisation, there is and must be a passage from subject to object. It connotes the state of separation. In the self-union of the Divine Nature there is no such passage. I suppose that this is why God is all in all. That which lies behind the reveries of ascetic self-sacrifice is the escape from our separate state, to enter that which is called union, being the God-state of self-knowledge.

The Mystical Experiment

"there was silence in heaven," being half an hour, is one of the longest on record. It seems impossible to maintain the tense state of ineffable exclusion, leaving out of consideration a likelihood that the most ineffable bliss ascribed to such Divine Experience would put an end to the interaction of soul and body.

Maeterlinck has mentioned the "extension of consciousness" in terms which recall us to that which is our true work upon the self within us. The Christian mystics did not use this language, but it was the subject in which they dealt—and none else. Their methods had no other effect than to extend consciousness. Whether they overcame themselves, whether they contemplated perfection, until something new passed into them or was by them attained, they were widening the field within them. When they emptied themselves of all sensible images and all the forms of thought, when they rested in darkness and silence, it followed that they were alone with themselves—alone in a simple, fixed, hypothetically unimpeded realisation. And if there came into them, or was there enkindled, that which they called the very love-light of God, the Divine Presence, it was declared in their desiring consciousness. This it filled and this it enlightened.[1]

If the consciousness can be held in this simple, empty, undefined mode, apart from object—the self-object included—and if in such mode the wordless, imageless love-concept of God be maintained—as a result of long training—it may be that the immediacy of union will

[1] It comes about in this manner that certain mystical alchemists were right when they affirmed that the one subject of the Great Art and the Great Work is man, that he is at once the vessel and the matter placed therein, and that whosoever goes outside himself in the Hermetic Quest wanders far from the way of wisdom. It is the search after knowledge in the self-knowing subject; and perhaps these alchemists encompassed their art with mystery and wrote it in baffling cryptograms because they knew by their own experience that it has heights and deeps before which the natural and unprepared man has cause to quail.

237

be then realised. But it should be remembered that light and darkness are also images of the mind and that the Presence of God in the soul is after neither of these modes. We look for an illumination in the Spirit as we look for light in the eyes, and we must destroy this pair of correlatives if we would attain the Presence within—meaning here its awareness on our own part. The only word—as it seems to me—by which we may be set free from the image-maker is—realisation. There is no doubt, further, that realisation of the Presence is not attained apart from what Brother Lawrence calls practice of the Presence of God. This then is the primary condition. I care nothing if criticism should term it a habit of self-suggestion; indeed the explanation may be accepted with no demur whatever. Auto and hetero-suggestion rule in all our lives, and I have no call to doubt that under the most saving aspect of their catholic law they take us also to God.[1]

This is how the process begins in consciousness. It is as nearly as possible apart from all sensible experience. It is still growth in love and all growth is silent, by stages which in themselves are imperceptible. I do not know whether to suggest that those about us may see the great divisions of its stages better than we ourselves do. I should say, perhaps, not so much those about us as those who meet us on terms of intimacy at intervals, and then not too frequently. It is by no means, however, my intention to conclude that we are unaware on

[1] Auto-suggestion or otherwise, the first key is self-immersion in the Immanence about us for the transmutation of life in the external and for the preparation in this manner of all our vehicles of consciousness, so that there may be nothing to hinder subsequently the realisation of the Immanence within. It is not so much a work of meditation and contemplation as that which I should call literally a suggestion made to ourselves and maintained within. You can rise in this state at morning, saying: "I in Him and He in me." If you maintain this in the midst of your daily work, the light will come to you. Do you know—can you not see indeed ?—that it is a work of daily joy ?

, our own part. The growth is not like a child's physical growth, which goes on in a measure imperceptibly. The consciousness must be alive to that which is at work therein. But it is in a high region of the mind and not in our sensible part, as I have just intimated. This is why it is much too slow and apart from all flashing evidence to suit the impatient side of zeal.

If it is certain, for the rest, that the turning of consciousness inward upon itself opens a new world of experience, it is not less true that the value of such experience must be judged on its own basis, in so far as it is common to catholic mystical life, but with due recognition (*a*) that a new element has been or may have been introduced by individuality, thus, and for the first time, integrated in mystical experience ; (*b*) that the criterion is not infallible and not beyond appeal—if only because of the imitative character of psychical states, which assume so often the aspect of mystical states. It is really the life of the seer which is the one true ground for judgment. It is sanctity alone which is qualified to sign, seal, endorse and deliver the evidence. There are, unquestionably, some high intellectual modes which make no especial levy upon sanctity *per se*, and they also are to be judged on their proper warrants. A very large reflective part of mystical literature belongs to this class. There is also that which comes by the poet's inspiration, and is great and true after its own kind. It is full of intimations belonging to the real order, but it is only rarely of the order itself. It must be recognised, however, that the poet's experience in Nature may pass into partial union with the Divine as immanent in Nature.

This is how it seems to me in respect of the Quest in Consciousness, and so far the word itself has helped us on the way. It is not well to postulate that some high wisdom of adeptship is at the bottom of the making of words, especially when they happen to be of Latin origin ; but for myself I shall always understand " Consciousness " as intimating at its highest the state of union between the soul and the Spouse, or cosmic Christ. It is obvious that in such union a transfiguration takes place in consciousness, the root or beginning of which is where consciousness has been realised as the place in chief of the Immanence, and in a sense the one place. Pseudo-Hermes says that God is a circle of which the centre is everywhere and the circumference nowhere, which is a great truth couched in the form of a paradox.[1] It is by such realisation that the truth of the symbolical expression is illustrated, for therein is every individual consciousness a Divine Centre and indeed the centre of all things. We can, moreover, complete the image, for if we are the centre all that is about us is the circumference—I mean, the manifest universe, where God is immanent also, so that we find Him in and through all.

Let us recur in the last place to two qualities of testimony—being that of man to himself in the presence of the external universe and of the universe to man. It signifies nothing in respect of the great issues that placed as we are in the manifest order, we are dependent for our experience thereon, or even that out of such experience our realisation of things essential arises. Without us—who can learn, know, understand, realise— there is a living reality as an object of knowledge and understanding, which object communicates to us through the senses. The means of communication are part of the objective world, towards which—through such channels—our consciousness is turned. Outside the senses, by the turning of consciousness other where and inwardly, we can receive testimony of a more direct order, in the exploration of self, and can reach that side of our own nature which opens on God. We are poised therefore between two worlds and both are fields for our research, though as to their essentiality both are

---

[1] It is paradoxical because it is obvious that in the absence of a circumference there can be no circle.

veiled and both communicate through channels. The character of the testimony borne to our consciousness by the physical universe is sacramental, and there is a sacramentalism of our inward life—as we shall see. The reflex act by which alone we realise our consciousness is the veil on self-knowledge ; the intermediary of the senses through which we communicate with external things is the veil on those. These veils are media ; the media are channels ; and it is through such channels that we receive graces from within and without. This is that mode by which the immanent noumenon of the world outside ourselves bears witness concerning itself to the noumenon which is immanent within us. It testifies to us through a veil, and we testify through our own veil thereto. So does that which is within us pass into expression without ; so does the grace without come within to those who can receive it. We are learning the world's meaning all our lives, by the help of its true interpreters, which are religion, poetry and art. They are three that give testimony on earth, and these three are one—one in our personal humanity, from which all interpretation comes. Man is the witness of all things, and herein is his chief title of nobility. This is why our thoughts about Nature may be even more important than Nature, as she flows to us through our sense-channels. Yet it is she whose kisses awaken us. We are immersed in spheres of symbolism, which are interpenetrating spheres. It is desirable and needful above all things that we should seek to understand the language of this symbolism, which not only speaks to us everywhere but has been put into hieroglyphical writing everywhere about us. There is nothing in the whole wide world which is so eloquent as the voice of the symbol, when that which shews to the eye and the other senses begins to speak in the heart. The most hopeless of all hypotheses is to propose that Nature is illusion. As such, it would be without meaning ; but if Nature signifies, Nature is true and real within its own measures. I conceive at least that, even within the fantasia of such philosophy, no one has suggested that it is a lying witness.

It comes about in this manner that whatsoever is beautiful in external life, in literature and the other arts is a shadow of the beauty of one thing variously declared and manifested within and around us. The ideal and perfect beauty is a fundamental implicit of the mind and is of our part in that one thing. The extent of our realisation concerning the external beauty is in proportion to the stages of our growth in the experience of the one thing: it is thereof and therein. So shall spiritual desire after the House of Beauty take shape within us: so shall the House be built.

CHAPTER XII

THE REORDINATION OF LIFE AND MIND

WE have considered in previous sections the entire field of Mysticism in respect of path and term. Points of palmary importance have been determined successively, and it is well to summarise them briefly because of the further field which remains for exploration. (1) The theology called mystical differs from other theology because it is a teaching of experience and not *ex hypothesi* obtained by processes of the logical mind, though it is without prejudice to these and indeed confirms some of them. (2) While the experience comprised by the term is not *per se* more secret or incommunicable than other qualities of experience, it is distinguished from all normal modes because knowledge of God is communicated at first hand. (3) The records of mystical experience furnish material which can be appreciated by the intellect, but nothing more. The bridge between such appreciation and personal realisation is the awakening nature of mental sympathy and the insight to which it leads. (4) The analogies and identities of experience in East and West throughout the centuries offer provisional presumption concerning the truth of this experience. (5) At no time and in no place does mystical experience contribute to debated doctrinal points. It has one doctrine only—the communication of God to the soul. The vedantist remains vedantist and the Christian a Christian. All the terms are transferable. I represent the Christian tradition in Mysticism, but I am not a Mystic necessarily because I am a Christian, nor a Christian because I am a Mystic. (6) The Christ is God immanent in the universe and man. The Father is God in the transcendence. The Holy Spirit is the bond of unity between them. But these points are of personal understanding. Those who look at the Mysteries in other respects may have equal warrants with myself, and some of them greater warrants. (7) The processes which lead up to union and end therein have been depicted under two forms of Christian symbolism, that of the Christ-Life in Nazareth and that of the Mystical Marriage. They cannot be apart from one another, being symbols of one subject; but they are distinct as formularies, subject to one bond in common—that neither of them must be pressed too far. Above all, both are symbols. (8) As regards the personality of man, there are the body of this world, the psychic body, the soul or self-knowing part, and the Divine Presence. Regeneration is a birth into consciousness of this Presence and the beginning of Divine Life in the soul. The end of this life is Union, and—from first to last—path, process and attainment, Kingdom, Heaven and God are within the self-knowing part. (9) The self in man is the vessel of reception for all experience. Once beyond the field of discipline, all the old self-tortures for self-extinction were motived by a vague and misapprehended feeling that there was something in the natural mode of our self-hood which hindered union with God. Ascetics accounted for it by ingrained wickedness consequent on the fall of man—or by an assumption based on doctrine—and by personal acquired depravity. I believe that I have defined the true barrier for the first time in the literature of mystical religion. It lies in the reflex act necessary to our self-realisation. Why do we know ourselves by a reflex act only? It is a law of our manifestation. So long as this remains there is passage from subject to object in respect of our selves and much more of God Who is within. This is separation and not union. St. Thomas Aquinas knew all this most surely, but the Thomist philosophy of things regarded the Blessed Vision as the term of all, not unification with God. The Blessed Vision is separation, all its engulfing rapture notwithstanding. (10) If this barrier is not irremovable, it is taken out of the way by love. All mystical practices, however denominated, lead in this direction, and that work especially which is called contemplation, but is properly a constant and undistracted preoccupation of all-engrossing love. Within this measure lies all sanctity, and all discipline lies. One is love itself and the other its consequence. It is this life of love substituted for the ascetic life that I propose to question, for the most practical of all purposes, being the possibility of its incorporation into our own lives. The present chapter will be a clearance of the path by a consideration of some old counsels which have prevailed therein.

That which we are called to understand by the need for denudation of spirit, and that which we can accept as lying at the root of counsel, is in respect of false knowledge, or the antithesis of knowledge of God. The poverty of this world is no help in the *ex opere operato* sense, nor are its riches of necessity a hindrance. The artificial love of poverty may be like the world's love of respectability. The cultus of poverty may be nothing better than the worship of an idol in the heart. Here, as elsewhere, the danger of asceticism is centred far less in its peculiar congregation of practices than in its set of moral principles. No man has a right of criticism over the methods by which others may look to gain their individual amelioration—using this term in its legitimate sense. A considerable degree of hard schooling may be a rule of prudence in some and in many cases. Such disciplines are of all virtue, if found to serve in practice. But they are a public nuisance if they, or any of them, are erected into standards of perfection and irrepealable laws. They are moral charlatanry when they form a ground for superiority. They are blasphemy when they are identified with Divine Law. They are a virus and an abomination when they are incorporated into some art of self-torture in order to please God. They are at no time a part of sanctity, as they never leave the category of precautions without passing into aberration.

The question of conformity arises for consideration in a more particular manner, and out of it in turn arises a question of the will,[1] wherein is a great mystery. The secret which begins in conformity is that secret which encompasses Divine Union. In this connection there should be no need to say that the mental habit itself is a rule and not a motive. Love and desire for God are postulated as antecedents. I put aside, as not needing discussion, that elementary sweet reasonableness and condign ordinary sense which dissuade us from " kicking against the pricks "—as the terminology of horse-craft has it. Assuredly it is idle to quarrel with any law that is part of the mode under which the universe manifests, and it does not enter into the present contention that conformity of this kind is a counsel for our own good. Such is the case, of course, but the motive of that counsel covers the whole scale, and it is a little confusing to allocate especially to a part that which belongs to the mass. A better and simpler reason lies in the notion of utility, and this has a higher aspect than appears amidst the departmental shibboleths of cheap ethics. Even at the heart of heroic renunciation there lies a question of utility, and the one is not justified apart from the other.

[1] The rule of mystical attainment is the concurrence of human will in the work of regeneration, and that work is by following the way of faith, which has its term or fruition in the knowledge that comes with experience. The word concurrence signifies an act of the will, which may be moved slowly or spontaneously, e.g. by an irresistible inherent impulse—as, for example, at the truth or reason of a point submitted for concurrence.

The Reordination of Life and Mind

Utility is a question of conduct and calls as such to be regarded from the widest point of view. We cannot overcome, nor can we even adapt, certain laws by rebellion, and in such cases it is therefore useless to rebel.[1] On the other hand, there is very often, and more than often, a transient advantage in ignoring some higher laws, our concurrence with which gives the true meaning to conformity. The difference between those laws under which the universe is maintained in expression and those which, by an artificial distinction, are termed Divine Laws is that rebellion against the one tends to be (a) impossible, (b) disastrous utterly, or (c) in some sense disastrous and this quickly, while rebellion against the other is (a) possible always and (b) not obviously disastrous in an immediate sense.[2] As regards the artificial distinction just made, it is understood, of course, that the mode under which the universe passes into

[1] It follows that those who are not in conformity over evils which are by them irremediable are not in a state of reason ; but if it be said that we must be content also, this is a misuse of words, for content is not connoted by conformity. There is, however, the state of active discontent, which is rebellion in one of its aspects, and this destroys conformity. In one sense or another, the state of content denotes ease ; and as ease belongs to the order of relative goodness it is right to desire this state, unless a higher relation intervenes, for we should desire goodness in all its grades. We must never cease to hope and to work for the remedy of all evil. But though suffering is not in itself good we must be prepared to risk and even to court it, supposing that it has to be accepted in the search for some greater good. These considerations are a touchstone for the judgment of asceticism, renunciation, abstinence : they belong to the path of life, in so far as they are aids to very life ; otherwise they are ways of unreason. All life is a quest of joy and bliss ; but the search after God is of these things in the absolute.

[2] For example, if the ordinances of the Church Catholic are literally those of God communicated through a channel created for that purpose, then its commandment to hear Mass on Sundays and other days of obligation cannot be ignored without peril to the soul within that church, yet negligence in this respect carries an apparent impunity in the visible sense of things. It is of the soul and not of the body—of the world unseen, not of the world manifest.

expression is not less Divine essentially than the mode under which grace operates in the soul of man. To go still further, it may be only in a fluidic sense and for purposes of convenience that I have distinguished two laws. However this may be—and I feel certain that there is but one conclusion—it remains that in respect of both there is the high counsel of conformity. That which is understood as natural law enforces and imposes itself; but—as things now are—the Divine Law has to be taken into the heart by an act of will. This initial act is the beginning of a life of valiance, and there is much, under the best circumstances, which must be held to go before and lead up to it. I think that the whole process might be symbolised in terms of chivalry. That which precedes the act corresponds, among other things, to the watching of the arms, though we could search out earlier analogies. The act itself is like the sacrament of knighthood, and it is followed by a life of warfare. Many knights died in warfare, and the glory was with them therein. But some reached a term when they laid down their arms in honour, and then they dwelt henceforth in castles or palaces, as barons and princes of old. In the life of spiritual valiance many die on the way, still in the season of warfare, and the recompense hereof is with them whose face is set towards Jerusalem. But there are some who have so striven that they can lay down their arms—surely in more than honour—because they have attained the outer courts and precincts of the Holy City. The strife has ceased, for the reason that conformity is established and the higher law has been engrafted within us. This suspends the active exercise of isolated will, seeing that we will in God—even as we breathe the ordinary air of earth. So also denial of the personal will is not necessary henceforward for those whose will is with God. This is the case of all who have become living stones in the sanctuary, according to another form of symbolism. To them has the Christ said: "My peace I leave with you: My peace I give unto you." Therein is the life of perfection, albeit among the saints of old it was not realised as such. I see no reason why it should be far from the life of this age of ours.

The mystery which is described as that of resignation to the will of God is much deeper than appears in those lamentable recitals of renunciation with which we are accustomed to meet even in the books of great masters of the spiritual life. Böhme tells us, for example, to hate our own will, and here all natural inclination is included by a single sweeping implicit.[1] The true counsel is in the contrary sense, for if we continue to use the word will in this mode of convention, it is obvious that it stands for our true, proper and only instrument for the great work of being brought into conformity. The first thing to do therefore is to recognise its natural sanctity and high vocation, while the next is to make quite certain that on such account we shall do nothing to debase it or contaminate. It is much too great in possibilities to be put to the lesser uses or set to feed with swine. It shall be the object of our high reverence, not of our common hatred—according to bourgeois counsels of ascetic life. There is, however, another point of view, from which it has to be treated as a child and led in the

---

[1] Jacob Böhme is particularly extravagant in his terminology, which does not arise always from personal disqualifications but occasionally from the literal reproduction and construction of the old conventions. He says, for example: If thou lovest thy life, then thy life is in that for whose sake thou forsakest it—taking in this manner a divine figure of speech at the foot of the bare letter. "He that loveth his life shall lose it," has a literal application in the proportion of one to a million of the application that is figurative. But the justification of the figure of speech is in the admitted fact of the exception, as, for example, in the rare case when it may be of vital import to die for the sake of conviction. In all ordinary and ever recurring circumstances, it is much more serviceable and may be still more heroic to live for conviction—which, I should suppose, has been said often before, and I ask pardon of the high canons.

way that it should walk, that it may grow into the likeness of God, remembering always that it comes of royal lineage. But in the last resource this symbolism is rather of the fanciful order, as if one mode of the will could be set to school another in lower classes. If it be said alternatively that will is the matter for transmutation, according to an alternative sense of images, being those of the Hermetic Mystery, the same criticism applies, or again there is something which rules behind the will and moves it there or here. The whole is really a work of the mind conceiving a given purpose and shaping all its powers to the end defined.

Resignation is only one side of conduct in the path of perfect life, and it is a negative or passive side. It may connote simple suspension, leaving the work altogether to Divine Will; but this, in its separate understanding, is a precarious and usually a false quietism. It was carried of old to its logical conclusion in the literal practice of forsaking the world, though I do not suggest that there was no active side to the life of solitaries—even to the life of Trappist or complete recluse. Conformity is on the active path and differs therefore from resignation, as the etymology of both words will shew. It is a work of formation with the will and activity of God.

But it has been pointed out by a modern writer that the really philosophical word is not will but liberty. That which we have to effect should become more intelligible at once if it be said that the work postulates a change in the axis of our purpose. The idea of will, as it is understood commonly, does not give expression to the necessary initial passage from subject to object; but this is provided by the word purpose. I am speaking of the work at large in normal fields of activity, knowing well that there is a state of the will fixed at its own centre when there is no such passage, since it is set on God Who is within. But this is a Sabbath of the mind, and there are *feriæ* and service-days which make up those of life, till " He giveth His beloved sleep."

The difficulty is not so much to do the will of God but to know it, and this knowledge—when the desire of the heart towards the great and true things has entered into a grade of life—bears little if any relation to the recompense in educated conscience which results from obedience to authority that may have imposed its rule upon us in the youth of the spirit.[1] The true monitor is within and obedience to this voice is the secret of purpose and attitude.

The importance on life of attitude, and of purpose which really animates, is incalculable in this respect, for it means that our election is written over everything. Such attitude and such purpose are, however, like those of the poet, the painter, the musician, whose dedications do not mean, in the working sense, or even in the conscious sense, that the artist in verse is thinking poetry for ever, the maker of pictures seeing nothing but pictures, or the " tone-poet " awake only to music. But these things, besides being their special avocation, do actually tincture their whole existence ; and this is the standpoint from which they look at all. The followers of the call to God, of the Divine vocation, will know that He is the poet, the artist and the maker of all music. For them will life itself be a realisation of these and all the arts. If I speak of my proper election, I know that

---

[1] Marsay did not express it in this way, but he did recognise that there was a difficulty about knowing the will of God, though it goes deeper than perhaps he discerned. The sense-images and the mind-images were the chief things which, in his view, confused the issues. He spoke of "the many voices that call themselves the voice of God," and of " things that often have the appearance of being very good and profitable," but in which it is difficult to distinguish the Divine Will from that which is in the mask of its likeness. His counsel was one of prayer for the leading of the Spirit of God.—See *Discourses on Subjects Relating to the Spiritual Life*. Translated from the French. Edinburgh, 1749. Disc. XXVI.

it is those only who cry out to God that have the true sense of literature, and for them the expression of this sense is everywhere—in all the tongues of Nature and all of Grace. The workings of the mind enter by its aid into worlds of glory.

It remains that doing the will of God is doing our own will, while the only renunciation involved is that dictated by universal good sense—being the subservience of lesser to greater interests. But the word interest brings us back to the word reward, which it appears to connote inevitably. There is a good deal of false or artificial reasoning on every side of these subjects, and here is one among them which has peculiar tendencies in this direction. Our first duty is therefore not to be afraid of consequences in the region of common opinion —as, for example, the vulgar charge of commercialism, utilitarianism, and so forth, in following the high things. It must be said, in the first place, that the word reward, being that which presents itself for use rather obviously in such a connection, and which I have there-fore adopted intentionally, is not an accurate word. We must recur to the question of purpose and remember that this connects with the attainment of some end discerned. There is an object in view—in the sense, for example, that martyrdom has its crown. The recom-pense of those who seek God inheres in the promise of His attainment. The consequences of our purpose are present implicitly in our minds, if not otherwise. We undertake a journey with the intention of reaching a goal ; we desire that goal, for itself or its concomitants ; otherwise, we should not begin the journey. All action must either presuppose motive or it is not under the law of reason. It follows also that, speaking in human language, God desires the union or He would not open the path. Eckehart goes further and says : " God can as little dispense with us as we with Him." The attainment of union is the reward of all, or the motive is destroyed.

Willing co-operation with the purpose of God, by the very fact of the hypothesis behind it, carries no doubt of this kind, because the course taken signifies that the hypothesis is accepted—namely, that God is and that He recompenses those who seek Him out. Now, recompense is in respect of self and the will therein. It is said indeed that " though He slay me yet will I trust in Him," but, at least as we adapt the affirmation, all that we understand by trust and self goes on after the slaying. If a time comes when the will and the purpose of God are pursued for their own sake, by a definite and conscious separation of the reward motive, this depends from the postulate of absolute goodness resident in Divine Nature and on an advanced state of union therewith.

Some Quietists of the eighteenth century darkened counsel by the supposition of fantastic cases, for the sake of an argument *per impossibile*. They postulated in this manner the love of God in the state of an eternal outcast. There is no call to consider such a possibility, as a God Who can cast out love is not the God of the mystics, nor are His people their people. A more serious confusion arises from postulating a stereotyped set of actions to represent our own inclinations and another set, still more stereotyped, which are held to stand for the will of God. A sharp distinction is instituted between both, and in the case of the natural man it is inferred that he ignores the one to follow the other. There is thus established an entirely false canon of the criticism of conduct. The difficulty is that on the one side, or in what is termed our natural manhood and the environment thereto adjacent, an imperative voice is speaking close at hand, while another and unfortunately a reflected voice, an external authority, imposes another course, but too often bestirs no real conviction, though artificial conscience is on its side, prevailing from time to time. When people decide to try and obey this voice they are led usually by a very imperfect instruction, and the last thing they learn is to realise that the voice of God can, as it must, be heard within themselves. But if a time comes when they listen and hear, redirection of purpose follows, and they may, as they should, be taught how it is their own better will that they are following in that of God. There can be then awakened within them the sense of (*a*) vocation, (*b*) election, (*c*) valour of high ambition ; and presently it may so happen that new purpose will eat them up. Their souls shall be taught to magnify the Lord in the fulfilment of their own intention. It will be testified to them that it is theirs and no other's, that no one shall take it away from them. If they can receive into their hearts the life of this election, they will be crying : " O temptation, where is thy victory ? O sin, where is thy talisman ? " For the scales will have fallen from their eyes. The difficulty about this kind of inward fire is not so much in its maintenance as in its kindling.

It may be thought by those who look not beneath the first sense of things that I am exercising a gift of subtlety for ministration to pure self-hood, by its consecration in the name of God ; but I am affirming a truth of intelligence from which no escape is possible. It is we and no other who go to God ; it is we and no other who profit in the soul-sense by doing the Divine Will ; it is we and no other who lose all things by setting up a transitory will against that which is truly our own.

The expression which has obtained so long may be excusable in one sense, but to talk of giving up our own will in obedience to the will of God is a contradiction of its own implied motive. I may give up my will to a fellow-creature for this or another reason, so that he may take the place which I have sought, possess the treasure that would perhaps have been prized by me, and so forth. The gain is his, the presumable loss is mine, and to what extent I am compensated by the ministry of unselfishness depends on a disentangling of motives which are often exceedingly involved. I mean that in much seeming self-denial he who gives up may be left in a state of uncertainty as to whether (*a*) he was actually making a renunciation, (*b*) and if so whether he was impelled by the heroic motive, or (*c*) the supernatural motive ; (*d*) whether it was natural goodness ; (*e*) whether it was a question of personal weakness, (*f*) so that he was persuaded in the end ; and (*g*) how far the will as a definite cause of purpose entered into the matter at all. But in the order of Divine Things there are no complexities ; by the essence of things, and not in our mind's refinements, there is no loss possible, and it is only in the creation of false issues that the motive can be deemed doubtful.

Speaking in harmony with the truth and beauty of the whole subject, Böhme says : " When thou canst throw thyself with That where no creature dwelleth, though it be but for a moment, then thou hearest what God speaketh." He says, further, that where no creature dwelleth is within us ; that when we stand still from the thinking and willing of self the Eternal shall be revealed within us. We shall become the organ of His Spirit ; our Spirit will hear His voice ; and in the silence of that state we shall be as God was before Nature and creature. This suggests that the whole *negotium* consists in suspension of action rather than in its redirection. We have to make unto ourselves the image of a Divine Prospect and the after-work is one of conformity in all things.[1] Resignation to the will of God is exercised rightly over all that which, being inauspicious on the surface in respect of our personal selves, is beyond our control or adaptation. It is really a marriage of our proper intent

[1] But conformity in its highest understanding is what is called in Zoharic symbolism the bed of Solomon, a place of peace, which—in other terms—is desire in its fruition. It is the peace between the Lover and Beloved, having one heart and one interest.

with that of the universe, on the faith that there is good behind the groaning and travail of the whole creation. Redirection of our own purpose is for integration in the purpose of God, and at the beginning—as we saw much earlier in these pages—it is like an undertaking to keep the Law before it is declared in our consciousness, because the Divine Purpose is not written at large over the manifest order of things, because we need the direct witness, and because that of our fathers before us is neither perfect nor first-hand. It is certain, however, that union with the purpose of God is the end of our being and a realisation in advance of all that we understand by the catholic term of union. Hence it involves nothing that can be called renunciation, save in the most relative sense. It follows a law of exchange; it is giving old lamps for new, the stable in Bethlehem for the High Palace at the Centre.

The design of these intimations is to shew that there is a very true and real sense in which we can say: *Facilis ascensus superni ;* and if it be true also, but in another way, that the soul of man

> "Mounts and that hardly to eternal life,"

the initial hardness is that of grasping the real interests and losing those which hinder and yet, as we are placed now, have too often a more direct appeal.

The way of ascent is set forth in the old counsel to grow in the likeness of God; this is also the whole mystery and the whole work. There are various constructions of that great Biblical mythos which says that we were made in God's image, but for us it is a question of rehabilitation therein, since the likeness abides no longer in our normal consciousness. This notwithstanding, whatsoever perfection and similitude were, by the hypothesis, once inherent there are still lying deep in our nature, and mystical practice is a work of finding it within. Be the turbid waters stilled and the thickened waters cleared; then the eye which is turned upon them shall see that image in great depths of the well of our being. We shall know it because of its shining. But this is a work of purification and of great devotion.

There is, however, to the high desiring spirit of man, a sense of inadequacy in likeness. There may be many maidens who, at their several distances, are like unto that one only who is crowned in the heart of the lover as queen of beauty: the similitude is one thing, but other is the state of her who is that radiant lady enthroned. Were there any in the outer courts who might be termed her *alter ego*, it would be well indeed for such; yet the heart has a single throne and one can sit thereon—one and no other of all in the world of love. It is to be thought, however, that more than likeness is suggested by the passage of Genesis, where the word " likeness " is supplemented by that of " image," and both are applied subsequently to the begetting of a son by Adam. There is a distinction, moreover, between the likeness, presumably accidental and partial, of A and B and the creation to a likeness and in an image by intent and will. On the deeper side of this subject a great truth is expressed by Tauler when he says that " the living fire of the Holy Spirit burneth up all unlikeness."

Growth in this image of God is a process at work in and through all the faculties. It is married to the purpose of life; it is joined to the will of man; it is in desire and emotion as the hunger after godly things; it is love in and through all; it fills the life of the mind. The time comes when there is no longer an appeal to the intellect, because the intellect has laid down its arms in reverence before another mode of consciousness. The holiest of all natural terms is that of sovereign reason, and in the mystical life the highest act is one which leads to its suspension. The great act on the path is the conversion of reason—not, however, by an intellectual process but one of love.

So rises in this place the question of the mind, a word that we are apt to use as if it were synonymous with the material brain; but this is its vehicle. There is a sanctification of the intellect, by virtue of which it may enter into realisation of the mystic term—within the intellectual measures. The logical understanding may be in one sense our consciousness morganatically married to outward things, working through them and in them confined. But the point is that we do work therewith, and this also is to be treated with great reverence.

Some modern mystics are disposed to weight it with the burden of all our intellectual sins and then drive it into the wilderness as an emissary goat.[1] But in the last resource it can be brought into such a state of prepara-

---

[1] We hear a great deal as to the failure of the logical understanding, and I have borne witness on my own part. But it is too often loose terminology and breeds much confusion for minds not rooted naturally in high reason. Understanding is an essential quality of consciousness, for this is a mode of knowledge. The mystical stilling of thought is in understanding, but it is no longer in logical bonds because it is not working processes. The logical understanding, the reasoning faculty, operates in the exercise of meditation, in the outward thinking processes; but in-thinking, but thinking in the heart, the true contemplation work, or the work of love, is in another region of the mind. Holy and beautiful and high enthroned is the imperial Cæsar of our natural human reason. May the great hosts encompass it; but—speaking with the tongue of symbolism—there is a realm behind wherein another monarch reigns; and he is hailed as King of Peace. The grand key-word of this Grade in our progress is truly *Pax*, and when He of Whom I bear witness is awakened within us, or we are awakened in Him, it can be said that Shiloh comes. Solomon is also peace and peace signifies the mystical bed of Solomon, mentioned as a refuge and security in strange pages of the *Zohar*. But in a sense there are two Solomons, who are aspects of our man within: one of them has a thousand wives, being interests, concerns, processes, ways through the world of thought, activities without end, and he works through the brain with these. The other sleeps with the faithful and awakens with the just made perfect: it is given to him that he should know the things of God in the land of the living. He is peace, and he brings peace—peace and light to the realms of the King of reason, and the heart's desire to the King.

tion that it will say of its own accord: *Ecce ancilla Domini*. I know therefore, and well, that the head is uplifted in holiness and that the eye of mind, as well as the heart's eye, sees Zion on the eternal hill.

There is a question indeed whether the mystical experience is not another state of the intellect, the rational faculty, the *mens*.[1] But all the terms must be redistributed.

The splitting up of the mind and its processes leads into no less confusion than the divisions and subdivisions of personality, and it is precisely the manifold misconceptions on this important subject which give us cause to be thankful for the sovereign reason in that part of its domain which belongs to the logical faculty. It continues to save us from deception when verbal formulæ and shibboleths rise up to testify.[2] The soul, the knowing and self-knowing part, and the mind are but various aspects and modalities of our one individual being. In respect of external things, of all that is connected with and arises therefrom, this being operates through the brain and is under the limitations

---

[1] According to Rabbi Salomon Ibn-Gebirol, in his *Fons Vitæ*, the intellect was (*a*) the most direct emanation from the Divine Will; (*b*) an intermediary between man and God; (*c*) more simple and unified than all other substances. Above the sphere of the intellect was the Throne of Divine Glory, before which the intellect was brought to a pause, unable to penetrate further. I mention this Jewish poet and theosophist of the twelfth century, because of the influence which he exercised in the West under the name of Avicebron. Albertus Magnus and St. Thomas Aquinas were familiar with the *Fons Vitæ* and are said to have combated certain heterodox doctrines to which its great popularity had given rise in several schools of Christian thought. See Salomon Munk: *Mélanges de Philosophie Juive et Arabe*, 1859.

[2] It has been well said by Rouse, speaking of the Light of the Spirit: " The reasonable light of man continueth in man, even when this supernatural light shineth. It knows what other men know, and knows what itself knew and thought before this light came to it; but this light being come it yields willingly to it, and surrenders both itself and the man whom it formerly guided."—*The Mystical Marriage*, p. 239.

of its instrument. In such relation the mind is a maker of images. These and their antitheses, opposites and the pairs of these, are all part of the pageant. But it is in communication also with the Divine, working sacramentally upon us, and is that point whereunto all natural sacraments converge. Now, there are stages in the mystical work when the external offices of mind must be suspended, if we are to attain experience instead of symbols. But that which brings about the suspension is mind and no other. Therein is the motive, therein the sense of the end and the processes which lead thereto. It is mind which empties itself, and if—in the consequent state of denudation—God enters to take possession, or remains and manifests within, that which He fills is mind, the knowing and self-knowing part. But these three are one, and their other name is soul.

There is, of course, a very clear distinction between Practical and Intellectual Mysticism, which is a recognition of the law of unity as between God and the soul. The mystical process is an integration of the soul in God. The direction towards Mysticism is on the threshold— or in the majority of cases—an intellectual consequence. It begins to be alive when it becomes a work of the heart. Such intellectual recognition is assuredly a great advance beyond the natural materialism of the mind, but by itself its characteristic is insufficiency. The mind of man goes in quest of the great things, and this is well; but there are conditions of grace and sanctity when the great things come down to the soul. This is to say that, after all excursions of thought, after the intentness of ordered thought, we must recognise in the last resource that there are moments when truths which seem to exceed us naturally begin to irradiate our consciousness, coming we know not whence and entering we know not how within us. It would seem that we are placed in communication with universal harmonies in an exalted state of receptivity. We know then that to see all things in God and to discern God in all things are not opposites but correlatives—both sides of the sphere which symbolises the All being true sides, and this equally.

Unfortunately, in our partial inhibition, we meet with many complications—as, for example, those instances wherein the grace of understanding seems to go before complete sanctification. It is these, in addition to sin, which make the way to God a *Via Dolorosa*. The path through sin is at need a way to God, and *Via Dolorosa* surely; but it is such only in the sense that evil is trodden down—like rough stones on a road. Otherwise, it is comparable to Egypt—a place from which we must come out. And hereof is our journey at the beginning, in the case of each and all. We have to come forth from our own Egypt, our land of sin and of bondage, the place of much food in fleshpots, remembering that he who overcometh is he who, having set forth on the quest of God, is at length able to say : Where Thou art, lo, also I am. It rests with us whether we shall abide in the desert or enter the Promised Land. It rests with us whether the desire of the House shall pass into the Presence of the King. The King in His presence is not apart from us, and the House is ours.

The Blessed Vision is within, even when we postulate the object-lessons of the Paradise in Dante's Dream, for the gift of sight is assuredly one that flows outward from within. That which we call the Divine Union is above all things a state in consciousness. But we are taught, and wisely, to cast out the images of mind, at least in the sense of physical forms of thought. We must deal only with pure thought in consciousness. I believe, further, that a true counsel cautions us to be very careful about modes of sensible experience in these matters, for psychic feeling goes much deeper than is supposed generally. We have always to remember that the work is one of love and desire, but there is no sense-body to these qualities in that world with which we are dealing. The love and desire are to be understood, firstly, as in a state of dedication and, secondly, as in the law of necessity, because the term is for us inevitable. I am not reducing the importance of sensation, in the external world, or the office of material thought. These are great, and, being great, are full of natural holiness. They can and muss be sanctified in the supernatural sense, which means that they should be pressed into the service, when and wheresoever possible, of that quest which I have delineated as taking place in our self-knowing being. I do not think that anyone is fit for the Kingdom of Heaven, or can attain it as understood in consciousness, who does not receive, if indeed he does not know by his own experience, the glorious intimation of certain lines written by Aubrey de Vere. The lines are: " Blessed are they who kiss thee morn and even "; and " Blessed are they on whom thy hands alight." Granted this, or granted at least its capacity in the ascent to the Kingdom of Heaven, all good things belonging to all the worlds within and without are of necessity superadded. The mystical contemplation, so called, of which Ruysbroeck says in one place that it is knowledge without mode, but immediately after that it is modeless sight without knowledge, is an uninterrupted preoccupation of love, a state in which the Beloved possesses our whole kingdom and, thinking or not thinking, is never out of our concern, never apart from us, do what we can and will. The way of salvation in this respect is to keep our hold upon consciousness, letting the crowd of psychical and cognate faculties pass by in their native disorder.

A man is that which he thinks, and, as an old Scripture intimates, his heart is in the house of his treasure. If we think God in our hearts He will dwell within us, and we shall abide in Him. The mind is tortured continually over the choice between speculative alternatives concerning modes of subsistence in a land that is very far away ; but if we enter that Land of Promise we shall know where the milk flows and where also the honey. We shall know in what quarter of the Palace the King has His Supper-Room and where His nuptial bed is dighted. We shall know where the Matins are chanted and who sings Mass in the morning—when it is the time of the Angelus and when of the Vesper-bell.

CHAPTER XIII

THE MYSTICAL STATE IN THE WORLD

THE history of Israel is like unto that of our election as postulants of the mystical life. We went down very early into Egypt, for we thought ourselves in need of its sustenance ; and we were bondsmen in that region, being under the tyranny of material life. We came out of Egypt in the guidance of a great leader, and because of our high vocation. We began to follow the call of God; but the way was hard and the way was wild and long. We grew sick of the spiritual food which came from Heaven—of which the Eucharist is a symbol, like the manna : we did not receive worthily. The law of our election was promulgated on the mountain summit of our spirit ; the lower nature heard it with lower ears: it was not taken into the heart. We came at length into the Promised Land of spiritual experience, so that we know the workings of the Lord within us ; we know also how good it is to dwell in the House of the Lord ; but, all our dedications notwithstanding, we have been ever a stiff-necked generation : we have fallen away from that election and have gone into many captivities. The greatest of all has been the age-long thraldom of the thought-life apart from God, for that of Egypt was more especially the yoke of sense, but this is the bondage within measures of the material mind. At the present time we are lifting up our eyes, believing that our salvation is at hand: but we know not, indeed, we know not.

I am not reading allegory into the Pentateuch but

offering at its proper value a certain analogy between things within and without. It is again Jeremiah's thinking in the heart that converts the wilderness of Sinai into the Promised Land, which does not mean that the wilderness is not a blessing, as it is truly, for it is the place of arduous toil. But I am also postulating the term of quest in thought, for the simplification of all the issues, because we have confused ourselves overmuch with the ideas of indrawn states and the expression of spiritual experiences in the language of those that are pyschic. The labour is that of love, and the term is love in fruition. We are in a state of confusion also respecting things within and without. If we say, with *The Book of the Man from Frankfort*, that we have two eyes, one of which looks upon this world, the other on the world to come, they are in a serious state of astigmatism, and our dealings with one in the cause of the other, on the faith of past authority, have destroyed the true focus.

The old counsel was to forsake the world, as if it were not the raw material of all redemption. That counsel is rich in grave misconception, and at the risk of expressing a platitude I must say that it calls to be translated into a higher sense than any which obtains normally ; then it is true counsel. Qualifications of this kind signify a vital need for re-expression which obtains on every side.

It must be remembered, however, that St. John, that master of light and sweetness, once said on the part of Christ Jesus : " Love not the world, nor the things that are in the world," which requires, however, to be contrasted and at need qualified by another teaching, according to which " God so loved the world." Now, there is no question that we are all ministers of salvation to ourselves and others, or are as such intended, and that the root of salvation is in love. I want therefore (*a*) some principle of understanding in respect of the Divine Love which, by the hypothesis of Scripture, sent the only-begotten Son of God into the world, so that it might be brought into harmony with the counsel first quoted; or (*b*), in respect of the second teaching, a canon of distinction for that element, part or aspect of the world which we are directed not to love in view of that counter-aspect, element or division, the love of which is, from diverse considerations, incumbent on us, and is by other texts imposed.

The most obvious answer will be to speak of that spirit of the world, called otherwise " the prince of this world," in whom Christ has not anything. There is, I suppose, no need to indicate that it is not a personal spirit, as if a legendary leader of the so-called powers of the air, which notwithstanding it is a very real force and essence, permeating and encompassing humanity. If we say that it is a misdirection, an evil, a subtle virus, we are within the truth assuredly. This is a diagnosis of condition ; and it is for those who have the spirit of Christ to provide their theriac, which—*ex hypothesi*—they carry about continually. It is therefore a condition to be changed, removed, dissolved, and is obviously not to be loved or suffered, much less permitted to integrate within us. In another form of symbolism, which belongs to the most obvious order, and must have been used incessantly, if we are soldiers of Christ we are not prosecuting His campaign when we go into hiding so as to keep out of range of the enemy. The danger is here and now, yet is it the place of opportunity and of the grace that dwells therein. It is the field of the soul's warfare, in which cometh the victory. So also, while we must not love the possessions of this world *per se* and accumulate them for the sake of possession, we can and must cherish signally all gifts, endowments and properties of things which—from any point of beginning—may enable us to do the Divine Work on earth ; we must take pride in them and in the doing, or we shall fail.

Our life in the world is sanctified and a new mean-

ing enters it when the vision of Divine Life, which
has been formulated by the mind, is kept by the will
not only before but within it. The vocation of most
people may not take them further, but a grade of
partial illumination, a foretaste, some blessed quality of
certitude can be attained therein. At least such souls
are fed by the crumbs which fall from the King's table.
For others it may prove a gate of the mystical life and
it is a work of joy to enter thereby. It is a gate which
opens on the infinite of all good, for those who have or
shall receive the call and power to go forward therein
shall enter into the consciousness of Divine Things. It
is the office of consciousness, when it has been opened,
to receive; and it has never opened towards God in
vain.

That we have been intromitted into the universe for
the working out of a glorious destiny[1] I believe utterly,
and it is the purpose of this book to declare our destiny,
its reason, circumstances and manner of fulfilment.
Assuredly the direction—unceasing and irrecusable—of
the soul along one line is a testimony—or shall I say at
least a predication ?—as to the truth of direction. The
path bore witness to the soul before it set foot thereon.
So also is there ground for believing that those who
love the highest shall come into that which the love has
in some sense made their own already. Leibnitz did not
express it in these words, but he rooted the truth of
of Nature's evidence on the truth of God. I am mystic
rather than philosopher, but if I cite the truth of God
before the mystical tribunal, I know that it will witness
for those who look to end in God. The many forces

---

[1] This follows therefore : That which we need is here ; all that we
can expect is now. Here in a certain sense is a plea for some direction
towards the concrete. Attainment is a vague prospect, so long as it is
kept in the abstract ; but we can take God into our heart, in no " creed
of the phantasiasts " but in a living and vital manner, when we receive
His world therein.

which seem without mercy are forces which drive us toward the great end.

All things good belong to us by the legitimacy of our dedication: there is even no part of the gods which is not a part of us. We may read in *Tristram of Lyonesse* how the knights of King Arthur's court elected to go in search of the Graal for a year and a day. They swore to maintain the quest upon holy relics and Eucharistic elements, after hearing Mass and seeking remission of sins. We also have heard a Mass in our hearts, in our hearts we have sought to be purged, that we may go in search of the high things. This quest we are pledged to follow for a year and a day—as it might be for all our life—if therein we may reach a term. We have had enough of that knowledge which is a storing of minds with treasures gathered from without: the true treasures are within. It is for this reason that the office of real books is not to assist us in collecting and ordering facts but to awaken that which is in ourselves. The key is: Christ liveth within me. Divine Consciousness is awakened; it is no longer the I which is known in the ways external: it is God abiding. But it is certain that the mind which is filled with God is in some grade of the union; and as union is union we have not to seek out a new process but go forward with that which we have. Let the Divine State be free to deepen within us. Unfortunately the life of mystical quietude has been placed by common consent at the opposite pole to a life of action, and the life of action has been understood as scarcely to be followed concurrently with what is called a life of contemplation. There is a sense, however, in which we can reverse the terms. We have to understand and follow the one in the sense of the other, to attain activity in the mode of contemplation and thinking in the heart as activity at its uttermost and highest—on the old analogous principle that the wheel's hub is the point of greatest rest and greatest activity. Herein is that doing of things as if we did them not which is a counsel in respect of external work, but it leads happily to a better understanding thereof. Indeed I do not know that any true rest of the spirit is apart from activity: there is nothing in the whole wide world like repose in the work which is of God, and this may be the whole travail of life. The man who is wanting in efficient faculties for the full use of time is not in a prepared state for the riches of eternity. Time is a sacrament of eternity and is to be received in the sense thereof. *Cæteris paribus*, the best use is the fullest. God and His world both love a generous and free recipient. A greedy nature is to be preferred before one that is stinted.

In the past also it was not understood adequately that the way is a way of joy, though the bare principle has been affirmed from time to time, or indeed frequently. We have not realised further that the mode of attainment in contemplation is a mode of intentness in love. The preparation in external life is by abiding on the bright side, the fair side, the side of mercy and peace. This is the luminous reflection of an eternal brightness, an eternal beauty, the *beneplacitum termino carens* which brought the universe and all its glory into being.

Another counsel is to use the gifts of God in purity, and on this condition the freedom of all is ours. Let us receive with our eyes and the other senses those ministries of beauty which are communicated through all the senses with the same aspiration after worthiness that is self-imposed in approaching the Eucharist. That which is called " hidden things of the spirit " shall be then made manifest to our own spirits ; and the activity of life in all degrees shall not hinder the " secret continu-ance " of that inward intentness with which we look not only into the heart of life's mystery but come to abide therein. The worlds merge one into another ; the two are indeed one. The other world is the inwardness of this. Time is *signum* and eternity is *signatum*. Let us get at that heart of the mysteries which lies behind common things: we shall see the rareness of all rareness in that day.

One of the characteristics of *mystæ* is a sense of Nature's beauty and her symbolism; yet all the old processes of religion have offered, or claim to offer, a way of escape from Nature. It is time that we sought to realise what is put into our hands. The stars in their courses move with the man who moves through the pageant of the universe with realisation of its glory and dignity, and with a sense of the dignity and glory native to the discerning heart which can see the splendour without. The beauty without is part of the beauty within; they give to one another, and each receives from each. This is the higher understanding of that adjustment of the senses to the external which is the condition of our manifest existence. Nature is a perpetual Rite, and it is for us to take our part therein, understanding what we are doing and that which is done about us. The mystic Saint-Martin mourned over the silence of the world, but the truth is that it is we who awake speech in Nature. There is no verbal communication until there is a common language. It is by arriving at a language on our own part that we enable Nature to talk. There is no doubt that the world will begin to speak for us on its own part when we furnish the medium on ours. Meanwhile it communicates vaguely and we communicate with it through a common bond of sympathies. Nature's loss and inhibition will cease when we come into our own. It awakens in our awakening and speaks in our speaking.

If from one point of view it is we who question and we also who put our answers into the mouth of the universe, from another it is Nature who gives us music and love that finds the meaning. Nature and love, love in Nature, Nature working in love—indescribable superincession : here lies the way of all true interpretàtion, till God gives up His sacraments. And true interpretation unveils the life of God which is hidden in the world and within us. This is the sense in which there lies everywhere about us the first matter of that great work which is called redemption. The testimony of the external world comes into our consciousness through the senses by an operation outside ourselves, our part being to contain as much of the world in consciousness as we are able to receive. We assist the operation by going in search of testimony. It is only in proportion as the cosmos passes through us that it can be said for us to exist. When we are gifted like the poet of faërie, so that we can see the same thing everywhere, we shall not only be integrated in the Divine Immanence but shall discern after what manner that Immanence dissolves into Divine Transcendence. Let us strive therefore to see as with his eyes, that we may find the secret soul manifested amidst the glory of the world, from henceforth and for ever.

It follows that the world is pageant and symbolism— is sacrament, that is to say. The true mystic is priest, poet and interpreter, but artificer above all therein. He is the minister of every sacrament, and in virtue of his office he raises Nature by its spiritual realisation into the world of grace—not indeed that there are two worlds, for they are made one in him. The Church is pageant and symbolism ; the mystic is he who holds the key to its meanings. Certain Instituted Mysteries rank third in this glorious triad. The aspiration is : Abide with me ; but its value is as an aid to realisation that God abides essentially. When we discern it as the place of Immanence, Nature is transfigured. This is also, and more than all, what happens in respect of our own consciousness. The evidence pours in through all the human senses, and concerning it consciousness testifies to itself in the stillness of reflection therein. So also the consciousness of Nature's beauty is within us, and this beauty is convincing enough to justify our faith that when the present veil is removed we shall see that Isis either under a more glorious vesture or apart from all drapery in the form of absolute beauty. Once more therefore, the world is a great pageant, a glorious manifestation of the Divine, and those who have the gifts can see and hear and read—the open things and the secret, things simple and deep, the great and high things. The gifts grow with the meanings, both from more to more : they open for ever and ever. It is for us to adjust the lens through which we look at the universe. The passage which we make through it is a sacrament of the great quest. It remains with us to change the natural sacraments into those of a higher order by the power of our inward priesthood ; but this is a kind of ministry which comes not with the laying on of hands : it is of another order and validity. It lies very far away in comparison with the official ordinations, but its attainment seals us for ever, as the deacon is sealed by the bishop on the altar-steps. There is one word more hereon. The pageant of the universe requires no miracles to substantiate its glory and its promise.[1] The case against miracles does not depend upon their falsity but rather upon their veridic nature. The use of the term veridic in this connection has the same relation to truth as gentlemanlike behaviour has to gentle life.

Sanctity is the operation and effect of that law which is called dedication to the work.[2] It takes up all parts

---

[1] Another title of greatness belonging to the instituted sacraments is that they tamper in no wise with Nature. The Real Presence in the Eucharist does not make void its veils.

[2] The sum of sanctity is to know all things in God and to realise Him as manifested in the sanctuary of our inward nature. The reason that we know Him so little is that we have sought so little in ourselves, so little attempted to live that life which would enable us to know so much.

of the personality into the life of redemption. It does not exterminate these parts, which would be a literal understanding of the counsel to pluck out the right eye, if the right eye should offend us. The Christ within us does not come to destroy the parts of the personality, but to fulfil them. They are fulfilled by the graces of the sacraments, when the dispensation of the sacraments is understood and when they are received in a realising mode. But the consideration of this subject belongs to the next chapter. The counsel which I have mentioned is not, of course, taken literally, but it has been understood as connoting the tortured life which has been held to lead into sanctity. If it must be said, the five wounds of Christian Mysticism are Asceticism, Celibacy, Divorce from Nature, Miracles and the Doctrine of Physical Resurrection, but the last is only skin-deep, for it has never entered really into the life of the subject.[1] It does not seem easy on the surface to save the counsel, but it may obviously be reduced to a simple rule for the elimination at all costs of the things which hinder.

Subject to such qualifications, the counsel to which I have alluded is that also of contemplation; its synonym in mystical language is the casting out of images from the mind. It should be realised further that it is the condition, and so utterly (*a*) of monastic life and (*b*) of life in the world. It can become also the union of both in a common cause and work—though I think in my heart that if it had been construed properly from the beginning there would have been no monastic life, though there might have been manifold Houses of Retreat. As to monastic life, it is easy to see its shortcomings—much more easy perhaps than to discern its ground in grace.

---

[1] I speak with a certain reluctance on this official doctrine, but if it be needful to define my standpoint, I regard physical resurrection as a simple misconception of St. Paul's teaching concerning that which is raised out of the tomb of mortality for a vehicle of the soul at the next stage of the life to come.

It has been with us for two thousand years in Christendom, and they are foolish in things of the spirit who think that it has not served. The highest graces may be outside such a state *per se*, by which I mean not that they are unattainable therein, but that they are not of the state itself, because they can be reached apart from it. We know that any good path is good enough to initiate a quest of God, though none are free from difficulties. The celibate state is one of those which belong to monastic life. It was inevitable enough on the ground of policy, but it has been erected into a counsel of perfection, the false implicit of which is that chastity connotes celibacy, and this cries for vindication to the body and soul of Nature. Fortunately it has never been tolerated by the Orthodox Greek Church, as its marriage-service shews. Regarded in itself, celibacy is regrettable as a fixed principle, but it enters into the region of iniquity when it becomes part of the interdict which is laid by ascetical theology on natural affection.[1]

And now as regards the external and internal states considered from the standpoint of our place as citizens of the world. We do not turn to the presence of God simply by turning inward; we do not turn from that presence simply by turning outward.[2] The presence

---

[1] We can happily correct such writers as Gerard of Zutphen by others with higher claims. Ruysbroeck admits that it is good to have some solicitude, though not too much, about external things and those who are around us.—*Book of the Twelve Béguines*. Even a pious merchant in the commonplaces of Christian life, like the excellent provincial Pagani who wrote *L'Anima Amante*, had eyes enough to see that human affection has to be subordinated to Divine Love, not eradicated. If Louis de Blois says that " you can never be united to God perfectly till you are set free from all that is not God," it is obvious that this can take place in two ways, the second being discernment of God in all that is. We must remember also that if that which is done for another is done for God only, that other counting nothing, it is unlikely to rank with God. The true motive is—for others' sake in God.

[2] The initial key to the Union is perhaps intention, which means a marriage of wills. There comes a time when we are conscious of attain-

of God abides within and without, and Christ is in the public streets, in virtue of the great truth of Divine Immanence. That Presence—as we have seen—will speak to us in the universe, if those words are ours by which the universe is questioned fittingly.[1] We can also awaken that Presence—as I have said elsewhere—so that it will testify inwardly concerning itself. The word of understanding is in both cases expressed in the language of the tongue by the term realisation—with the practice leading up to which we need never go astray from God's Presence.

Brother Lawrence gives one key when he says that we should feed and nourish our souls with high notions of God. That which shall follow herefrom is condign views of the worlds within and without us. Nature will be transfigured in their light, and we shall be ourselves transfigured.[2] Both worlds are now under a cloud, but within the cloud is a sanctuary. This is how we quicken ourselves and that which is without us. At the beginning it is a work of faith, but the life-value of faith is increased to the extent that it exceeds its own measures. It is an aid to the fulfilment of what is hoped for and

ment in this direction. It is called otherwise, but perhaps less adequately, an union with world-purpose.

[1] This is the word which is sought in the later Instituted Mysteries, which is spoken of as lost, which is found in other Degrees and is there communicated in a form which always and of necessity suggests and is indeed, in one sense, a substitute. It is lost because man is incapable commonly of realisation in the direction where his search would obtain its recompense. In the truth of things, it is hidden but is never lost : it is nearer than all things nearest. It is in the sacred heart of the beloved and in the lover's eager heart. It is like the pearl of great price in alchemy, and although a quest is involved it does not need seeking, for it is here as well as there, and a man must find it in himself before he can find it without him.

[2] I think, therefore, that Dr. Rudolf Steiner is right when he says that " the knowledge of Nature is not enriched by the knowledge of God but transformed." In such transformation it is, however, enriched for us.

to the sight of things unseen. It is on the assumption of faith that the great quest begins : to walk in its light is to enter the path of quest. Again, it is by realising the matter of faith that we reach to the grade of experience. If the primary condition of understanding the Law is to obey it—and this is true demonstrably—the condition of knowledge in all Divine Things is faith, implied also in the other, and this is really an annunciation of the same mystery after a variant fashion of terms. Hereof is the purpose and end of the inward life—that a man should know in fine Him in Whom he has believed at first. This itself is the justification of that faith, whereby it is said, in the beginning, that we are ourselves justified.

Brother Lawrence also directs those who are in the press of the great world not to seek for joy in the false glitter of things that encompass them. The counsel is sane and true in so far as there is a glitter of falsehood, but we need a canon of distinction in this respect, and it is precisely because of its absence that the counsel is suspect ; it may intend to caution us against the holy joy of clear seeing into the great pageant of creation. So also we have heard much about vanity, and vanity is great in the world, but the vanity of enlarging overmuch on that vanity is not less great as vanity.

It is of course true that although the sense of God is communicated by external things His perfect realisation is in the transcendence only. Where is the path ? He is immanent also in us ; once and again, " that is best which lies the nearest " ; there is our path to Him. Our normal consciousness is of the manifest order, but to explore consciousness is to enter our unrevealed, latent or immanent self, between which and the normal there is no arbitrary dividing line. Here also is a journey in love. At our own height is He. We do not leave ourselves in order to find God ; and I would add to this that in the stages beyond our present manifest life we do not leave the world but explore it further. The next stage is one of deeper indwelling.

On another side than was touched by Lawrence, our brother in God, there is truer counsel and higher doctrine. That doctrine recognises the value of all life, while the counsel is to seek and find—and those shall find surely who seek truly—even in the press of the great world—that hidden but not invisible splendour which is reflected from the things that are eternal. Before this point is gained it is possible that the word " action " and the word " contemplation " will both have come to be understood in a different and unifying sense ; and it is then that we shall turn " hardly ever " from the practice of the presence of God. It will abide with us in life and in that which we call death, which is a new form of the Presence, or as Hellenbach expressed it— with another intention—it is a change in the form of perception. The secret is " life in God and union "— not " there," as Arnold said, but here. It is union in the waking ways, and then the door of sleep may open after another manner into a new aspect of the mystery of life in God. The day is for mystical life, sleep is for mystical death, and each morning is for an awakening into life of resurrection. All formal contemplation is for our ascension into heaven ; each emptying of the mind is for a descent of the Comforter, and therein are tongues of fire.

The external side of the work remains that which it is always, namely, the co-ordination of daily life so that it shall offer not only the least hindrance possible to the purpose, but shall become a part thereof. The inward science is that of the realisation of our presence in God, for perhaps this expression is preferable to the alternative of Brother Lawrence, the practice of the Presence of God—his simplicity and winningness not-withstanding. More correctly, they are complements of one another, the first giving expression to our relation with the Immanence in the universe, and the second to our consciousness of that Immanence within.

These things remind me of another counsel of prudence. The mystic should never say that God is unknowable. He is that in the knowledge of which we grow for ever in ourselves. These words give expression in the categorical and literal sense to the great mystery. Growth therein is growth in the only reality—which is the true self. The same unity, the same self-hood is explored by all who grow and in proportion as they do unfold in this manner. What is the higher pan-theism ? The state in which God is all in all. When does it begin to be realised within us ? When we have begun to be all for God.[1]

The work of Mysticism in our daily life is to prepare the way of the Lord, so that He may dwell within us by an intimate realisation. The *desideratum* is the reign of God in the soul. The state mystical is one in which God is our knowledge, our will and our deed. Thought at the beginning is best fixed on God by way of general intuition. It is in such a manner that the fire is kindled in the heart. On the assumption that this fire is kept burning, it will follow the analogy of fire ; wherever there is food of fuel there it will find nourishment. The general intention will become particular, and the desire of the House of the Lord will eat up the heart. I am seeking here to indicate after what manner the thought will be with us always—by implication, when not expressly.

The state of peace is not beyond the cultivation of any ordered mind, and it is the first step to be taken towards that art which is scarcely to be called an art of thinking in the heart. I am not speaking to the mere

[1] The life-process in true mystical work is the absorption of God. This is the path and the term. It is contemplation, Divine preoccupation and self-emptying : it is love also and the attainment of the God-state. It is the whole doctrine and the whole practice.

worldling, but (*a*) to those who have, on the simple question of values, survived the common temptations and (*b*) who know that all the duties of daily life can be performed efficiently by using the external part of us somewhat as an instrument, in this sense standing in an innermost, apart therefrom. There is a great and saving secret in such a kind of aloofness. Those who know it can stop, or may learn to stop, easily and at will, the working of the instrument which I have named. The powers of our humanity sink down thereby and thereat into a simple repose of consciousness, and we can learn to abide therein, for a shorter or longer space, apart from the external vicissitudes. It is as if the Word of God had uttered its " Peace, be still " upon the deep waters of the soul, so that the soul is for a certain period sealed with peace. But I would counsel the seeker not to be deceived herein, mistaking the beginning for the term ; and he should understand further that it is not to be regarded as in any sense a state of permanence. Things of this kind are aids to reflection, lodges of rest by the way, opportunities for the light to enter consciousness, for the Presence to declare itself.

To declare itself : this also is a statement of the true case ; it has the advantage, moreover, of leaving the question open as to the how of the occurrence—by a development within the consciousness or an infusion from without. John Tauler, or the mystic who wrote under this name in the *Following of the Poor Life of Christ*, gives us certain instructions for the subject here in hand, when he says that communion with God is attained in the unity state of our nature. It must be confessed, however, that the terminology of the context seems exceedingly vague, especially as regards the drawing of the senses inward. It is commonly in our solitudes more fully than in our crowded life that God speaks. In a manner, He is speaking always, but we cannot or do not hear. The language of the senses is

misleading in this respect. The speech is not speech
and the hearing is not hearing. That which is realised
divinely is in a timeless state of consciousness—by which
I mean that its realisation comes in the putting aside
of the time-condition. The essential is stillness of the
senses, and therefore inhibition of the external. The
state is thus silence without, and as God does not speak
within us after the manner of men, the Divine Communication to consciousness is in correspondence with silence
rather than speech ; but we are in reality outside the
pairs of opposites. The only adequate words are that
there is a realisation of God in consciousness, where
realisation can occur alone. Here is a school in which
we can all be graduates, whether we are male or female,
in virginity, espousals or widowhood ; whether we are
men on 'change or a writer like myself of poems and
books through all my days and years, in which memorials
I have forgotten for a moment if the grace of God and
His union are not mentioned on every leaf. The effect
of this spiritual regeneration on the vehicles of our mortal
life is that they cease to be a hindrance on the path of
our inward progress. They do not become arch-natural
or glorified, but they have entered into the rule of
peace with our higher nature.

CHAPTER XIV

SACRAMENTALISM OF OUR INWARD NATURE

THE relation of man to the universe is in analogy with his relation to God. It communicates to him and he is in communion therewith, owing to certain media, channels or sacraments ; but it is to be noted that the last term is not used, or anywhere throughout this work, in its strict philological sense, except in so far as the sense mentioned implies a guarantee of fidelity in a given bond, token or pledge. This in the present connection would signify that the communication of the universe to man after its passage through the media or channels has not undergone such a distortion that it does not represent its source. The media are the senses, and the hypothesis is that of Leibnitz applied in a particular way. We communicate one with another sacramentally through the same channels, and we know in this manner—on the basis of experience—that there are others in our likeness, while they know that we are in theirs. The instituted sacraments exist and are valid in virtue of the same implied representative bond. All sacraments are mysteries, because their communication is of necessity under veils. By the hypothesis God is veiled in Nature, and if there is a distinction between the universe and God, His communication through the senses to the mind is in virtue of a twofold sphere of sacrament and is exceedingly indirect by consequence.[1] Mysticism has

---

[1] The Immanence of God in material things is notwithstanding a chief channel of grace for the overwhelming majority of men. It is in virtue of this that the whole world is sacramental.

postulated, however, the immanence of God in the soul, as through one sacramental channel, which is the bond of the reflex act involved in self-realisation. Practical Mysticism seeks by the suspension of this act to establish direct communication, and its records over the whole world claim that the object has been and may be always accomplished—at least *Deo volante*. While the channels through which we are related to Nature differ therefore from our mode possible of union with the Divine, it is recognised that there is a natural theology in virtue of which we can discern God in His works. The truth of this can be realised apart from formal systems of thought, and gates may open upon great vistas in this manner.

Now, there is another side of the same subject which carries us to a deeper ground. We are manifested to ourselves through two broad channels of thought and feeling, yet are we profoundly conscious that we are not comprehended or exhausted by these modes of being. It is as if our reality exhibited to ourselves in these manners, while leaving inexpressible suggestions behind or beneath. There is no need to specify that feeling is of the sense-world, of our relation to external things rather than to the world within, but it is an inclusive word which represents states of the soul in addition to those of the body—intellectual joy, sorrow, gain, loss and so forth—with love as the crown of all. But I have said that we are shewn forth to ourselves through these two modes ; they are sacramental channels in respect of our proper being, and it is through them also that we flow forth in the attempt to establish relations with God, though the work *ex hypothesi* is effected in their suspension. Whether there is complete suspension is another question—whether we ever really cast out the images of sense and mind or reduce them to a minimum only. The state called that of abiding in the Cloud of Unknowing is one of utter stillness, and may seem therefore to be not less liberated from feeling than from thinking; but we must remember the counsels of the text which lead to that state, and we shall come to see that the Cloud is not one of unfeeling—that it is rather emotion at white heat. Those who depend on emotion almost exclusively do not understand that the quest after knowledge, including the joy of its attainment, has a deep root therein. " The glory of going on and still to be " in a mere bliss-state is one thing; but the beatitude which corresponds to a notion of knowledge possessed in fulness of all completion is another, and to some at least it comes with a higher appeal. There is a further point. The conception of love as desire of union in the satisfaction thereof is apt to overlook the truth that such attainment is itself a world of knowledge set open for our inquisition. The loving contemplation of manifested beauty is a study in suggestion only; beyond it there is the world unknown—yet knowable— of the undeclared beauty within. Of such is Divine contemplation, and God opens to the soul—depth within depth for ever. These are the riches and the beauty of the knowledge of God ; and to know in this sense offers for those who can receive it a greater intimation than to feel simply. Yet the one is not without the other, for the parts and faculties of our nature do not stand alone.

I believe with Plato that the senses are avenues, through which a measure of reality comes in. This is why the conventional mystics are wrong when they seek to arrest and deny the channels of communication, just as ordinary men are wrong when they depend on those channels entirely. In respect of the Immanence, I believe that God is behind the world and that the world shews forth God, there being no other ground for its existence. The veil is thin, for the light is seen everywhere, whence it can be said that the world shines in God and is irradiated by Him. But the veil is dark and thick because of that which we call evil.

I do not intend, therefore, to set aside the offices of emotion, as one who should say that there is nothing further from feeling than the mystical state; but I know on which side—for the time being at least—we can avoid the errors of enthusiasm. The work is one of experience in the soul of man for the attainment, after our separation in the manifest order, of a Divine Union with the One and Eternal Nature. It is ineffable union, and it is not adequately represented by any analogies which we can find among external things. The term oneness is preferable to that of union, and it is of course loosely synonymous with unity—not, however, with identity.

I suppose also that the emotional side of Mysticism—but this is a reverential term, not one of disparagement—would say, and has said indeed substantially and truly, that it is in God alone that desire is attained for ever, without being ever satiated, and that herein is eternal beatitude —the blessed rapture as well as the blessed vision. In sense-language, it is a fruition through all fibres of being of the ever-desired object, above all things desirable. Hereof also is the kind of union with fellow-consciousness which I hold to be the only true realisation of our make-believe unions here below.

It may be asked what remains when thought and feeling have been alike expelled. I speak here in terms of hypothesis only, but that which remains is *mens nuda*, set with undeviating purpose towards God. By the mystical hypothesis also—if I am right regarding emotion —it is then that God manifests. Observe, however, that *mens* does not signify the mind working through brain organs. It is our knowing and self-knowing part alone with itself for the purpose of finding God Who is within, the postulate being that whatsoever is outside consciousness does not exist for us, and we can neither posit nor imagine it. This is why God is realisable only within. Everything that is for us is either rooted in consciousness—e.g. our individual selfhood—or its image abides therein—e.g. the pictures of the universe.

Emotion in its highest form is understood as that which we call by the gracious name of love, though none can pretend that this definition includes its subject. Love is one thing, in whatsoever direction it moves; therefore the love of man for God has this bond of union at least with the love of man for man. There are other likenesses. I think, for example, that the mystery of Divine Life in humanity is a mystery of possession: we have to let ourselves be acquired; all unions are exclusive and jealous as such. The mystical rest in God is in analogy with that ineffable ecstasy when the eyes of the Beloved are open to full light and are looked within. But I have said—in analogy only. Love is catholic in the proper practice of the presence thereof; but in the narrow way of our passions it is made protestant, and we belong to a sect therein, not to the church universal of faithful hearts. The practice of the presence of God is the practice of love's presence. But in all the higher walks of love the suggestion of the senses should be absent, or come only from a very far distance, like the confusion of images amidst music.[1] The fear of God drives many, and this is well; but God's love drives the elect, and this is better. The love of a little child in the sense of Christ is better than all the houses of initiation that are apart from charity. Thus, and in every way, from outward to inward the appeal always moves. We have heard that heaven is a state, and so then is the King of Heaven. Love is also a state, and this is how in its attainment it sets reflex personality aside by suffusion. It is a bliss-state, and so Divine

---

[1] The secret of attainment along this path is, I mean, a love above sense and its quickenings. Yet it begins in sense. Human love may be the nearest way of the desire after union which ultimately reaches out to God. We have to realise after what manner He is there. The Holy of Holies is within the arms of love.

Espousals are not to destroy but to fulfil. The state of aloneness is separation, and the Doctrine of Union was proclaimed when it was first said : " It is not good for the man to be alone." The motive of mystical love is not so much the glory of God as the satisfaction of a mutual need. The central union of the soul with the Divine Being consists, according to Fénelon, in the maintenance of an unbroken continuity of love ; but that which is wanting hereto is the manner of his understanding love. It is obvious, above all things, that love must be on both sides before the term union can be used in respect of it, while the union of mutual love postulates very much more than inheres in the notion of intercourse. Intercourse is, however, in all cases an operation in consciousness, and this is why the nuptial act in physical life is the threshold of a mystery which has been hardly ever crossed in the wantonness of sensuous quickenings and amidst the deadness of emotion towards the higher side. The contemplation of absent beauty is not union, nor can it be postulated indeed of intentness on merely manifest beauty, however absorbing and absorbed. I have spoken of the condition of eye to eye, which is vision in the uttermost degree thereof ; but the only fruitional word is immediacy.

We must be very careful to interpret rightly the counsel to love God only, and the first requirement is to remember His immanence in all things.[1] Love is religion in the beginning of its operation ; religion in its attainment is love realised. God is like all lovers—or rather they are in His likeness—and He wills to be present for

---

[1] We hear of selfless love, impersonal love, and the general love for every one ; but love must be centralised in order to know itself. We need self and more self, that there may be ever more to give, and we need also the object, so that it may be drawn within us. This is true in both the worlds—of God as of man. Here is the path of realisation—as it comes to me in the stillness. But there are many aspects. Let us give no narrow name to " a science both ancient and infinite."

ever in the minds and hearts of those who love Him.
It comes about in this manner that the love of God is
the most personal of all offices. God is immanent
within us,[1] but is asleep for us till we awaken Him, and
it is often a work of many years to learn the secret of
the quickening kiss. It is a secret of joy and tears. The
joy arises from the certainty of His presence in some
chamber of the palace that is within. The tears are
those of sorrow—sorrow for separation and all its ways
of loss, sorrow for the evil which has come about thereby.
The tears that are precious to God are surely such tears
of sorrow; but these also, and surely, are tears of
longing. It may be that we shall yet know others,
which will be tears of bliss in possession. For in the
things of love—both human and Divine—the key-
word of attainment is this holy word—possession. The
Divine Union is a great mystery of ownership, a great
mystery of everlasting giving and receiving. This
mystery is reflected downward. The work which is
good and true in one grade of life is true and good in
another, and herein lies the first ground for the consecration of human love.

All those are far from the truth who say that love
ceases if it be true love in any degree thereof, and I
testify that human love is only lifted higher.[2] If in
God we attain all that is real and pure and holy, it is
certain that human love finds its fruition in Him, so
only that it is pure and holy and real.[3] The triplicity
of these qualities is not voided by the fact that love is
human on the plane of humanity. That is in the law

---

[1] His immanence is His love for us, from the beginning, before the
world was, in His very self.

[2] So it is true in a sense undreamed by Southey that " they sin who
tell us love can die."

[3] Here is another way in which *Dieu est le lien des esprit, comme
l'espace est le lien des corps,* as Malebranche affirms. The extension of
consciousness within this bond is a way for human union.

and the order ; each thing that is capable of consecration receives its hallowing within and without according to its proper nature and the measures thereof. It follows that the true love of the creature is in God and is so attained.[1] Do we counsel a man in his search for the Divine to cease from his love and his duty towards wife and daughter and sister ? Yet this is the love of creatures. The virus of celibate life and its assumptions or implicits has disordered the views of Christendom and confused the true issues on the whole subject.[2] There is one passage in the Apocalypse which seems at the root of the trouble. I know not whether it has another meaning concealed within it, but I do know that I have not as yet found it, and so far as the interdict obtains, my conclusion is that those who *cum mulieribus non sunt coinquinati*, by their own dreams and longings *coinquinati sunt*. The high counsel is to keep the ways of Nature in cleanliness, for these also are ways of grace.[3] In this case, what is the office of love and why is it so essential in the quest ? The answer can be only that search presupposes desire and that there are no true dedications

---

[1] Dean Inge has said truly that the maxim is not " each for self " but " each for all." Let it be noted, however, that " each " is postulated. Before I can work for another, I am. Whatever is implied or expressed by this formula of the self asserted is that which *ex hypothesi* can help the world by holy service and is that also which is looking towards God for its own fulfilment.

[2] Those who have considered the burdens of ascetic tradition under the yoke of the Latin Church, and the confusion of issues therein in those authorised handbooks which constitute the Church's canon of criticism, may well call, in place of the celibate life, for the substitution of the life of chastity in sacramental marriage. I am offering no law for the priesthood, though the intervention of a semi-monastic rule among the secular clergy of Rome, who have taken no monastic vows, leaves much to be said thereon.

[3] While it is not good in itself to abstain from those sex-relations which are part of the law of life, there are cases obviously in which they should or must be renounced for reasons distinct from any common counsels respecting sense-indulgence and so forth.

save in respect of love. We cannot seek properly that which we do not want lovingly. The desire of the House must eat us up before we can look to enter the House. It is love of the world which leads us to quest in the world; it is love of possessions which makes us seek after our own in objects; it is the love of sense-delights which maintains the craving for delight in the sense order. The root of the mystical work is alike in desire and thought; the search is nourished by both; both are in the path of search; and if at the end ✳attainment is reached—as I have said—in a state of *mens nuda*, that state is in marriage with *desiderium nudum*.[1]

The Ven. Augustin Baker has pointed out that the love of creatures which must be overcome is the love✳for themselves without reference to God, " as if we thought them to have a being or subsistence of and in themselves, and not of God only." It is questionable whether such an implicit can be postulated, but the state of unconsecrated affection arises from the materialism of our normal nature and the rule of the senses in darkness of mind, so that God is ignored. The light which shines in such darkness is uplifted by that counsel which I have given already—to love God immanent in human beings, and these utterly therein, for this is the only mode after which one can become, and can deport ourselves, according to the true heroism of love.[2] A world of pure devotion can be opened in this manner, and if thus did

---

[1] If it be advanced—and it has been advanced often—that the attainment of this state has been reached in the past chiefly by people in enforced sexual abstinence, it is not for such reason suspect. It may only accentuate the fact recognised by the Zohar that the mystery of sex is the supreme mystery.

[2] The great need is that we should contemplate love *sub specie divinitatis*. It is everywhere the *latens Deitas*. But love is catholic and therefore *sub speciebus humanis* it is very sure that we are contemplating nothing else.

every man love the woman of his heart, I know scarcely
what paths might be travelled.[1]

The state of rest in God is described by Böhme as that
in which no creature can molest us ; but this notwithstanding, it is assuredly a state of service wherein we can
do good to all that is capable of goodness, while that
which is goodness itself can minister also to us. " If thy
will go into the creature," he says, and it is the beginning
of a discourse on creaturely affection which is in the
common manner of those who would glorify God by
depreciating the work of His hands.[2] But all that this
and the rest come to is that the desire of the heart must
be in God and all other desires must lie within that
union as in a supersensual world. The alternative and
true counsel is to love all things in God which are
capable of being loved in Him.

The face of a beautiful woman contemplated with
eyes open to the Divine Immanence within her is a way
of attainment in God.[3] And if it seem to us in her case
that the veil of manifestation is thinner, be it ours—as a
chief ministry—to awaken that Divine, and we shall
then behold a light which was never on the natural land
or sea. Love is a great transfigurer, descrier and inter-

---

[1] I mean definitely that the path of human love may be that which
leads to God.

[2] We may compare Dutoit-Mambrini, who, Hugenot—or something—as he was, lived, like many Catholic devotional writers of his
approximate period, in an enfeebled quality of ascetic atmosphere. He
says : " The friendships of this world are a reciprocal commerce of self-
love, an exchange, a giving and receiving. They cease when reciprocity
ceases."—Op. cit., II, 242. Another dealer in wholesale statements
mentions that " the friendship of this world is enmity with God."

[3] I mean that the soul of the beloved is part of the blessed vision.
Woman is sacramentum ineffabile. Having tried many ways, we have
found that man is all things ; all things are in man, and a great secret is
to know ourselves in one another. He who looks in the face of his beloved can recite with a full meaning his nosce teipsum to himself. So is
the Home ever near ; the Palace is at hand always ; the garden is behind
our dwelling—could we only realise the proximity.

preter of beauty. In respect of its object, one may say truly: *Vel incomparabile invenit, vel incomparabile facit.* Before we had love we were blind; in love we see.[1] The metamorphosis of the object is in its contemplation, and this is not self-deception but discernment. I hold also that it reacts on the object outwardly by awakening that which is within, so that love beautifies visibly.

I conclude that there is a consecration of human love which raises all ties and relations of this life into a gate and part or mode of our longing for the Divine.[2] Its lesson is to do unto others what we would that in a Divine sense God also should do unto them, remembering that in this manner we look to be a third party and to be joined with them in Him. The love of man and woman in purity may become, along paths like these, a School of Divine Love, so that the body of desire is transmuted. The integration of two personalities in one consciousness by love would be, I think, an unknown door to God.[3]

[1] The eyes that see are the eyes of love, and it is by casting out evil from desire that we can become like God, seeing and desiring only that which is good. The counsel is therefore to love the good things of the Lord in the Land of the Living and to hunger for the beauty of the House. But the Land of the Living is here and now, and this is the House of the Lord.

[2] Between the manifest active and passive of love on the physical plane there lies hidden a *tertium quid* which supersedes and transcends the physical act, and this is that narrow way back which is symbolised by the Garden of Venus. See the essay on this important symbolism of Pausanias in my *Studies in Mysticism.*

[3] There is another point of view on which it is possible to touch here only under reserves, obscurely and as if from a great distance. That secret mystery of union which is accomplished, by a certain hypothesis, between man and woman mystically can be no other than a deep intercourse in mystical consciousness, seeking the same term. This again is the "narrow way" back, and its term is Divine Union attained in common. It is a work upon the Immanence, at first hidden but afterwards manifested in the two natures jointly. It is the uttermost height of attainment open to human love. Of the state itself there are hints

The Way of Divine Union

Sex is therefore a great mystery of grace when it is understood in holiness and when its work is so fulfilled. It has been said that "from the influx of God's love into our heart results the overflow of our love to others," and this is true mystically, on the warrant of the doctrine that "in Him we live, and move, and have our being," as on all the other warrants.[1] But there is also an approximate cause in the humanity of our nature on its physical side. On that side it seems to be true imperatively that the root of love is in the sex-relation, out of which appears to have arisen that love which is not of sex but is still of the human order—love of fatherhood, motherhood and friendship.[2] If this be so, we are brought to the redemption of sex-relations as the first work. It may seem to us that the highest love is sexless, that its place is where there is "neither marrying nor giving in marriage"; but after reflection in the heart we shall see that this phrase has a deeper content than appears in the accepted and tolerable surface-meaning. We must acknowledge in any case that love, as postulated at its highest, has many substitutes among us which are not to be called counterfeit, and they have been hallowed by sacramental law, with its plenary power of indulgence.[3]

but no records, and my testimony must be understood as that of the seeing mind and a speaking state of heart. It is of the poet's vision, for the poet knows and sees, both with and above experience.

[1] St. Bonaventura says that the perfect love of the creature is attained subsequently to the perfect love of God.—*The Goad of Divine Love*, ii. § 6. The word perfect means in kind, degree, depth and height : it is greater and fuller than is possible in the natural states.

[2] Its higher correspondence is Divine Love, or the love for that which is Divine.

[3] We read in many books of the Mysteries, and we find the same thing everywhere ; but as it is variously expressed so there are diverse degrees of perfection. I do not know that those can rank as the highest which are offered like a garland of roses from the rose-garden of Sufic mystics and poets. It is well to remember that the bread and wine which are the veils of the Eucharist are pure and beautiful. But should any one discourse of these semblances too ardently there would be for him and

Sacramentalism of our Inward Nature

The mystery of sex is part of the cosmic mystery. The keys of Nature are male and female. The union below is a sacrament of the union that is above.[1] Manifestation is male and female, illustrated by a thousand analogies, from the beginnings in active and passive to their loftiest expression in man and woman. That which is sympathy in the lower is love in the higher kingdom. Love is the secret on earth, and it is the secret in the Kingdom of Heaven. For us and for our elevation, the human affections are the base of all, working from the manifest to the unmanifest.[2]

I conclude hereon as follows: The Kingdom is below and the Great Crown is above; between them there lies the high path of attainment. The lesson is that our

those who followed him a cloud on the sanctuary of the sacrament. It is after the same manner with those who seek to express the Mysteries of Divine Love too obviously in the terms of the outward body of the beloved. The desire of the union had entered into the Persian heart but it did not absorb the heart entirely, because in spite of great transmutations the roots of the house of emotion remained too deeply in the sphere of sense. However, the Persian poets have not been so far translated by one who is also a poet, and they have not therefore entered into the manifestation of literature, so far as the western world is concerned. We are waiting for the voice of the cushat dove to be heard in this land.

[1] We are ever passive to God, and ever the soul of man is in search of her bridegroom.

[2] It is true, excellent and perfect in its own degree when " they two " become " one flesh "; but the true marriages are when male and female become one soul. The body is the gate, and that gate must open. It is thus that the union in flesh can become an efficacious sacrament, through which souls may be intromitted into another union. The *signum* gives place to *signatum*, but the point is that *signum* is the way There may come a time when it has served its purpose and is thereafter suspended in a perfectly natural order. I do not affirm that this is the only way : it is the most difficult of all to follow because of the over-ruling power of the sense-life. That which it secures by my hypothesis is the co-attainment of two in Divine Consciousness—the union of one with another, each in God and God in each, so that this one is not on the path when the other has arrived, nor is one in the depths while the other has scaled the heights.

marriages—being all our loving relations—should be made on earth so only that they may be ratified above by a fulfilment in the divine sense. We take our lawful pledges in this life, and while we keep them in faith here God is, in our regard, performing His covenant in Heaven. There is a common root of human and Divine Love, and all life is a symbolism of marriages. Beyond those kindlings which belong to the sphere of sense another consideration of love is possible. I have spoken elsewhere on my own part of that love which is without the body of desire, but love has a spiritual body in another region of our nature, and this is a vesture and organ of divine desire. The conclusion is that there is a sanctity of the body of our humanity, considered as the place of the sacraments, the place of the manifestation of sacraments, the place of their reception. The doctrine once and again is that God is within, and by virtue of this—as I have sought to indicate otherwise—every man is a centre of the universe, a centre for the immanent God.

CHAPTER XV

OF SAVING GRACE IN THE CHURCHES

THE great rites of the great official religions go on without intermission from season to season through the years and generations. It is now nearly sixty years since the Abbé Constant, commenting on the same fact, said that more and more we feel the need of religion. There is a sense of vacancy, as if the House of God were empty and the high offices made void. The consciousness of that something which seems wanting is keener to-day than it was at the period which has been mentioned. It is indefinitely keener than when Matthew Arnold observed that we could neither dispense with Christianity nor be satisfied with it as it was—or, let me add, as it now is. The five wounds of the Church which were diagnosed by Rosmini call—as we have seen—to be understood at the present day in a different and wider sense. In that sense they are not all characteristic any longer of Latin Christianity only, but of all the ecclesiastical forms. It might be said that the Churches have not changed, except that some are more earnest; and the inference would then be that the conditions have altered in humanity. The reference in any case is not to the common indifference which prevails still, nor is it suggested that any vague personality which is described as the Man in the Street is either conscious of deficiency in ministration or aware—to a marked extent—that he is somehow wanting in himself. Nor again is the reference merely to scientific materialism in its strongholds, for certain trumpets have sounded and these forts are falling.

The growing craving and the growing sense that there is somehow no adequate nourishment characterise other classes than the man of science and the people of the crowd, though among these also it is found. The *fides quærens intellectum* goes on its quest in vain for the most part, and a search for the ground of faith finds it less and less possible to discern that ground in authority. The zeal of the House of Theology is a sincere and holy zeal. It is receiving exemplification continually in memorable works and in many more which are good within their especial limits, even when they can scarcely lay claim to a high place among intellectual achievements. They offer much that one is glad to have seen, much that is of wholesome and cleanly service in the lesser ways. Nearly all of them raise inevitably larger aspects of the problems with which they attempt to deal, and this is likely to continue until some great new angel of schools unknown to the past shall furnish a more perfect and intelligible statement of Christian doctrine. It has long ceased to embrace the whole field of spiritual consciousness: perhaps it would be more true to say that a vast part of it does not enter the field. Those of us who continue to love it, and in some sense to hold thereby, are ever seeking—but so far in vain for ever—to stretch the old glorious canvas so that it shall cover that which over-laps the embroidered veil. It is rather like faith itself, in the common and insufficient understanding thereof. We have heard of the venture of faith and its possible confirmation by the findings of reason ; but we know in our hearts that the great need is a light on that clouded way wherein and whereby the high speculation of doctrine can reach some term of demonstration in experience within.

With the official churches we may lament by the waters of Babylon, seeing that they are rather there than in Zion ; but we need not desert them in Babylon, though we may not only remember Zion but may have seen it in visions of our own on the high hill. It seems to me, further, that much current criticism of religion, in its recognised sphere, including the higher criticism, is the valuation by those who do not know—in the sense of interior experience—of that which above most things calls for inward and direct knowledge—or, in other words, for the criticism of mystical perception. As such, it is no part of our concern. It may be that dogma is passing through that kind of dissolution which will lead onward to its resurrection in a new or transformed body of our desire after Divine Attainment. In any case, the spirit of so-called liberal Christianity sets us free from more than it designs, including the yoke that once was sweet and the burden which was once light. But it is comparable to physical science *per se*, because it cannot offer us the true charter of our liberty. If it could, we should be rather in the place of attainment than in that of search.

Let us look at it from another standpoint, for in a wider sense than was included by the old phrase there is a *consensus omnium sanctorum.* Whether in the East or the West, like " the fairy-gifted poet," we may behold the same thing everywhere, in the things of religion— as in the world outside. All Christian churches are an external symbol or type of that church of plenary grace which is entered only from within. All other great faiths are spokesmen, after their own manner, of that ancient, ever new, truth and beauty, the subsistence of which has been declared to us from the beginning of things. There is not one of us who—in deeper or higher moments—has not heard its voice speaking in the centre of his heart. The record of the experience of religion is everywhere : there is no place too low or too exalted, no path too far from ours, but the still witness is there. Above all, in the most unexpected manner, we may find it at our own doors, in the house of our neighbour and in the room which is next to this. We may find it, as I have said, and suddenly—perhaps outside expectation—in the witness of our personal hearts. Sometimes it is heard audibly even at the corners of our streets, as a clouded testimony rising in the consciousness of some Salvation Army or other itinerant preacher. These things shew that there is a Holy Spirit in the Churches which gives life to the valid forms ; here is the warrant of the mystic for maintaining the official forms in the light and grace of the Spirit, leaving the official spokesmen of authority to go their own way.[1]

On the other hand, we have known from the beginning the inadequacy of merely literal doctrine, though it is not for the current reasons. The root goes much deeper than any common plummets of the mental sense. We have known also—how often !—that the preachers have no office and their audience have no ears. Yet the Christian mystic can still say his *Credo in Unum Deum* and the whole of the great symbol, without one tittle of variation. The truth is that Christian doctrine—and that, moreover, of all the great religions—is a sequence of sacramental phenomena in the mind-world—like the material universe itself. But, fortunately for the life of the soul, it is not so difficult to approach the noumena which lie behind it as it is to enter the noumenal world which is behind things that—being physical—are outside ourselves. The door of religion is the door

---

[1] The consecrations of personal life have been in Church care through the centuries, and preparations for the path generally. The churches constitute the path up to the point which I have mentioned. Thereafter it is of Christ and God—as if one said man to man. For us in the West, the beginning should be, therefore, in the churches, though a few who travel far are joined on in the spirit only and not in the letter. In other symbolism, they are united in the soul, not in the body. But the normal and more natural way is *per signum ad signatum*—as the soul of the beloved is reached most easily, most fully, and perfectly through the body of her.

which opens, most naturally into the region of reality.[1] But its outward doctrinal forms must be so re-expressed that every thoughtful man who is disposed towards spiritual things shall be able to take them into his mind's life, that they may work like a leaven therein.

It may be said in this connection that Christianity is not so much a doctrine of theology as the high history of an experience. The Lord Buddha preached a doctrine and Zarathustra taught a philosophy, and Krishna's legend is great, glorious, wonderful. These and that which they represented have held high offices in the leading of men ; they have drawn myriads into salvation ; but the Christ is a path and a life in the palmary sense of the words. It is as if the remote, magnificent myth and symbol of Osiris had taken flesh in a sense unrealised by symbol and by myth. Whether we regard the Christ story as that of an historical personality or as an expounded gospel of experience in the inward spirit, it is equally true to affirm that all the grand old myths have found their centre in Him, and in Him were all preceding Masters incarnate. He silenced the old oracles because He fulfilled them. The reason is that the story of Palestine is that of every soul in its progress to life in God. The incarnation is the great mystery of true witness in Christendom : it is our title, our warrant, our earnest. That as which the soul must be reborn is Christ. This is the mystical basis of all Christology, and this is the sacred sense in which it stands apart from merely official doctrine.

The Churches—as I have indicated—are a means of salvation to the world at large, and considered as a gate they are scarcely less essential than that of morality,

[1] It was said by R. Greaves Pitville (quoted by Walton, pp. 28, 29) that creation is an appendix of the Church, following which Walton said on his own part that Christ is the substance, while the rock is a shadow. There is assuredly one sense in which the Church is the Divine Immanence unfolding at a specific centre.

which is equivalent to affirming that our path—in the great majority of cases—lies through the official temples. It is best for a man to begin in his own spiritual home, and it is so much the harder for him if he have none from which to start. The prayer that he learned at his mother's knee is no doubtful point of departure for a journey which ends in God. There is certainly no better mode of entrance offered than that of the Churches, though we can at need be joined on to the path from other points. There is a sense, as we have seen, in which all roads lead, on the understanding that where they lead is to the path. Progress along that path is not a forsaking of the Church but an entrance into its higher ministry. Yet the Church transforms with us—for us and in us.

As regards the question of authority, we must remember that this is of necessity within a defined province—so far as authority is external—and there may come a time when the soul proceeds beyond it, which is without prejudice to its rule within the province. In that illimitable region beyond one has to say, with great reverence, that the external authority passes into automatic suspension, or rather exists not. The keepers of the literal word rule in the world of the letter, but beyond it there is another kingdom. If there comes a time in the experience of the individual soul when the living Christ is found abiding within and—seeing that He has been known by other names in all ages of the world—if then the historicity problem has ceased to signify, the witness of the Church has been superseded, though it may have borne true testimony on the historicity question.

The Churches are therefore—as I have said also—the Wardens of Holy Gates, great witnesses to the logical understanding and guides for normal life in the world. Their pageants are fruitful aids to reflection and they are means for the communication of that grace which flows in from all quarters ;[1] but there is a stage at which these offices either end or are changed over. This stage is indicated by Molinos in terms that differ from mine, and his condemnation is instructive as an object-lesson, though the statement in no sense signifies that the Quietists were in all things right, or that the Church was wrong utterly in the action taken—if considered as a question of policy. She regarded her titles as in jeopardy, which in any real and essential sense was far from the fact, but Molinos was liable to misconstruction, and this was the danger of his teaching. It would have been not less dangerous had anyone come forward to establish a distinction between literal Church doctrine and its mystical aspects and understanding. Such a distinction may be right—as indeed there is no question, for the letter is not the spirit—and Molinos was right, in essence if not in accidents.

Sacramental Nature being the normal minister of man, and religion being also sacramental, that Church which possesses the fullest ministry of sacraments is the one that is most in harmony with the Divine Order. Here, in this material age, amidst the clash of modern interests, it is very difficult to speak of these high inquiries. They sound fantastic, as if a man should set forth to find Avalon in the West-Country, or the enchanted City of Hud. It is, however, with the antithesis of such an enterprise that I am concerned here. As a mystic I carry an eirenicon in my heart for all the faiths, and I have undertaken no speculative or extravagant quest. I believe that the sacramentalism

---

[1] I might tell those who would listen how the chief offices of the Church are symbolised and its Holy Hours. Great things lie hidden in the whole period of its schooling, in those classes and degrees which are distinguished as Faith, Hope and Charity, in Cardinal Virtues, Counsels of Perfection, Gifts and Fruits of the Spirit. These things and many others call to be studied after a new manner, in the living sense and not in that of conventions and of formalism.

of the Christian scheme holds up the most perfect glass of reflection to the mystery of Divine Attainment in consciousness, and in this sense that the Church comprehends — however imperfectly delineated — the catholic scheme of our return into union. But I know that there are mysteries which are not of this fold, and that it is given unto man to find the jewel of redemption in more than one Holy Place. Unfortunately, the people who listen in the churches and frequent their Rites are not as a body qualified to do more than take Rites literally, nor to receive sacraments in a deeper sense than that of their official administration.

The greatness of the Christian Church centres in this fact, that it is the first religion which has taken the offices of human life and has shewn forth those graces which may abide within them. It has left much to be done hereafter along this line by the way of extension ; it might have done more and better within its own measures ; but it has made a good beginning. Explicated by ecclesiastical observances but implied in Nature, all Church offices constitute a great sacramental system of the instituted kind, and yet with all the devotional and all the teaching literature there has never been a full . grip of sacramental doctrine. Much has been missed of this character in the body-general of ritual and in all the hills of symbolism with which the Church has stayed up spiritual life. Protestantism is not worth speaking of in this connection, being a lean method of observance and worship which finds the soul in nudity and cares for it without clothing it.[1] The system reached its apex in the set of social, artistic, moral and religious sentiments, thought and atmosphere belonging to the early Victorian period.[2] It is now exanimate, though the *corpus vile*

---

[1] The beginning of our salvation from the all-wretchedness of this state and system came about unquestionably through the Restoration of the Roman Hierarchy in Great Britain and Ireland.

[2] I suppose that the Reformation was governed by a certain awkward

suffers an occasional galvanism. It is in need of what it will obtain scarcely, that is, decent burial, for this kind of dead is left to bury its dead, and there are no places of consecrated thought wherein it can be put to rest. Occasional memories concerning it recall us the more urgently to those great things, intimations of which have been with us from the beginning.

In contrasting the natural and instituted sacraments we must remember that the latter depend from the former in virtue of the outward sign. By the doctrinal hypothesis concerning them, the latter transcend the former, and this is a case in which doctrine is reinforced by higher understanding of the rational mind.[1] There are two grounds hereof. Recognising the sacramentalism of Nature, the mind has raised up certain material elements, certain offices of life, and has sanctified them in a particular sense and manner. In other words, the

and clouded instinct over its reduction of the instituted sacraments to the Water of Baptism and the Bread and Wine of the Eucharist. It realised in an obtuse manner that these matters of sacrament are among the most direct types in Nature. It might have been forgiven for a comparatively honest attempt to improve the circle of belief by curtailing its dimensions, and for characterising as abuses whatsoever did not happen to coincide with its particular scheme. Having excluded marriage, however, from the harmony of the instituted sacraments, it published unconsciously the full value of its titles. It is understood, of course, that, except for a small number of the elect therein—and these had tongues of silence—the Churches, orthodox and otherwise, knew nothing officially at the period. Had they known what they held in their hands and the treasures of which they were guardians, it is obvious that no reformation would have stood one chance of an audience. But on the external side at least the Church had become a worldly institution in competition with the other institutions and seeking predominance over them in their own worldly sense.

[1] The instituted sacraments can be received after two manners, of which the one is as signs only but the other as living channels. The one is a communication of the symbol, the other of an efficacy within. The Eucharist is the greatest of all because it is the sacrament of mystical marriage. In its symbolism therefore it depends from earthly marriage, is rooted therein and arises therefrom.

chief instituted sacraments are those of Nature exalted to what is signified by an arch-natural degree. This is in all respects the office of the Divine, as the Divine is realised in man, and it speaks with golden tongues concerning the transfiguration of Nature which can be operated from within ourselves. It comes about in this manner that the worlds of art and literature are ranged about the sacramental concept as about a centre.

From another point of view, all the sacraments are natural and all are instituted, whether in Nature or Grace, for it is man who constitutes them by recognition and reception in his consciousness. The distinction between Nature and Grace is a symbolical distinction, and is significant of the essential correspondence and necessary communication between the Divine Immanence in man and the universe. There is hence no need to say that the distinction does not illustrate a line of clear demarcation, save in respect of usage, and here it is a false distinction. When properly understood, Nature is in all Grace and all Grace is in Nature. God is implied in His own orders everywhere. They belong to one another, and they interpenetrate one another. In a certain degree of our consciousness the things which are of Nature are raised above that which for others is their normal sphere, and they shew forth the undisguised offices of Grace. But it is not they which have changed; it is our perception.

The *signum* is the outward meaning and *signatum* is the meaning within: the use of these words indicate, a relation according to the mode of analogy and the doctrine of correspondence is recognised by Christian theology as fully as in the Hermetic writings or Zoharic literature. It is natural sacraments which have become instituted in the sacramental scheme of Christendom, and I have mentioned that there are many others which still await institution. We may be priests all of us after this manner, and some of us do so institute continually, according to our personal and temperamental needs and insight.

Each of the seven sacraments is a certain gate of entrance to a world not realised, and perhaps there are none of these worlds so unknown in respect of possibilities as that which can be entered by marriage, though it is implied of necessity in sacramental doctrine that it is a Divine Path. The ineffable world of union and the whole scheme of redemption are the *signatum* affirmed by this *signum*. It is destined yet to become a peculiar work of sanctification, if the hope of manifested perfection is not of mere dream. In the solidarity of our human personality, the hand is not apart from the eye, nor the foot from the seat of the will; the physical centre of sense is rightly and sacredly the straight road to the heart, and the act of communication therein is an arrow's flight thereto. It is the most holy sacrament of chastity in the work of natural union. It is the abiding and indwelling sacrament; it is the exemplified mystery of love. It is the meeting-point in consciousness of instituted and natural sacraments, and it is herein above all that the Sacramental system of Nature may be taken up and transmuted. It shews otherwise that the life of true mystical doctrine does not destroy, but fulfil the offices of Nature and the senses.[1]

That which is foreshadowed *ex hypothesi* by espousals is *ex hypothesi* communicated by the Eucharist. That which is externalised on the physical plane in marriage by two becoming one flesh is internalised in the Supper of the Lord.[2] The sacraments are not therefore isolated one from another, but rather support each other. The intimations which it has been given me to express on

---

[1] The language of highest intimation concerning the state of interior union was derived by St. Thomas from the analogies of nuptial union, and it represents the completion which is only yearned for here.

[2] It is the great significator of solidarity, communion, the redemption of one by another.

the Eucharistic Mystery will be found in some other books, more especially concerning the field which lies beyond the normal consciousness of literal Church doctrine. I wish only to add here that this sacrament— nor is it the only one—is in its proper realisation a daily ministry.[1] There are indeed seven great sacraments which enring all our life. He Who said " Do this in remembrance of Me " can be remembered at the morning meal, and every evening refreshment may become a Supper of the Lord. In our days of fast they will keep us in the path of the Cross, and in our festivals they will remind us of the life of glory. Truly the Eucharist can be taken by the elect in all their daily bread, and for them the universe itself is as a Sacramental Rite. There is nourishment through all the channels of the senses, and it depends upon us whether it shall prove living food. Man is his own priest when he knows how to consecrate elements unto this high end ; but his inherent office is without prejudice to other priest-hoods. It is the same with the natural sacraments, as these have been distinguished here. If owing to the changing power of consciousness operating upon those which have been instituted for the more especial needs of the soul, these others are for the most part like shadows of those, he who has been sanctified by the one sequence can take up the other and transmute it. The efficacy of every sacrament depends then upon us and on no priest other than ourselves. The Eucharist is but an outward sign if we are only an outward sign to ourselves. It is valid if our realisation is valid, and it is super-efficacious if we have attained ourselves. The great Masses are to come for each one of us.

There are high issues of dedication and of hallowing in Holy Orders by the realisation of which we may be ordained—all of us—a holy people and an elect priest-

---

[1] Because the possible transmutation of life is typified by the Bread and Wine which become the Eucharist.

hood—again without prejudice to the Orders of official priesthood. I am speaking of a particular and perhaps rare attainment in the spirit and the mind, wherein we can maintain for ever the grace of this sacrament. The doctrine of Apostolical succession implied in the instituted Sacrament can be understood mystically as a type of that sanctity and sonship which belong to the personal self, as a type also of the consequent dignity which abides in our human nature. Both are set forth by the sealing, the anointing and other ceremonial processes in the Rite of Ordination. As regards the expounded word in connection with priestly ministry, we know that the vocations cannot be limited and that there are therefore many priesthoods. There is an apostolate and priesthood in literature which are great and true and holy. But, once more, the special priesthoods should not be open to intrusion, because each legitimacy has its inherent titles and rights. I believe in my heart that this statement has a deeper side than that of *la haute convenance*, to which it will be ascribed, and there may be exceptional calls that suspend the implied counsel.

Of the seven sacraments two are particular in their present administration and five are catholic. Those which are particular, being Extreme Unction and Holy Orders, have a wider field than is recognised by the mind of the Churches. There is another spiritual side of Extreme Unction, by which it is applied to the health of the soul in the sense of the forgiveness of sins, and it is connected therefore with Penance. So also the Unction which flows upon us in contemplation can have the grace of Extreme Unction and can prepare us for mystical death.

Of the five other sacraments there are three which cover the whole ground. Baptism is a sacrament of life : officially speaking, it is received once and for all. Being perhaps of all the most obvious, it is that which most enters into the hiddenness. It belongs really to the higher understanding of *Lavabo Inter Innocentes Manus Meas*, about which it may be said (*a*) that while it does not belong to the accepted side of instituted sacramentalism, yet (*b*) it exceeds the simple symbolism which may be held to inhere in the ordinary washing of hands and other lustrations. All these are types of cleansing and purification within. For such reason did Christ wash the feet of His disciples. It is the purgation of the life of offence. The use of holy water in Churches signifies the renewal of baptismal vows. The life of the Christian mystic is a life of baptism, as it is—in another sense—a life of crucifixion. It is the custody of the baptismal robe and the priestly character therein, as shewn by the laying of the priest's stole on the body of the infant.

In conclusion, our aspirations must confirm our works, as our works must confirm, realise and then enlarge our aspirations. When we say in our hearts, " Come, Holy Ghost, Creator, come," there may take place that Descent of the Spirit by which we shall be confirmed in sanctity. There is no need that I should speak of Penance and the repentance implied thereby. The axiom concerning it is always that the Kingdom of God is at hand. It abides with us in every stage and aspect of the contrite heart, and this is the Gate of the Kingdom of Heaven.

Such in brief outline is the life of the official sacraments in man. It is by us that they exist as such ; it is in us that they are made alive ; and of those who follow this path it is said that they are seekers after God. In fine it is of very truth that in this path they shall find. They shall find The Seven Gifts of the Spirit, which are in correspondence with the seven recognised sacraments. They shall learn after what manner The Twelve Fruits of the Spirit are born from these, being Twelve Stones of that Holy City which is built up within us.

CHAPTER XVI

THE WAY OF ATTAINMENT

LOOKING back upon the last four chapters, they will be found to constitute a preliminary survey of the field which lies before those who are conscious within them of a call to the realisation of Divine Things, and that they offer no impossible task to anyone who feels that call. They are of states which can be attained in this world, with a little love in the heart for God and His realities—almost an elementary dedication. They are addressed more especially to men and women who are drawn already to self-culture on the spiritual side and are either God's lovers or desire to be written down in their own hearts as such. I believe that there has been actually a promised clearance of the path in this respect. I have not meant to shew people how we can make the best of both worlds, but to this it comes of necessity, because the one is not without the other in the true things of our spirit. They will see that to attain the very end of Mysticism there is one thing only needed, and this is love.[1] The old counsels are clothed by it in another body of language. Whether they concern denudation of spirit, conformity of mind, the state of resignation, attitude towards God and the world, the

---

[1] The beginning of all is in the loving thought of God; the continuance of the work is in the loving thought of God; and out of that loving thought does the work never move. The prophet Jeremiah calls it thinking in the heart, and he adds that all the land is desolate for want thereof. This is an exact diagnosis and a statement of the whole difference between "the desert and the sown."

redirection of purpose in life, one and all are—in their proper understanding—the work of love. It is this "inner impulse" which rends the veil of the "old husk." Love conforms the whole man with its object. It is in God's love that we know God's will, and the difficulty would be not to do it. There are no conventional ordinances and no practices. Love has no part in formalities. The work is to become love, and then naturally, sweetly, insensibly all the self-fulfilment which is our motive through all life is changed over into the love-object. An utter consecration follows, a re-ordination of life and mind, and the state which is called mystical is maintained without let or hindrance in the world and its cities, even as in the House of God and the Secret House of the Heart. For love transforms the valid and efficacious side of all its sacraments.

It follows that the master-key is in our hands,[1] and here at the end of all we must seek, under God, to open the door of the King's Treasury. The intimations of this final chapter are addressed to those who are so stirred and quickened within them that they are with child of an all-embracing Divine Love. I must tell them how it shall be with them when the Child has been born within. There are no two worlds for them. There is one world of love. There is no dividing line between the love of God and man, for man is loved in God and God in man. There is no distinction of present life from life to come. There is one life of love. Even that gulf which separates time from eternity for the rational intellect gives signs of

[1] The transmuter also is within us and the Watcher. There are gates to be opened within us which lead into the attainment of all desire in the order that is called absolute. It is so called because after its attainment all that we understand by the soul's dream has passed into the soul's reality. The soul has wings as the white ship has sails, and the art of all arts is their unfolding. This secret is part of that loving mystery which is called contemplation.

closing up, because love is in the now-state and without change or vicissitude as regards its inward essence. In these and in other respects, on every side of us, are barriers burned away. We can take in succession the most cryptic aspects of mystical theology, as it has been studied in these pages, and the fact will be illustrated by each. With the key of love in our hands we shall find that direction in which the solution of Dionysian problems was said to lie.[1] The so-called nullity mode and the voidness are not an intellectual but a love-state, and the stillness is that of love. So also the transcendent manner in which God is said to be known is a manner of love.[2] It is the love of love, for and within love, the contemplation—or worshipful loving—of the absolute Loving Beauty.[3] There is no casting out of images in this state by an unrealisable act of concentration—as if *per impossibile*—but more and more they "fold up their tents like the Arabs." It becomes unnecessary to investigate that almost desperate question whether they are cast out in reality. Amidst an ever-increasing love and engrossment in desire of God, they have withdrawn, as of their own accord. They are people of the threshold and intrude no longer to interrupt the one preoccupation. The one Image remains, and if it be true that this also must dissolve, that in which it dissolves is love. In the sense of the logical faculty there are of course no "imageless ideas," but there are realisations or states of being; there is an abiding in God as love, and in love as God, which is a being-state, and it "gives up no form." Hence it may be said that there can be no image in perfect love. It is then *mens nuda* and that *desiderium nudum* which is *per ipsum et cum ipso*. To reach over to the meaning of this is to understand what was intended by the strange Dionysian formula concerning Divine Darkness and that which supervenes—which is not light, though the mind, ever moving

[1] See p. 50.   [2] P. 52.   [3] Compare p. 67.

between the opposites of things, is so driven to formulate
—that is, love in its living essence. The truth about
this empty state—which is found, as I have said, to be
not void but *plenum*—is that the image becomes us, and
by an ineffable exchange we become it. This is to say
that we are love henceforth, and we stand then unawares
on the threshold of the Great Work.

We shall discern what is meant by my allusion to a
Higher Pantheism ;[1] it is not that of Tennyson but an
all for God in love. The experimental act of love to
which St. Thomas alludes is an immersion in the love-
object until thinker and thought are one. It is this
which opens what I have called—speaking in symbolism
—the Door of Union.[2] We shall understand the deep
sense in which I have said that the self contains that
which it conceives[3]—e.g. Love—not as a picture in the
mind but in its own being.[4] We conceive God in love and
within us He abides as love. In proportion as we grow
in His love, it may be said that God increases within us
—we in His knowledge and He as our knowledge in Him.
To the depth of the riches of this knowledge the great
witness has been given. We shall understand also after
another and better manner the multiple confusions on
lower and higher personality,[5] which are simply modes
of our being. This too is a question of separation and
union. The lower personality is being which is not in
the love-state. In the latter we dwell on what the Ven.
Augustin Baker calls the Height of our Spirit. The
higher personality is literally in love, and this is union,
which grows from more to more, until that is reached
which—albeit with a full sense of imperfect expression—
we call attainment, a state final of being, and therein a
still beatitude, a realisation of all. So does that God

---

[1] P. 111.   [2] P. 131.   [3] *Ibid.*

[4] We may conceive an image of some person whom we are about to
meet for the first time, only to find that it is very far from the truth.

[5] Pp. 147, 148.

Who Is recompense those who seek Him out. It is love in spiritual consummation. Preparation,[1] path and goal are all modes of our one being. The threshold is love possessing all the fibres and raised into a white heat of stillness ; but when that threshold is passed I can say only in my poverty what was said by him whom the Spirit inspired, that " it hath not entered into the heart of man to conceive what God hath prepared for those who love Him." But I do know the veil of what is prepared and where to seek it, for out of his own sanctuary shall no man go onhis journey Godward. Castaniza calls the state a transformation in God.[2]

Now, we have seen further that sanctity is the condition of attainment, while growth therein is indubitably what has been called growth in the likeness of God. But the qualities of sanctity—about which I said that we must seek a canon of criticism[3]—do here unfold themselves without search upon our part. They are qualities of love. There is no holiness apart from love, and all holiness is therein. So also are the fulfilled counsels of perfection[4] in the second birth of these. (a) Voluntary poverty, because love empties itself, is filled and empties again for ever. It possesses all things in its own attained state of being and gives all things always as the condition of that possession. (b) Perpetual chastity, because the soul can have no other spouse than God, and in that mystical marriage can alone fulfil the valid earthly unions. (c) Entire obedience, which is the direction of the will towards union and the performance of its covenants. These things are mysteries of regeneration,[5] from the birth of love, which for the soul is rebirth therein,[6] through that regenerate life which is love and is led in

---

[1] P. 149. [2] P. 150. [3] P. 151.
[4] P. 152. [5] Compare p. 187.
[6] Compare p. 184. It is obvious that Christ can be born in the soul only as a regeneration of the soul itself. This is one of the defects in the Christ-Life formula and symbolism.

love, to the mystical death that precedes the union, being the dissolution of all that hinders, and self-realisation in God as love and in love as God substituted for the normal reflex act, so that there is a virtual becoming into God, which orthodox theology has not feared to call deification. Thereafter is a resurrection in love, for I pledge my life that at this point, and all about it, things which exceed expression come to pass " in a moment, in the twinkling of an eye." We do not all die—except mystically—to reach this point, but change only therein.[1]

Finally, the sinking of the self-will in the will of God is only a work of love. We cannot escape it in love, and outside this we cannot proceed to any part of the work, not even if we had that kind of inclination which sometimes assumes but does not deserve the name of will. The reason is that then the Divine Will is to us as a sealed mystery. The difficulty is to reach the super-eminent grade of love. It is this precisely which has justified me

---

[1] There is a certain crude analogy between these symbolical stages and the alternative sequence in spiritual alchemy, which affirms that the power of all transmutation is within us, and there is the Tingeing Stone. But that Stone itself must be tinged before it can communicate tincture, and the tingeing is called Grace. There are three stages of the process : (*a*) Mortification, for that which can die must die ; (*b*) the Black State, being that of death completed, and these two are the work of sufficing grace ; (*c*) the White State, which is a work of plenary grace ; (*d*) the Red State, or the work of super-essential grace. In the Black State the unredeemed life of sense reaches its term ; the White State is the manifestation of pure soul through all the vehicles ; but the Red State is that of the Spirit in its splendour, and this is the Christ-Spirit, working also in the vehicles, the state of espousals and union, of redemption by the mystical blood of Christ. This is the Great Mystery of the Sanctuary, the Second Advent, the return of the personal Christ. But all things are within, the matter and the principle of tincture, the Spirit and the Redeeming blood. So also sanctity is born within and does not enter from without. This is why the alchemists said that gold grows, and that from which it grows is an inward seed. Grace grows also; sufficing, plenary, super-essential, it moves from state to state in a grade ascending. When some mystics speculate whether their term is attainable otherwise than by a free gift of God, the maxim that God is within still remains and obtains.

from the beginning in affirming that the mystical work is the hardest enterprise which can be undertaken by the human soul. But the grade reached, it is then *ludus puerorum*. Then *facilis* indeed is the *ascensus superni*.[1] The supernal is with us and in us.

It is clear at this stage that the work of deification is the work of love, and that we have passed beyond anything with which it can be said that the world at large is concerned when it would put itself on the side of God. That which must follow can be addressed only to those who either see or are devoted without reservation to the attainment of a state in which they should see with their own inward eyes that God is for them all things, is the one desire, the one love-object, the one intent and purpose, while that whatsoever which belongs to them in the external ways—life and the call of life, duty and state therein—is understood as belonging to them only in God. The postulants for this grade of being must realise that they can reach it only in love. It is neither a matter of doing nor of not doing, though something of both may follow by way of consequence.[2] That is in the hands of love and is meted to no two persons after quite the same manner. The question is—can they so love that they can enter and abide in this mode ? Until this question is answered in the affirmative sense by very experience they are in God's porch or sanctuary, not in His Holy of Holies. But if the preoccupation and absorption are such that they stand upon the threshold which I have mentioned, or have indeed crossed it, the secret work of the Great Experiment is actually going on within

[1] P. 256.

[2] There can be no arbitrary formulae, either as to path or attainment. The mystical work is the most individual of all operations, and the dealings between man and God can never be comprehended by one uniform process, because on the side of humanity, no two operators are in more than general likeness. For each of us the Holy of Holies, or place of attainment, is within, but the mode under which it is entered varies with every soul who follows the path of attainment.

them, and this means that there is something in the course of removing its difficulties—as it were, an insensible change in what I have called our mode of self-knowledge. On the authority of the Angel of the Schools, I have said that God knows Himself immediately in an essential activity of cognition, without passage from subject to object, and He is therefore in a state of absolute unity, while we are in separation from ourselves, because transition from subject to object is involved by the reflex act in which the self is realised.[1] It will be seen that these two modes are in analogy by their opposition only ; we are in separation from God as well as from ourselves therein ; but another state of being is possible for us if Divine Union is possible, as all mystics testify on the basis of experience. This is the metaphysical crux which lies behind their records and the solution of which they found, though the records on their intellectual side spell only a confused understanding of the metaphysical question.

After long consideration, it is clear to me that Dionysian mystical theology had no other problem in view and that its " supernatural flight upward," or plunge into " the mysterious brightness of Divine Obscurity " meant that the difficulty was overcome and the " mystical experience " of God attained " after a transcendent manner " in a complete mind-suspension. So also the way of solution was being indicated through the centuries by the counsels of practice concerning sacrifice—though in the wrong sense of the word[2]—and the renunciation or

---

[1] P. 227.

[2] Sacrifice in its proper sense is a process of saving or hallowing and self-sacrifice is self-realisation. The things that can be given to another do not belong essentially to ourselves : we can part with accidents only ; essential things are inalienable. The most of all which we can give to one another is the effluence of love, but love's inward capacity no one can bestow. All goodwill lies within the correlated opposites of giving and keeping. Of such is the law of our espousals with the world to which we belong. It is a communication from our inalienable centre to the circumference of the

casting-out of self. These things are insisted on everywhere ; but the cloud over all the memorials is—as I have suggested—that the mystics do not seem to have grasped their metaphysical ground. They saw only what must be called the ethical and ascetical side, rooted in the implied hatefulness of the natural man in the sight of God. All this matter of motive had nothing to do with the transit of faith into experience. In so far as the practices helped those who followed them it was in spite of the underlying motive, or postulated cause and reason, and in virtue of another principle at work.

The last secret of attainment is also the first secret ; the end is like the beginning; and the change in our mode of self-knowledge can be reached only by such an expansion of love that the self is in God only and we know with Him and in Him. It is consciousness operating in God, and we shall realise therein for the first time— vitally and infinitely—the capacity of the word *conscire*. The love of the lover in *Locksley Hall*

" Smote the chord of self, that trembling passed in music out of sight " ;

but here the self passes in God. The realisation ceases after a self manner, to be transformed and enlarged in Him. It is in looking towards this state that I have called mystical life " an exploration of self," and after its attainment the soul continues to explore its deified self in God, in the everlasting, ever-deepening love of Him.

manifest, and it is imposed in virtue of solidarity. If I may use another symbol, which is not to be understood as doctrine, the Divine Nature is like a tree which is one thing from root to leaf. The root is unmanifest Deity, the trunk is God in manifestation, the branches are worlds, the leaves are hierarchies of intelligence : they are all joined together ; yet the leaf is not the root. I am not laying an emanationist mine for the unwary, but explaining by an image the solidarity which binds all together. It is a key also to the path of universal love and service, by which the Divine Immanence does pass in us into the Divine Transcendence by realisation, and this is the state of union. Its maxim is all in all.

This is what St. Teresa, choosing her words loosely,
spoke of as rapture beyond union. When in far-off ages
of the individual soul such a state becomes that of being,
the better term is absorption. Hereof also is the deeper
sense of Jacob Böhme's " discovery to be made in man."
God knows, and all His mystics, that such absorption is
not attainable now ; but there is a deep and undistracted
preoccupation in God which is not beyond some of us,
and therein are moments, brief periods, certain halves
of hours, when that preoccupation is " lifted higher,"
when the love becomes so transcendent that the knower
and the known, subject and object, are wrapped up
together in an indescribable unity, and this is that attainment of which we possess the precious records in Mysticism.[1] Its barriers are burned away and all the barbed
wires of intellectualism are melted. *Quod tenet nunc
teneat donec de medio fiat.* The great problems are taken
out of the way very easily by a true solvent, and this is
ready to our hands in a very simple adaptation of certain
words of Fénelon.[2] When Divine Love fills the soul,
the thought of self is not possible. And this is God in
the soul ; the only reaction on self is that of God, in
whom our knowing part abides. Reflex act, distinction
of subject and object—these things have passed.[3]

[1] The terms used here are intended to reiterate the difficulties of this
ascent in the scale of love on which I have insisted previously. They
may be compared with the indications of Cardinal Bellarmine in *De
Ascensione Mentis ad Deum, per scalas Rerum Naturalium.* There is an
intervening gulf, representing all the difference between the life of
devotional piety and the apex of mystical life. The difficulties notwithstanding, whatsoever a man has done it remains that a man can do. He
who can conceive holiness at this day has no door shut against him, so
that he may not from his present standing-place go up where others have
gone of old—the cloud of holy witnesses. We who are heirs of the ages
—but I mean ages of sanctity—have a right therefore to set the term
before us, seeking to realise what it was, is and involves, in the general
light of our heritage.

[2] Compare also St. Ignatius, as cited at p. 80.

[3] Those who can enter, even intellectually, into all that this state

There is only one point more. If love is the secret of the change,[1] and if the love of man for God, and in Him, be the silver side of the shield, while the side of gold is God's love for and within man, there is no question—such as that proffered by theology—whether the intervention of God is necessary to draw the soul across the threshold of union. It is all the work of love in mutual continuance. This is the Divine Act mentioned by St. Bonaventura[2]—the drawing out of the soul in God. In the work of Divine Love, He is always intervening and the soul concurring always, so long as that work goes on. Nothing at any stage is apart from the soul, and nothing apart from God.

This is how it comes to me in respect of that which I have called, with utter precision, " the most difficult enterprise which can be undertaken by the human mind." And now there are certain things that remain over and must be touched on briefly, though at least in one case I should prefer to leave it, were that indeed possible. This is the problem of essential values in the Christian element of Mysticism. We know that the great experience is catholic to all ages, and what therefore is the canon of criticism regarding Christ as the Way and Term ? Does union with the personal Christ signify Divine Union ? If so, is the vital implicit that union is possible only through Christ, that mystical experience is illusory over the whole world, apart from Him ?[3] Alternatively, did Egypt, India, China, Araby the Blest,

involves will understand at once both how and why the mystics never contributed anything to Doctrine, and how in attempted delineations of the state they mixed their language-symbols wildly, combining theism and pantheism in a Mænad-dance of words. They will see also that such intellectual extravagance may be very often a note of the deeper states and that Eckehart in his exercise of the free spirit may well have gone further than St. Teresa, amidst the trammels of Medusan " directors."

[1] P. 225.   [2] Pp. 11, 28.

[3] See Clement of Alexandria, as quoted, pp. 56, 57 ; St. Augustine, p. 59 ; *Theologia Germanica*, p. 81 ; and Molinos, p. 106.

in attaining union also attain Christ under the veils
of other names ? My answer is that whether the story
of the Christ is taken as it stands in the records or is
held to be projected upon the material plane from
a hidden place of sanctity, it is the whole story of
the soul in its second birth, its spiritual life, its mystical
death, resurrection and ascension or return to the
Father. As this was either actualised or symbolised in
Palestine, so in many a religious mythos and in every true
Mystery process it was put forward under a great variety
of veils. Everywhere therefore we see the working of
one spirit and discover one bond of union, to which each
religion furnishes a particular vesture. There is no
question that Mysticism is much simpler on a pure
theistic basis than on any Trinitarian hypothesis, but the
Christ-process remains the Way, the Truth and the Life
from either doctrinal standpoint. Out of the Christ-
Idea and the gospels which incorporate it there has arisen
the great body of theology ; but the divisions between
East and West, with all later sub-divisions, have left us
without a canon of criticism on the subject of theological
final values. The churches and sects must be left to
settle their claims in respect of such values. One certitude that emerges from the witness of the mystics is
that they were concerned with a way in life and not
with doctrine. The deepest states of loving contemplation and the highest beatitude therein brought mystical
saints no particle of new knowledge in departments
which belong exclusively to the rational intellect. Hereof
are the official theologies. The thing called everlasting
loss was still loss to everlasting for those who were
taught in the youth of their spirits that this was one of
God's dealings with man created by Him. No one
passed from one to another system of doctrinal belief
under the Christian ægis as a result of following the
mystical path, for the inward experiences cast no ray of
light on the wide fields of contention. And that which is

true of Christianity is true of the other religions; but because each mystical attainment took place within some particular circle of faith it is unquestionable that intellectually this fact rooted each mystic in that faith which was his originally. Out of the experience of union he who had been nourished on the Vedas came forth a more convinced Vedantist and the Thomist a more assured Thomist. Only at this day, when it is possible to encompass the whole field in our survey, are we in a position to establish that the mystical experience contributed nothing to the warrants of the Vedas and nothing to those of the *Summa*—for the same reason—as we have seen—that Eckehart tending towards pantheism does not contribute to its defence, nor does the most pronounced theistic mystic offer anything of value to his school. We might as well expect Ruysbroeck to return from the *pelagus divinitatis* with a demonstration on the historicity question. This notwithstanding, had it existed at his day, he would have thought intellectually that he did. It follows that he who attains may never have heard of *Vedanta* or—except at a far distance— he may have heard of nothing else. So also the *Summa totius Theologiæ* is a true and potent aid to reflection. It has served as such through the centuries; but he who has not read it can still go forward. There is yet a further point, for it must be held to follow that people who do not accept the historicity of Christ are not, for such reason, to be excluded from the Great Quest. I hold no materials in my hands in virtue of which it is impossible for an earnest soul to follow the way of the mystics and attain its term, though he may ascribe Jesus of Nazareth to the sphere of purposed mythos. I understand the cosmic Christ as God immanent in the universe and this Christ takes flesh in the heart of every man who enters into Divine Union. Here is the scheme of redemption by the finding of life in God, and that life is called the Blood of Christ in Christian symbolism.

I should not alter one line that I have ever written on the Eucharist did the idle negative on the historicity of Jesus enter suddenly into demonstration. But I believe that the Saving Lord of Palestine is the Great Personal Master of Christendom and the prototypical example of those in whom Christ takes flesh. If, however, any man on the living quest of God is intellectually so ill-advised as to reject the historical personality, because the external data are in the cloudy state which might have been expected, he may still in Divine Union attain the life of Christ's blood. The historicity question is important from every point of view except that of essentials.

The other questions concern the problem of evil, the fall of man and evolution from the animal into the lowest human type. It is best for those on the quest of God not to waste themselves at the beginning over these problems. They are unlikely to reach firm ground. Those who say that evil is over-ruled by good, which turns evil to its own purpose, and that if we could look at the sum of events we should not distinguish evil, but only Eternal Goodness, do not deal with the problem. I know well that we must go far before we can understand the discords, their unknown language, their symbols, and how within the power-sounds there are the grace-sounds, or in what sense God is less in the tempest than in the still small voice. I know also that in order to understand evil we must have put it outside ourselves, until which time it adulterates all the messages.

As regards the fall of man, that which began in mythos and has been since erected into doctrine is no simple dream of some past event but an explanatory theory respecting a burden of present life. Is there need to say that we enter this manifest world tainted by the mistakes, follies and wickedness of our progenitors— going back through all the ages ? There is a congenital tendency towards the side of death and evil. The testimony of Nature tells us that it was never otherwise with the body, which belongs to the animal kingdom and is accounted for, roughly speaking, by the law of the genesis and development of species—though that is still on its trial. But the spiritual part of man " cometh from afar," and the spiritual race of man began to take up its residence in the present manifest order when the nature-body—anthropoid ape or what not—was ready to receive it in the course of physical evolution. Why did the spirit-race come down to inhabit such vehicles and take " dejectedly its seat " upon the throne of such a mournful kingdom ? It must be admitted that true Mysticism has no theory as to the circumstances under which we arrived in the manifest, because doctrinal speculation is not of its subject. When I affirm that physical evolution has prepared an organism as a working instrument for the spirit, I present the only view concerning it which can be entertained, even provisionally, by the mystic, but I am not intending to suggest that Mysticism has borne witness on the subject or can speak authoritatively about anything but the soul of man. These questions therefore remain in suspension.[1]

[1] Yet it is the mystic more than all who is qualified by his dedication to deal with things as they are, and he least of any is called upon to seek testimonies of mercy in the ways without, if Nature cannot give them up of her own accord. Supposing that it is we only who from our yearnings and implicits read mercy into the universe, I hold that this is good ; we at least have conceived mercy and we are placed in the universe—which has no purpose apart from us and those who are like us, from those who are working to reach our own estate and those who have passed beyond it. The gospel of mercy is with us, in us, by us, and we can bring it into manifestation everywhere. This is the mystic's work in the world. It is in this sense that we are meant to be saviours of the whole society of Nature.

As there is one right point of view from which to inspect evil and thus reduce the problem to its due proportions, so there is another in respect of its manifest and imputed consequences, here and hereafter. In a work the design of which is to open heaven within the consciousness of Christians, I have no call to speak of hell ; but if one be the term attained in God, its opposite is the term missed—which may happen in a thousand ways, apart from all questions of stability and permanence. O place of

The Way of Divine Union

And now a word in conclusion to those of the great majority who stand in the outer courts, amidst the lights and shadows of the threshold, but not without hope of crossing. Let them look within their own hearts in search of that which hinders and believe when I bear them witness that it can be taken out of the way. The one step further is always possible, till at last the threshold is passed, and God still leading, it is always one step more. It is well for those who die with their faces towards Jerusalem ; but it is better, and of all things

many mansions ! Hell has a thousand cities, and not one of them is free from the worm of search or from the preaching of many doctrines of beatitude and salvation. It is the region where men dree their weirds and purge their Karma and work their redemption in a myriad figments of the mind, but the processes are false. The following of a true process is of course the path of escape. Apart from this, the worm of unrest dieth not and the fire of hunger and thirst is not quenched. Yet are they a process of concealed redemption, operating below the consciousness of the weariful world. If there were rest in hell the mouth of the abyss would close on all its hierarchies. We know too well what qualities of need and longing are taken by crowds of humanity out of this life into the next—as one might say, out of their hell here, God help us all ! For this world is hell or heaven, as we make and mould it—after our image and likeness. There is a sense also in which it can be said with a heart of gratitude that the holiest hell of all is the hunger and thirst after righteousness, for the state of separation is hell, notwithstanding " all its hourly varied anodynes." This is why hell's summit has above it the earth of Paradise.

Be it observed : I have not said that there are no hells of suffering ; all hells indeed are such ; but so long as consciousness remains—which remains indeed for ever—the Divine Witness is in hell, as God is in His heaven. Loss is separation, and I suppose that it may go from bad to worse, as if even into a world of uttermost loss. The analogue of the state therein would be madness in physical life. It would be self without love carried to the last term, and it must be surely the hardest of all bournes to reach. The proper word is void, antithesis of the *plenum* which is God. It would be the burden of all that is evil in all worlds, too great for bearing. Such pit of all is empty—meaning that it is a figment of the mind.

But God is in the heaven of consciousness, and if we are set firmly to look and see that this is so, we shall see indeed.

good, to die in Zion itself. The desire of the House is saving, but the House itself is redemption : it is the distinction between the becoming and the become. Blessed are those who look from Pisgah heights on the Palestine of the Promised Land, but it is those only who abide in the place flowing with milk and honey that have the nourishment of angels. To the aspirants and dwellers in the outer courts let us wish God-speed in their particular ways, hoping that some time they may come into their own and ours.

There are those who have gone up into the blue height and have descended into the black void. They have returned, like Dante, saying: " And have not our fathers told us ? " They testify that God does recompense those who seek Him out. But the height and the void are symbolism. In another mode of it I may add as a rider that it is not the saint who ascends the mountain, but the House of God and the four-square City and the Palace at the Centre, the House of David, House of Ivory and House of Gold which comes down and is built round him from within. The witness shows that those who are dedicated out of all revocation, with the whole heart of their nature, to the great things of love, find all the love-spaces peopled in directions where the normal sight of humanity, the eye of the untrained soul, sees and can see nothing. But they are all inward directions, or at least until we can see the Great Mysteries unfolded within we shall never discover them without, uplifting their own veils and revealing the shining centre. The counsel is therefore to remember that we are the *Sanctum Regnum*—the Holy Kingdom—the *centrum concentratum* of love and that it is for us to learn the Royal Art by which it is prepared for the Presence to abide in our love therein. The preparation is the Practice of the Presence, a will towards realisation of that which is always there, and this is a will to love. It is the Practice also of Peace.

The Way of Divine Union

That which the soul can repose in, even from the beginning of its dedication, is the naked hypothesis of the white peace in God, looking in the midst of our putative exile for that time when God will call us home. We shall come in this manner to find that there is no exile and that we are in the courts and gardens of an eternal home. So is the prospect ever extending, ever drawing into closer environment. So is the search after God a quest of joy and is not likely to be brought to its term otherwise. The proper mood of animate creation is joy, and it is the basis of adjustment between our senses and external things. The universe is the veil of the Immanence and its communication to the soul is the warrant of all beatitude. The opening of the inner sensorium to beatitude here and now is the best preparation for life in joy to come. This is also the way of love, for that must be sought in joy which we look to possess in gladness, or the still joy in the centre, full of peace and sweetness. There is a great art herein, and it is the last message which comes in the Way of the Union to close the book of these mysteries, written for the counselling and consolation of those who call upon God and seek to be renewed in His love. Creative and re-creative, may the Spirit of Joy quicken their hearts in these pages. I know that the mystical life is the great light of literature and the other arts. God is the sum of the arts, and all their grace is from Him. The well-spring of pure inspiration flows over the search after Him, and of Him are all books of life. Thou art the Pierian fount, O Lord. I have come to Thee as a poet: I have desired to drink deeply. I have looked for Thy revelation in the night and in the day I have waited on Thine inbreathing. Thou hast sent the gift of literature into the world as a voice of direction for those who would return to Thee. In the aspiration and hope that here may be one of its channels, I bring my task to its finish. That which stands forth at the end is the certitude of mystical attainment in the simplicity of Divine Love and a second birth of practice on the path which leads thereto.

And the path of Quest goes on. And the Quest, as it may be, ends in attainment—we know not where nor when. So long as we can conceive of our separate existence in any sphere and under any veils, I know that the Quest goes on—failures and victories, retardations and progress, raptures and agonies continued henceforward. And ever shall reflection on the ways followed by those who have passed in front be a help on our own path, so that the extension of our comparative knowledge of all that has been once attained is the most wise, enlightened and informed of all researches. Hereof is our encouragement and herein the spur of zeal, and with the grace of zeal in our hearts the sacred, vivifying fire aflame in heart and mind—may it be with us as was said by a great poet:

> The noble heart which harbours virtuous thought,
> And is with child of glorious great intent,
> Can never rest until it forth have brought
> The eternal brood of glory excellent.

INDEX *

Abelard, 173
Abelson, Dr. J., on *Jewish Mysticism*, 19–21 ; on *The Immanence of God in Rabbinical Literature*, 20
Advaita Philosophy, 136
Alacoque, Blessed Margaret Mary, 17
Alvarez, Jacobus, 12
Antonius a Spiritu Sancto, his *Directorium Mysticum*, 2, 13, 33, 40, 41, 42, 150, 161
Aristotle, 150 ; *Book of Theology*, falsely ascribed to, 40
Augustine, St., 9, 45, 57, 104, 173 ; the *Confessions*, 58, 62 ; *The City of God*, 9 ; some other works quoted, 58, 59
Autenrieth, 219
Avrillon, R. P., in *L'Année Affective*, 104, 187, 200

Baader, Franz von, 96 ; his *Fermenta Cognitionis*, 213
Baker, Ven. Augustin, in *Sancta Sophia*, 88, 165, 289, 312.
Balmes, his *Fundamental Philosophy*, 227, 228
Beatific Vision, 41, 48, 63, 65, 103, 202, 218, 245
Bellarmine, Cardinal, in *De Ascensione Mentis ad Deum*, 87, 318
Bernard, St., his *De Consideratione*, 10 ; *Sermones in Cantica Canticrum*, 10, 105, 192, 193, 195

Bevan, Frances, his *Three Friends of God*, 153
Birch, Una, 102
Böhme, Jacob, 15, 24, 25, 69, 89, 94, 95, 156, 176, 178, 181, 201, 249 ; his *Three Principles*, 95 ; answer to Isaias Stiefel, 96 ; *The Holy Week*, 96, 174
Bona, Cardinal, 6 ; his *Via Compendii ad Deum*, 12 ; *De Psalmis Gradualibus*, 88 ; *Principia Vitæ Christianæ*, 153
Bonaventura, St., in *De Mystica Theologia Speculativa*, 11 ; *Itinerarium Mentis ad Deum*, 196 ; *God of Divine Love*, 292
Book of Ceremonial Magic, 26
Bridget, *Revelations* of St., 198
Bromley, Thomas, 99 ; his *Way to the Sabbath of Rest*, 100

Çankara, 127, 128, 129
Cassian, John, in the *Second Conference of Abbot Isaac*, 59, 60
Castaniza, 149, 165, 210, 313
Catherine of Siena, St., 17, 31, 32, 199, 205
Cell of Self-Knowledge, 62, 146
Chrysostom, St. John, 59
Clement of Alexandria, in *Exhortation to the Gentiles*, 56, 57 ; in *The Pedagogue*, 57
Cloud of Unknowing, 31, 50, 52, 75–78, 87, 126, 155, 164, 165

* The Analysis of Contents furnishes a sufficient guide to subjects, and this index is practically confined to names of authorities and titles of books.

Index

Index

Index

PRINTED BY WM. BRENDON AND SON, LTD.
PLYMOUTH, ENGLAND